ARSENE WENGER

ARSENE WENGER

THE INSIDE STORY OF
ARSENAL UNDER WENGER

John Cross

**SIMON &
SCHUSTER**

London · New York · Sydney · Toronto · New Delhi

A CBS COMPANY

First published in Great Britain by Simon & Schuster UK Ltd, 2015
A CBS COMPANY

3 5 7 9 10 8 6 4 2

Simon & Schuster UK Ltd
1st Floor
222 Gray's Inn Road
London WC1X 8HB

www.simonandschuster.co.uk

Simon & Schuster Australia, Sydney
Simon & Schuster India, New Delhi

The author and publishers have made all reasonable efforts to contact
copyright-holders for permission, and apologise for any omissions or errors
in the form of credits given. Corrections may be made to future printings.

A CIP catalogue record for this book
is available from the British Library.

Hardback ISBN: 978-1-4711-3791-4
Trade paperback ISBN: 978-1-4711-5339-6
Ebook ISBN: 978-1-4711-3793-8

Typeset in Caslon by M Rules
Printed and bound by CPI Group (UK) Ltd, Croydon, CR0 4YY

Football is a comfort, even through the hard times in life.

My dad introduced me to football, Arsenal and the love of the game.

When Arsenal were losing the FA Cup final 2-0 to Hull in May 2014, I could almost my hear my dad – who passed away just two days earlier – look down in exasperation and say: 'Can't you do this for me just this once?'

Of course, Arsenal did it for him. And the magical part about Arsene Wenger is that he has done it so many times for so many people.

I couldn't have done this book without the support of my family. I would like to dedicate it to my dad. I miss talking to him so very much.

CONTENTS

INTRODUCTION

ARSENE WENGER IS HARDLY a run-of-the-mill football man-ager – and the Frenchman is proud to be different.

As if to prove it, on Monday, 1 September 2014, Wenger flew with agent Leon Angel to Rome for a charity football match. While the rest of football was glued to a telephone or watching transfer deadline day unfold on television, Wenger went to the Vatican to meet Pope Francis.

Arsenal chief executive Ivan Gazidis was desperately trying to complete a deal to sign Danny Welbeck from Manchester United. Gazidis was struggling to get hold of his manager on the phone and eventually he got through to Angel, only to be told that Wenger was talking to the Pope. Later in the day, the Welbeck deal was completed and Wenger got his man. But it just goes to show this is no ordinary football manager.

Wenger does not like getting drawn into transfer auctions. He attended a convention in Geneva while Arsenal went on their crazy supermarket sweep on deadline day in 2011 and that perhaps illustrates where his priorities lie. He plays by his own rules, is determined to win with style, would rather shun the money-mad transfer market and yet always ensures that he and his own players get very well paid.

Wenger breezed into Arsenal, the most English of football clubs in 1996, as a relative unknown but soon established himself as a genius, a football revolutionary. The beautiful style of his teams, combined with his charm and unexpected wit, was destined to make him one of the Premier League's all-time greats and the most successful manager in Arsenal's long and illustrious history.

When Wenger arrived, Manchester United were reigning champions, Newcastle their closest challengers. Arsenal had finished fifth the season before under Bruce Rioch and Wenger's greatest achievement over the next two decades was to bring trophies and a consistency that would ensure standards would never drop as low again.

Wenger delivered a style of football and quality of player which had rarely been seen at Arsenal before. He introduced new training methods, new diets and mastered the French transfer market. His brilliant one-liners ensured he made the headlines, and his jousting with Manchester United boss Sir Alex Ferguson – both on and off the pitch – established one of English football's great rivalries.

But, just at the time Arsenal were breaking records and enjoying the most successful period in the club's history, they were hit with a double whammy which would push the club to the brink and test Wenger's management skills to their very limit.

Roman Abramovich's Russian revolution bankrolled Chelsea from 2003, while Manchester City's new-found wealth also emerged as a major factor in the Premier League, just at a time when Arsenal were having to borrow heavily to move to the Emirates Stadium. Wenger was left fighting with both hands tied behind his back – and yet continued to deliver Champions League places every year, challenged for the title and, by 2015, had emerged out the other side, winning back-to-back FA Cups to become the first post-war manager to win the trophy six times.

Wenger still does not like spending 'stratospheric' money, as he calls it, but two world-class signings in Mesut Ozil and Alexis

Sanchez have helped change Arsenal's dynamic, ambition and outlook.

Perhaps more than any other recent big game, Wenger was able to bring it all together in the 2015 FA Cup final when they beat Aston Villa 4-0. The mixture of pace, power and movement showed Arsenal at their best. They had struggled under the pressure of expectation, the slow, heavy Wembley pitch and being favourites in previous games against Wigan, Hull and Reading. But here, finally, was what Arsenal were about under Wenger.

Ozil glided across the pitch, Sanchez revelled in the big-match occasion, Santi Cazorla orchestrated the play, while Theo Walcott's pace stretched Aston Villa's defence to its limit. Arsenal didn't just win, they won with style, which is so important to Wenger. There is always a debate in football about whether it really matters how you win – just as long as you win. Pragmatists such as Jose Mourinho or Rafa Benitez put winning before everything and, when they are lifting trophies, that seems to be all that matters. But Wenger believes it goes deeper than that and, talking in May 2015, he gave a fascinating insight into why he believes it is important to entertain as well as win.

'Let's not forget you can win and lose playing with different styles,' said Wenger. 'I believe the big clubs have a responsibility to win – but to also win with style. I believe our sport has moved forward a lot on the physical side, tactical side but we must not forget the values that it carries through the generations. One of them is the vibe coming out of the team going into the stand doesn't lie.

'I always like to think that the guy who wakes up in the morning after a hard week of work has that moment, that fraction of a second, when he opens his eyes and says: "Oh, today I go to watch my team." I like to think it makes him happy, he thinks he can maybe see something special. We can't guarantee that, but we have to try ... It's amazing the effect you can have on people's lives.'

That seemed to come together again in 2015. There have been many highs and some lows during Wenger's reign at Arsenal. The Premier League and FA Cup Doubles in 1998 and 2002, followed by the history-making Invincibles season in 2003/04 when they won the title unbeaten, were some of the best moments.

After that, however, Wenger became as much accountant as football manager during the move to the Emirates but, through all the disappointments and frustrations of the years that followed, he kept the vision of a glorious sunny day in May as the inspiration through the dark times.

His philosophy may frustrate some – indeed, it often annoys and upsets his own players. But Wenger sets up to attack and win; he rarely goes into games to defend and stop the opposition. When Arsenal lose, it looks naive and foolish, and he rightly gets criticised. But when Arsenal win, Wenger gets the plaudits. And when they play the beautiful game and win, Wenger gets hailed as a genius.

Over the last two decades Wenger has, without question, revolutionised Arsenal, changed the face of English football and established himself as one of the biggest characters in the Premier League. He provokes strong opinions, but that's the life of a football manager. It's an unforgiving profession when sometimes even your own fans don't appreciate you.

But that only goes to prove why Arsene Wenger's career in English football has been a fascinating ride right from the start. There has always been drama, entertainment, success and disappointment.

What follows tries to get to the heart of his achievement and assesses his methods. Based on detailed insight from players, backroom staff and the boardroom, as well as many years reporting on the club and following its every move, it places his remarkable story at the heart of the football revolution.

CHAPTER I

WHAT'S IN A NAME?

To UNDERSTAND THE JOB Arsene Wenger has done, you first need to understand the club he was walking into back in 1996. And only then can you begin to appreciate the scale of his achievement and the transformation he has made.

In 1996, Arsenal was a club resistant to change despite having been rocked by a string of scandals, from bungs to a destructive drinking culture and a dressing-room revolt. It was a club steeped in tradition, with Highbury's Marble Halls a reminder of the past, but also perhaps a symbol of why the club could not go forward. With a capacity of around 38,000, the stadium's listed buildings were subject to restrictions in terms of improvements and expansion. And in the boardroom, which lived up to the Old Etonian stereotype, port and cigars were the order of the day. It was a club known as the Bank of England. That was the nick-name given to Arsenal in the 1930s because it had wealthy ownership, broke transfer records and gave big contracts. The Bank of England tag stuck into the 1990s, not because of the club's big expenditure but more because of tradition, being old school and very British.

Appointing a foreign manager in those days was still a rarity. Perhaps surprisingly, the first foreign manager in English football's top flight did not arrive until Dr Jozef Venglos took over at Aston Villa in 1990. The Czech manager lasted a year. His appointment was seen as the exception to the rule, a bold and brave move that didn't work. That perhaps explains why Arsenal actually rejected the chance to appoint Wenger in 1995.

Arsenal were looking for a new manager after one of the most turbulent periods in the club's history. George Graham, a member of Arsenal's 1971 Double-winning team, was sacked in February 1995 after a bung scandal, following revelations that he had taken unsolicited payments on transfers. Graham had won two league titles, cups and brought back success to Arsenal. But his nine-year reign ended in disgrace and finished with a team in decline, a difficult dressing room run by egos, and a squad used to playing dull football which had revelled in the fans' chant: 'One-nil to the Arsenal.'

But the fans gradually fell out of love with Graham's cautious approach, which proves that success is not always enough. Arsenal needed a change, a different direction and new hope. The one member of the board who enjoyed being seen as different, a revolutionary, a mover and shaker in European football's corridors of power, was their vice-chairman David Dein. And the first meeting between Wenger and Dein – who remain as close as ever – tells you everything you need to know about Arsenal's history and traditions. Little did they realise then, but 2 January 1989 was to become a pivotal date in the history of Arsenal Football Club.

Wenger, then manager of Monaco, was at Arsenal to watch a game during a break in the fixtures in France. He had stopped off in London after a match in Turkey. An agent, Dennis Roach, had got him a ticket in the directors' box to see Arsenal take on Tottenham in the north London derby. Arsenal beat Spurs 2-0 and went on to win the title that season. Amusingly, the main thing that sticks in Wenger's mind about that game was the appearance of Arsenal's ginger-haired substitute. Perry Groves can be proud that he made such an impression on Wenger, even if it was more to do with the colour of his hair. Dein recalls:

[Arsene] was passing through London and stopped off to see a game at the old Highbury stadium. We had a boardroom, which on match day was the domain of the directors and their privileged guests, and next door was the cocktail lounge, which hosted managers, scouts and generally football people from within the game.

Since, in those days, women had limited access to the boardroom – that soon changed! – my wife and one of her friends camped in the cocktail lounge. She managed to get word to me that the manager of Monaco was there. At half-time, I introduced myself to this elegant man, wearing a long trench coat and what looked like bad National Health glasses. He really didn't look a typical football manager.

I asked him how long he would be staying in London and he said: 'Overnight.' I then asked him what he was doing that evening. He said: 'Nothing.' One of my favourite sayings is the motto of the turtle: 'You never get anywhere unless you stick your neck out.' I then enquired whether he would like to join my wife and me at a friend's house for dinner. The answer changed our lives and I guess the lives of every Arsenal supporter. 'Yes, I'd like that,' he replied.

Wenger stayed the night at their house in Totteridge, having been persuaded to go along to a small party being hosted by Dein's friend Alan Whitehead, who played drums in the 1970s pop group Marmalade. They had an evening of buffet food, small talk and rounded it off with a game of charades. Dein continues:

> Arsene didn't speak English that fluently at the time, which was just as well since it's a mime game! Within a few minutes he had the courage to act out *A Midsummer Night's Dream*. I thought to myself that he was not the usual football manager, an ex-player who has left school at 16. Arsene spoke four languages, went to Strasbourg University and had a degree in economics.
>
> During the evening I saw this vision written in the sky: 'Arsene for Arsenal!' It's destiny, it's fate, it's going to happen. Of course, at the time, George Graham was our manager and we were about to win the league at that unforgettable game at Anfield. But Arsene and I became good friends, and from time to time I would go to Monaco to watch their matches. I could see how he interacted with the players, the press, the supporters and his board. He didn't realise that he was auditioning for Arsenal.

That fateful meeting changed everything, and over the course of the next few years they cemented their friendship: Dein would courier a video tape of Arsenal's latest game to Wenger and they would talk, as friends, and analyse every performance. So when the Arsenal job became available in 1995, there was only ever one man as far as Dein was concerned. But, although Dein was hugely influential on transfers and the running of the club day-to-day, the rest of the board ignored his advice.

Arsenal chairman Peter Hill-Wood met Wenger in his favourite Italian restaurant, Ziani's, just off the King's Road in London. Hill-Wood recalls being impressed with Wenger, but had major concerns about him largely because he was foreign. 'I actually had cold feet about employing a foreigner at that time,' Hill-Wood said. 'Because we had a tricky squad, and one or two of them had personal problems, I wasn't too sure he would understand it. I liked him immediately. I was just nervous, and I think some of my colleagues were as well, whether we were ready for a French coach. We decided we weren't ready for it. We had a fairly difficult team. I was wrong, of course.'

Hill-Wood was later forced to admit that the man they eventually went for, Bruce Rioch, who left Bolton to take over at Arsenal, was 'not up to the job really'. But ironically – given the board's reservations about Wenger – the players were very mixed about him. Dennis Bergkamp was signed during Rioch's reign and the Dutchman speaks fondly of him, even expressing sadness that he left. And Martin Keown credits him for helping him start to become more expansive as a player.

But Rioch struggled with other big names and characters. The players used to laugh at him, particularly his habit of never wearing a belt on his trousers. Little things often amuse players, and if a bit of mickey-taking over not wearing a belt was all Rioch had to worry about then he would have been fine. But perhaps his biggest clash of personalities came with Ian Wright, the Arsenal fans' favourite and leading goalscorer. Their relationship hit such a low point that the striker put in a transfer request after getting fed up with either being played on the left wing or being dropped to the bench.

Just before the start of the 1996/97 season, growing unrest in the dressing room plus a dispute over transfer funds brought about the demise of Rioch. So, in the space of 18 months, Arsenal, a club renowned for stability and caution, had sacked a manager amid a scandal, sacked another after dressing-room problems and were suddenly thinking about bucking the trend by going for a relatively unknown Frenchman.

These were the days before social media, before foreign managers were well known on these shores, and no one was championing Wenger's cause – apart from Dein. Since their meeting back in 1989, Wenger's career had suffered highs and lows, which left him questioning his very future in the game. He had managed Monaco between 1987 and 1994, but had constantly become frustrated, repeatedly finishing second best to Marseille. The frustration came in the shape of Marseille's match-fixing scandal. He felt cheated by Bernard Tapie, the Marseille president, and his attempts to bribe opposing players, officials and the game's rulers. Marseille reached the 1993 European Cup final against Milan and only a few days before that needed to beat Valenciennes to win the French league title.

Wenger is still angry about it and, when match fixing became newsworthy again in 2013 after allegations of a plot involving non-league and lower divisions shocked English football, Wenger revisited the subject in an emotionally charged press conference. It would be wrong to say he was happy to talk about it, but he was eager to speak up in order to make his point and try to stop it happening again.

'It was one of the most difficult periods of my life,' said Wenger. No wonder. Wenger was carving out a successful career in France, and feels wronged by the Marseille scandal. He still wonders what might have been had they all been on a level playing field.

Monaco had Mark Hateley, Jurgen Klinsmann and Glenn Hoddle. Wenger had recruited George Weah and, with all the hallmarks of his management mantra, was on the way to turning the Liberian striker into one of the best players in the world. When Weah later retired and swapped football for politics, a Liberian journalist came to one of Wenger's press conferences. He nervously asked Wenger whether he knew Weah was running for office.

Wenger responded with an in-depth answer which almost became a lecture on the state of Liberia and the country's politics. Did he know? Of course. Wenger remains loyal to his players even after they leave him.

Wenger also made a lasting impression on German World Cup winner Klinsmann, who has achieved so much in the game as a player and a coach but says he owes much to those days playing under Wenger at Monaco. His admiration for his former coach is obvious:

I think every player can only learn so much from his managers, and I was so lucky. I had Arsene, Trapattoni, Beckenbauer, Ossie Ardiles, Gerry Francis, Cesar Luis Menotti. If I look back, I had many teachers and they taught me so many things off the field as well, not only the soccer stuff. Wenger was already a legend at Monaco; he'd stayed there for more than seven years, and he went off real quick to Japan and since then he's here [Arsenal]. But he's not only the football coach, who helps you to put the pieces together on the field; he is such a wealth of knowledge off the field that for a player it is like going to the best university in the world.

There are lots of little examples that you never forget because they catch up with you later on. With Arsene it was always the long-term picture on players. We had a very talented Monaco team; we reached the semi-finals of the Champions League and lost to AC Milan. He left players out that I thought needed to play in order for us to have a chance. One of the big names was Youri Djorkaeff; at the time he was a young player. He said: 'No, he has to learn to live the right life off the field.' It paid off. The kid learned his lesson and a couple of years later won the World Cup with France.

There I understood his vision was always long term. Yes, he

knew he had to provide results short term. But it was more than that – it was how should this player be in two, four and six years from now. He saw that already, he saw it in Djorkaeff, in Thuram, in Petit.

Wenger was clearly a deep thinker right from the start of his managerial career. That's one of the reasons why being cheated in the Marseille bribery scandal hurt so much. Four Valenciennes players were offered 250,000 French francs each (roughly £30,000) to 'take their foot off the gas' in their game with Marseille. The players turned whistle-blowers, French football was rocked by the scandal and suddenly Marseille's success – Monaco had finished runners-up in each of the previous two seasons – was called into question. We will never know whether the bribes won Marseille their trophies. Wenger recalls:

You hear rumours and after that you cannot come out in the press and say: 'This game was not regular.' You must prove what you say. From knowing something, feeling that it is true, coming out publicly and saying, 'Look, I can prove it' is the most difficult. There are little incidents added one to the other. In the end, there is no coincidence.

It is a shame. Once you don't know any more if everyone is genuine out there, that is something absolutely disastrous. I think we have absolutely to fight against that with the strongest severity to get that out of the game. It was a period where European football was not clean, for different reasons, but I hope we have that behind us.

Look, you know what it is when you're in a job like mine. You worry about every detail, about who to pick for the next game, to prepare the next game, and when you go to the game you know all that is useless, it's of course a disaster.

I didn't feel like walking away [from the game] because even when it was happening in France or in Europe, I always felt that in the end the game will come clean again and the love for the game from everybody will take over.

But out of the Marseille scandal one unbreakable bond was formed. Boro Primorac was the coach at Valenciennes and he stood up for what he believed in. He gave evidence at the resulting trial in 1994 and was promptly ostracised by those in the sport in his country. French football did not enjoy having its dirty linen washed in public.

Wenger said of Primorac: 'He did very well because it's not always the fact that you stand up against it, it's the consequences of it after. I can tell you that story one day and you will be surprised.' Wenger enjoys dropping nuggets like this into conversations and press conferences. Rarely does he go back and complete the story, however. But what followed was a move to Japan – and he took Primorac with him.

It has been a strange career for Wenger, whose upbringing was in many ways unconventional. He was born in Strasbourg in October 1949 to parents Alphonse and Louise Wenger. Strasbourg is the capital and principal city of the Alsace region of eastern France, close to the border with Germany, and is effectively a bridge between the two countries. The family owned a bistro and a car spare parts business. Despite his nationality, he did not speak French fluently until he was about seven. And instead of watching football matches in his homeland, Wenger was taken across the border to games in Germany. He recounts fond memories of crowding round an old black-and-white TV screen to watch matches, falling further in love with the game after the classic 1960 European Cup final when Real Madrid beat Eintracht Frankfurt 7-3.

Early memories of English football were formed when he began watching FA Cup finals. 'It was a dream when I was a kid to watch the FA Cup,' recalls Wenger. 'It was one of the competitions you could watch in black and white on television … What stays in my memory is exactly the place where I sat at school, because we had to pay one franc to watch. What struck me at the time was the ball was white and the pitch was perfect, because I played in a village where the pitch was a disaster. The ball was white and small and the pitch was absolutely immaculate. And the players had their hair well-combed, and the managers were relaxed at that time – they joked together on the bench. That always struck me.'

It is fascinating to think that, even back then, Wenger was looking at the body language and behaviour of the managers.

However, the first team he supported was probably Borussia Monchengladbach, the side he followed on those trips to games in Germany. The excitement was increased by regular chats in the family bistro, which he rather fondly now describes as a pub, showing just how much he has embraced English culture. 'There is no better psychological education than growing up in a pub when you are five or six because you meet all different people and hear how cruel they can be. You hear the way they talk to each other like saying, "You're a liar." And from an early age you get a practical psychological education into the minds of people.'

By his own admission, Wenger was a pretty average professional footballer. A gangly defender, he worked his way up with amateur teams, lower divisions and then reached the pinnacle of his playing career with RC Strasbourg. He did not make his professional debut until he was 29; he made only 13 appearances for them, but did play in the UEFA Cup, and made two appearances when they won the title in 1979. However, Wenger's playing career is rarely remembered.

Wenger does, however, recall that he always wanted to work in England. 'The first time I came to England was when I was 29 years old; it was during the summer to learn English at Cambridge University, during the football holidays. I didn't want to die without learning English as I felt that I always wanted to have an international life and I thought that it would be impossible without speaking English.'

Even then, he showed a fascination and determination to coach which led to him becoming youth-team manager. From there, he became assistant manager at Cannes, then moved to Nancy where he was relegated and yet still gained admiring glances from Monaco.

Wenger does, however, remember those early days were incredibly stressful – even prompting him to be physically sick after games because of the tension. 'I started at 33 as a manager and sometimes I felt I wouldn't survive. Physically, I was sick.' Those who know him now say that, while he no longer throws up, his moods are just as bleak after defeats.

Relative success in those early days at Monaco turned to bitterness and, at the end of 1994, he joined Grampus Eight in Japan, taking Primorac with him. It was a new challenge intended to re-energise him, and yet initially it proved to be very difficult.

Wenger has an obvious affection for the Japanese people, often engaging them at press conferences, asking them which part of the country they are from. Despite this, Wenger didn't return to Nagoya until the summer of 2014, when Arsenal visited as part of their pre-season tour. There was an emotional reunion with his translator, who'd been on hand in 1995 when the club's owner demanded to see Wenger following his bad start. 'Come on, Boro, pack your bags,' Wenger said to his loyal assistant.

Wenger went in expecting the worst, and came out with a vote of confidence which was rewarded with one of the best spells in the club's history: they won two cups, were runners-up in the J League, and the Frenchman was voted Manager of the Year.

Wenger has very fond memories of his time in Japan – especially as the drastic change seemed to take his mind away from the match-fixing scandal that had severely damaged French football and Wenger's faith in the game in France. He comments:

> I had already coached for ten years in a top league in France. It was at the stage of my life where it is important, because to be confronted with a completely different culture was something that I think helped me a lot. As well, to be at the start of an experience like Japan was a very good experience because Nagoya was a very young club but a very professional club already at that time.
>
> They were very well organised and for me to experience that people give their best, which they do in Japan every day, was a very positive experience that I brought back to Europe. I could ... be confronted with a completely different culture in my job. That is fantastic. Not many jobs allow you to go to Japan and continue to do your job. That was something that is unique for me.

Japan seemed to reinvigorate Wenger and, in a rather understated way, seemed to help shape the way he is today. His experience there, the adulation of the fans, helped him realise the importance of embracing the culture of the country you are in, thus preparing him for his transformation into an adopted Englishman.

There is no doubt that his early days at Arsenal were a test. Wenger was a world away from what the players were used to. The board also. But the Arsenal hierarchy realised their mistake from a year previously and revisited their attempts to hire him. The similarity of his first name to that of the club must surely be a sign – a bit like the once-a-year punter taking a gamble on a horse's name in the Grand National, surely they could see that Arsene was the man for Arsenal?

But, of course, his name was not known in England, despite his record at Monaco. It's become an urban myth that the London *Evening Standard* carried a headline of 'Arsene Who?' to greet Wenger's arrival. However, according to those still in the *Standard* offices, the reality is that it was actually a street billboard to blame for one of the most fondly remembered parts of the story as Arsenal finally got their man.

The *Evening Standard* ran an amusing piece on 18 September 1996, which, while highlighting how much of an unknown Wenger was when he arrived, was further evidence of just how insular English football was at the time. The article asked: 'How should the name be pronounced – both of them? If you are French, you will probably address him as Ar-senn Won-jair. German? Ar-sehn Ven-ger, perhaps. North Bank regular, plasterer Trevor Hale, struggled slightly: "Arse-in Won-gah, innit mate?"'

Chairman Hill-Wood, for all his Old Etonian bluster, was a high-flying banker. He flew to Japan to talk to Wenger and the deal was done.

I liked Arsene very much from the moment I met him. He was very intelligent and personable and good fun as well, with a fine sense of humour.

Later, we went to see him in Japan and tried to persuade him to leave Grampus Eight a little early. He said he wasn't prepared to do that and I said I wouldn't try to persuade him. What he said was he'd tell Grampus Eight that he'd try to find them a replacement so they might let him go a little early.

That's just what he did and joined us about three or four months later.

I did mention to him that we had some fairly rough diamonds and asked him if he'd have a problem handling them. He said he didn't think he would because he'd had Jurgen Klinsmann and Glenn Hoddle at Monaco and he didn't have any trouble with them, even though they were quite difficult characters.

'Rough diamonds' was perhaps putting it mildly. Wenger inherited a dressing room with a drinking culture, big egos, strong characters and players who had proved difficult to control. In fact, Arsenal probably had some of the most renowned hard drinkers in English football. They were dubbed 'the Tuesday Club' because several of them would meet after training on a Tuesday and go on a drinking binge that could often last until the early hours of Thursday, if they had Wednesday off. New signings would face an initiation process and somehow play on the Saturday. Tony Adams had very recently admitted to being an alcoholic, Paul Merson had previously confessed to drink and drug problems and gone into rehab, and there were countless other examples of drinking incidents that had embarrassed the club.

Former manager George Graham had not eradicated the drinking problem and the players were big, loud and vociferous characters. Although they had respected Graham, some had mocked Rioch, and now they were being asked to embrace an unknown Frenchman.

John Hartson, a centre forward signed by Graham, who, by his own admission, enjoyed the big nights out, says Wenger was remarkable in the way he transformed the players, won the fans over and laid down the law.

It was very different. George was a fantastic manager, a Double-winning player, a successful manager – he won so much for Arsenal. He had the crowd behind him. The players were basically doing what they wanted to do in the afternoons. If they wanted to have a few beers then they could. If they wanted an 'all-dayer' then they could.

Everyone was drinking under George. I thought it was great! On the day that I signed, Merse had just come out of the Priory. I thought I'd missed all of the fun! But people were still at it. Merse was on top of his problems; he'd have a counsellor with him every day. Tony was trying to change his life around. But it was just a party when I first arrived. If you wanted to go out in the afternoon, there was always someone to go out with. It was very much old school.

Wenger got it through to players that that is not the way to live your life, it's not the way if you want to extend your career. If you look at Bouldy, Ray Parlour and, in particular, Tony Adams, they would have been finished and washed up at 32. They trained hard but they partied hard as well. Under Wenger, he wasn't having any of that.

It was both a massive gamble and a remarkable show of faith by the Arsenal board to bring in Wenger; and, furthermore, the appointment seemed to drag on because, having announced him as their new manager, he did not start officially for the best part of two weeks.

Wenger moved into a house in Totteridge, a leafy area of north London, near to the Deins. He recalls his first trip to Highbury, when he travelled by Tube and went unrecognised throughout the journey because so few people – even Arsenal fans – knew who he was or what he looked like.

'You know what? I have taken the Tube once, as Arsenal

manager,' said Wenger. 'When I arrived, Pat Rice told me to go to Potters Bar and take the Tube to go to Highbury. So I took the Tube – at the time nobody knew me. I sat there. It was when I arrived the first week. But it changed quickly.'

In actual fact, there's no Tube station at Potters Bar, but you can get the train and change onto the London Underground further up the line. Cockfosters is like a little village; it has a few cafes where Arsenal's young players hang out, one of the bigger football agency offices is there and many staff live there or thereabouts. It's sleepy, expensive, has big houses and is perfect for the football fraternity.

For most of the players, their first recollection of coming into contact with Wenger was when he watched Arsenal's UEFA Cup tie on Wednesday 25 September with Borussia Monchengladbach from the stands and then promptly came down to the dressing room at half-time to try to make a couple of tactical changes, then sat on the bench for the second half.

As Nigel Winterburn recalled: 'We just didn't know what to expect. My overriding thoughts and memories of it were that everybody was talking about "Arsene who?" – who was he, would he be a good appointment? My first recollection was from that European game. We were told that he was coming to the game but would just watch, wasn't going to be involved. But he came down at half-time and rearranged the team.'

Wenger's intervention didn't work. Arsenal lost to Borussia Monchengladbach and went out of the UEFA Cup 6-4 on aggregate. He will no doubt be thankful that the record books show he didn't take over until a few weeks later. Interestingly, Tony Adams has said on several occasions that he didn't appreciate Wenger coming into the dressing room then, didn't like his tactical changes, and perhaps that explains why Adams was cautious about him when he took over officially.

But Wenger was already working behind the scenes, even before he was free from his Grampus Eight contract to officially take up his job with Arsenal. In came Patrick Vieira, a lanky, leggy, yet tough French midfielder, who was plucked from AC Milan's reserves for next to nothing. Vieira's quality quickly impressed his new team-mates and that, in itself, had a reassuring impact: some of the players realised that Wenger, despite looking like a geography teacher, was extremely knowledgeable.

But the first meeting with the players was the all-important one. That is when lasting impressions are formed. Mess it up and you can be done for.

Arsenal, partly thanks to Wenger's own input, now have a state-of-the-art training ground. But when he first arrived, Arsenal shared their training ground with University College, London.

It was basic to say the least. When you came in from the big car park, there was a canteen in front of you and some changing rooms, but not much else; you'd walk into the main building and the treatment table was immediately to your right. As a young reporter, I'd stand there nervously – given regular access afforded to very few because I worked for the local paper and club programme – waiting for players to come through. It was loud, intimidating and tough. That old-school football atmosphere was hard to crack. Graham ruled it with an iron fist and commanded respect that way. The whole place went quiet when he walked by. It was an unforgiving atmosphere; there was no room for weakness or soft characters, which is why Wenger knew he had to make an immediate impression.

A through-door from the dressing rooms led to the immaculate pitches. Before you reached them, there was a small patch of grass with old, creaky wooden benches, two porcelain sinks surrounded by boot-cleaning brushes – where the youth teamers used to polish the first teamers' boots – and a little bit of raised ground which had, in recent years, been the stage for some of English football's biggest dramas.

It was there that Graham had to tell the players that he had been sacked after the bung scandal. For a man as proud as Graham it was humiliating, and the players were stunned as Graham simply thanked them for their efforts and said goodbye. Both Merson and Adams had chosen that spot to admit to their demons.

But, back on a sunny morning in September 1996, Arsenal's players were about to go out for a training session under the supervision of assistant boss Rice when Wenger, on his first proper day at Colney, announced that he wanted to hold a players' meeting to introduce himself. Wenger went smart casual, studious-looking in his glasses, leather elbow patches on his jacket. Yet he had an assured look on his face: his confidence and self-belief were all-important.

To this day, I've only ever seen Wenger in either a suit or a tracksuit – apart from one time. He turned up in beige chinos, a brown shirt and brown casual shoes. No doubt expensively assembled but he looked straight out of a Next catalogue. Wenger had been caught short. He'd clearly forgotten about a press conference; a press officer had called and reminded him, and he turned up the best part of two hours late. For any journalist who knows Wenger and goes to his press conferences, this is far from unusual. But it wasn't about keeping the press waiting – he'd just forgotten.

Back in 1996, Wenger's outfit did not stand out from the crowd and yet in a football environment it looked unusual as he set about his introductory speech to the Arsenal dressing room. He was strong, clear in his message and impressive. His English by then was excellent, doubtless improved through his friendship with Dein, and yet his accent and nationality still meant the naughty boys at the back were trying to contain the odd giggle as he spoke.

A few started doing Inspector Clouseau impressions under their breath behind their hands.

Wenger spoke about his desire for a 'culture of change' at the club. He told them he wanted to play 'attractive football, to win with style'. He assured them he wanted to take on the good points within the existing squad – the team spirit, togetherness and strength – and build on it to bring success back to Arsenal. Wenger also spelt out to the players that he would look to change training methods, to improve them as players, and he mentioned wanting to work on their diets, too.

His opening address lasted about 15 minutes, and the players who listened that day remember being impressed, as he announced he would tailor training to the individual and everyone would be given a chance. Wenger had something to say and the squad paid attention. He said he would be honest and, if the players trusted him, then he could bring them success.

Some of the players joked that Wenger was more like a teacher than a football manager, and it was clear that not all had been won over as many laughed at the end of his speech, still not sure he had the experience required for the job.

John Hartson was there and says: 'Arsene was and remains different class. He's the full package. He could talk in front of 500 people at the Savoy at a black-tie event. Then do exactly the same for big-ego players. What impressed us was that he'd done his research. It felt like he knew about all of us. At first, we were thinking: "What does this professor-looking guy know about football?" But I tell you something, he had the inside track on every single one of us.'

Midfielder Stephen Hughes recalls that day as well:

All the boys were getting out of their cars in the car park, saying: 'Who's this geezer?' I remember it very clearly, and he used to like to tell you what you would be doing in training that day, whereas George and Bruce would tell us to go and do a warm-up, run round the fields, then come back and we'll do the training. But Wenger would say: 'Right, we're doing this, doing this and then we're doing this.'

I remember us being nervous about it because no one was sure where we were going to go, what we were going to do as a club. I remember thinking his English was very good. He had all these eyes on him; he'd never admit it, but I think he was a touch nervous, too. I sat there thinking: 'His English is incredible. This geezer is incredible.'

Within a week, almost all had been converted – largely because of his training methods. They could see and feel a difference quite quickly.

Wenger's first training session was so different to what the players had been used to under Graham and Rioch – who were all about set pieces followed by small-sided games to finish off with – that many remember it vividly. 'What on earth is going on here?' they thought, as out came 30 mats which were placed on the floor. They had been used to standing stretches, touching your toes to stretch hamstrings and pulling up your leg to stretch thighs. Now, suddenly, Wenger wanted all of the players to lie flat on their backs, then bring up their knees and swivel their legs to do hip flexes.

Wenger also introduced plyometrics: sticks were placed across two cones and the players had to jump over; they did step-ups on to benches, lunges, ran in and out of poles. He really wanted to make the players move, increase their speed and power. Training was radically different; it was short, sharp, precise and always to the second, governed by Wenger – with a stopwatch around his neck. He would often stand over players, and if they weren't doing the stretches right, then he would get them to do it again.

One of the biggest characters in that dressing room was Ray Parlour, who recalls those early days and the difference that Wenger made on the group.

We didn't have a clue who he was. We were asking: 'Can he be successful here?' It was a bit of a gamble. We trusted David Dein because he loved the club, wanted the best for the club and went to every youth-team game, reserves, everything. It was David Dein who said: 'This guy will take us forward.'

His focus was the thing that struck me straightaway. He always looked to me as if he was very excited to work in the English league. He'd worked in France, Japan, but the English league was different for him and he was excited about challenging the likes of Manchester United. He knew he had a strong back four with David Seaman and a few others. Great players elsewhere, with Dennis Bergkamp who was there already.

From day one, he certainly had that focus and on the training pitch he was fantastic. We took balls out. Straightaway, it was about getting the ball on the floor, pass and move. No disrespect to other managers, but we probably as English players didn't work on that enough. It was an eye-opener for us as to how we needed to go forward in the future … He gave everyone a chance. Arsene stood there with his stopwatch and observed. That stopwatch changed everything – it made it interesting. He looked at everything you were doing …

He definitely developed my game so much. He gave me so much belief. Technically, I did lots more training with him. The training was so enjoyable that we'd stay behind and practise. Everything was just right. Everybody was at a good age. We wanted to improve for different reasons as quickly as possible. Suddenly, we had the platform to do that.

The foreign players he brought in were fantastic, like Vieira and Overmars. They were world class and made you a better player, there's no doubt. We loved the training. We'd have a practice even before he came out. He knew that. The sessions that he put on were amazing. The freedom he gave us was incredible. He'd want us to express ourselves; he wouldn't want us to complicate it. He'd say: 'Look, you all know your jobs, we've worked hard in training, let's go out and play.'

Veteran left back Nigel Winterburn, part of Arsenal's famous back four, was even more glowing about the complete sea change in training methods.

Within the first week, I loved the training sessions. They were short, sharp and intense. For example, in pre-season, we'd been used to lots of running, a hard slog, but he'd introduce a ball. He'd put you into your position, then he'd get you running up and down the line but then deliver the ball into the centre forward. He'd get you to do that five or six times and then recover. You'd then rest while the right back goes. Then he'd work with the midfield. Then you'd go again.

Yes, we'd run without the ball, but even that was on a stopwatch. What he'd do with the older players, the likes of Steve Bould, Lee Dixon, he'd give them an extra second on the run. Two or three seconds longer for recovery. It was fascinating to be a part of it. We'd get our base fitness. The younger guys, like Ray Parlour and so on, would work harder and get less time. Then we'd do the plyometrics part of the training – jumping through hoops, jumping over the hurdles. I'd never done this stuff before.

In pre-season back then, it was for hard running and hard work. Double sessions most days and running. But with Arsene, it was a light jog and a walk! We went in for lunch and thought: 'It's got to be harder this afternoon!' But we got out there and balls were out on the pitch. We'd do technical stuff and it was about easing us back into training after six weeks off. It was a completely different approach.

It was impossible, I believe, to be unimpressed with his training methods, the intensity of the training, how meticulous everything was in terms of the training. From my point of view, I bought into it straightaway with Arsene because I just loved the training, the movement of the football, the keeping of the football. He wanted to get everybody moving, everybody moving together, options with the ball, it was intense in training.

I have to admit that I wasn't always the best trainer early on. But Arsene came in, I was a bit older, there were a few rumours about him wanting to get rid of the back four and my mentality changed towards training; the intensity suited me. It was short, it was sharp . . . With the results that we started to get with the style of football, I think most players really, really enjoyed it. To be quite honest, I can't see a way that you wouldn't enjoy it.

Stephen Hughes said: 'What stuck out at first was that he would send us out on the pitch with a ball each, and Dicko [Lee Dixon] was saying: "What's all this about?" We were all going across the pitches, doing Cruyff turns, and I remember Tony Adams going: "I haven't done a Cruyff turn for three years!" Even Boro [Primorac] was doing Cruyff turns and we were giggling like schoolboys.'

Wenger also introduced mannequins in training. He would lay

them out in a formation, a 4-4-2 for example, then get the players to play around them. Often it would be a midfielder, full back, winger and centre forward who would be asked to do drills. They'd pass the ball in the middle, lay it out wide, back inside and out wide before the winger would hit a cross for the striker. It may sound an odd exercise, but it was done over and over again as Wenger tried to paint pictures in the players' minds. Next time they were in a similar situation in a match, they'd 'switch' the play, knowing where a team-mate would be.

Wenger felt the team he inherited was too regimented. He wanted the players to play with freedom but, at the same time, also to have potential moves in their minds. He sought to improve them technically, with fewer straight lines and more movement, and he believed the mannequins helped that.

He also wanted to get the players dribbling better, swerving and keeping the ball under closer control. Passing drills, players working in small triangles, passing the ball into areas where players were supposed to run into – these exercises were intended not only to improve them technically but also to increase their speed of thought. The players were meant to be on the move more physically and mentally. Gone were the days of hitting the ball long and into channels; Wenger worked in training more on ball retention and passing. The full backs, in particular, became instrumental in sessions, always making themselves available to receive the ball from the goalkeeper, who was urged to roll or kick it short rather than take a long punt forward.

In another drill, the players would form a circle with one player in the middle. The ball was fired in to him, he'd have to control it and pass it on. It was all done at top speed; the manager would be watching and the players really felt under pressure, but it certainly improved their touch and their technical ability.

Wenger would work with individual players as well. While Pat

Rice and Boro Primorac took over the training, the manager would be very hands-on. For example, one session saw two wingers put over crosses for centre forward John Hartson to work on his finishing. All the time, Wenger was standing next to Hartson, telling him how to work and improve on his movement to lose a defender or to get ready for the cross.

Despite the improvements he made, the joke among the players was that Wenger was 'pretty rubbish' as a player from the few odd occasions he joined in or tried to have a kick about while waiting for training to start. And it would be wrong to say that the players didn't question some of Wenger's methods. Back in those early days, Tony Adams – nicknamed Rodders after the *Only Fools and Horses* character – even went to see Wenger to complain that they were not doing enough in training to get them fully fit.

Hughes recalls how Wenger responded: 'We'd always end up finishing with a game of eight versus eights. He was the first manager to really talk about short and sharp sessions ... But he'd tell us: "Don't worry. We'll get stronger for the second half of the season."'

The other big change was in the players' diet. Wenger banned tomato ketchup and Ian Wright complained there was broccoli with everything. The quick transformation into a healthy, bland and very regimented diet came as a culture shock for some of the players, as Nigel Winterburn recalled:

Rehydration was so different: Drinking water. We got a new chef in. It was fish, grilled, boiled chicken and all the spices were taken out. Until 6.30 p.m. after games, the players' lounge was alcohol free. That was very important to him – refuelling straight after games. I loved a bit of chocolate, but Arsene would look to control everything. He'd like to travel on the train. He'd look down the carriage and see what you were doing. You'd have to be sure before having a cup of tea. 'OK, you can have a cup of tea – but no sugar.'

When we were waiting on the platform for a train and he wasn't looking we'd pile into the kiosk and get bags of crisps. I'm sure he knew exactly what was going on but we were performing for him.

John Hartson also remembers the new dietary regime: 'He changed all the methods. I didn't know much about the diet side of things. I'd come from Luton [where] there were old-school players ... who never really looked after their diets. Their diet was a gammon steak, egg and chips plus a pint of squash. But after I went to Arsenal, Arsene Wenger changed all that. We ate together; we all had to finish before we could leave the table. It was all chicken and rice. Pasta on a Friday night. There was steaks, fish, really good food and we were really spoilt.'

Of course, there had to be trust when it came to the players eating at home or even on away trips, and Wenger quickly had to introduce new rules after some players tested his patience. He banned room service on away trips and even ordered hotels to inform him if a player tried it on. Stephen Hughes recalls those early days and Wenger's new rules.

We were all gutted about the ketchup going. We were all trying to sneak it in. Big Johnny Hartson was a great lad. We'd have dinner, be away from home, and we'd knock on his door and he'd be having a pint of Coke, a club sandwich, and two hours later he'd leave all the plates outside of his room!

That didn't last long. I remember how he policed it – he pulled us all together and told us to stop room service and then stopped the hotel from giving us any extras. He'd tell the hotel to tell him and he'd pull whoever and say: 'Why did you try to order room service and a pint of Fanta?'

Wenger banned carbonated water at the training ground, because he claimed the fizz in the water restricted oxygen flow, as well as milk and sugar in tea and coffee, saying it was a 'disgusting English habit'. He relented slightly on that rule in later years, but told the players they must make sure the sugar in their hot drinks was distributed evenly.

While being interviewed at the training ground a few years after Wenger took charge, Sol Campbell sat down with a cup of coffee, glanced around to see if anyone was looking and then put some sugar on his spoon. He took remarkable care when putting sugar in his coffee; putting sugar on his spoon, he then put the spoon in the coffee and moved it from left to right until the sugar had dissolved evenly.

Campbell explained that Wenger had said: 'If you must have sugar in your tea or coffee you have to distribute the granules evenly in your coffee so it's absorbed evenly.' According to Wenger, that ensures it's also absorbed in an even flow in the body's system, and thus keeps energy levels stable rather than giving a sugar rush.

Diet is so clearly important to Wenger and is something he learned in Japan. Even now, he makes a point of following the players' diets. 'I think in England you eat too much sugar and meat and not enough vegetables. I lived for two years in Japan and it was the best diet I ever had. The whole way of life there is linked to health. Their diet is basically boiled vegetables, fish and rice. No fat, no sugar. You notice when you live there that there are no fat people. What's really dreadful is the diet in Britain. The whole day you drink tea with milk and coffee with milk and cakes. If you had a fantasy world of what you shouldn't eat in sport, it's what you eat here.'

Within the first couple of weeks, a nutritionist came to the training ground, gave a speech to the players and handed out leaflets on what to eat and what not to eat. Communication was a big thing for Wenger. Those early days were crucial for him to get – and keep – the big characters onside. Wenger could often be seen walking around the fields of the training ground with Tony Adams or Paul Merson, two players who needed a lot of support at the time, and Wenger's 'long walks' with them were a regular routine early on.

A further big change was the pre-match routine for home games. During the George Graham era, the players would gather at the South Herts Golf Club in Totteridge, north London, have a team meeting and then drive in convoy to Highbury. Under Bruce Rioch, the players would actually eat at home – most having beans or omelettes for breakfast – and then drive themselves to the ground and meet there.

Now Wenger insisted on them meeting beforehand (at first at the training ground and later it became a hotel, where they would stay the night before a match, even a home game) and eating a very strict diet up to five hours before kick-off. It would consist of mashed potato, vegetables and boiled chicken. Sometimes, the players would be desperately trying to force down a full meal at 10 a.m.

Under Rioch, the only pick-me-ups were jelly babies left in the dressing room. That also changed under Wenger. The players were put on the supplement creatine, which is supposed to boost energy and muscle strength. It is a legal supplement even if it has caused controversy down the years. Arsenal eventually stopped using it because it gave too many players upset stomachs. On top of that came energy-boosting supplements that looked like sugar cubes. The players used to joke that the physio, Gary Lewin, had become the dealer and that they were all on drugs. Players knew if they were in the first-team squad, because they were the ones to receive the supplements. Winterburn recalls:

The supplements that were there were never forced on anybody, so you didn't have to take them. I didn't take any of them, I have to admit. Everything was laid out in front of you; you were given a brief description of what they were for. But I had a set way and, with my stomach, I didn't eat lots before games anyway.

[The new diet] didn't really change, if I'm quite honest, my outlook or my perception of whether it helped me a lot. I went along with it because that's what you do if you're playing for a team. If the food is put there to be eaten then you go along with it. I didn't like cooked food at lunchtime. Sometimes when Arsene wasn't around I had a sandwich. I had to make sure he wasn't looking and I hope the chef didn't notice or I'd get into trouble!

The supplements you either take or you don't. A lot of the guys took it. You just got on with it. But as I've said before, that's the ingredients that are put there to try and help you. But the most important thing is what you produce in ninety minutes of football. In my opinion, it doesn't matter if someone is eating a hamburger, because if they're producing for you every single week then so be it. They can eat what they want, as far as I'm concerned.

Stephen Hughes added:

A few of the guys got into [taking supplements], gave it a go. I was always with Martin Keown and I remember him saying: 'Hughesy, I've got to be careful – I don't want to be too strong.'

He'd take it and after three minutes he'd be saying: 'I'm feeling better already.' Some of it, I'm sure, was psychological.

I remember putting on a bit of weight because of it and the boss saying: 'Hughesy, are you eating takeaways?' I said: 'No, I think it might be that creatine.' He said: 'Are you taking that? You come off it.' He watched whoever took it, studied it all; some of the guys liked it.

You could definitely see a difference in the players. Everyone was fitter, sharper and crisper. Not only would Lewin come round with little tubs of creatine, but he was also responsible for booking massages, which also became a key feature of Wenger's new philosophy. Suddenly, old-school players wanted daily massages. Lewin would have to warn off players as massages became more and more popular. 'Well, you might have to wait an hour, there's a big queue.'

Parlour recalled the rapid changes in match-day routine and diet at the training ground: 'There was no sugar at the training ground, only water with lunch. You'd have a three-course meal at 11.30 a.m.; you'd feel a bit hungry before the game. If you had sugar before the game, your level would go up and down and that's something he'd try to avoid. But at half-time, he'd come round with sugar cubes. Then water again at half-time. There was a little livener on the sugar cube – I don't know what it was!'

Hartson highlights the revolutionary impact all of these changes had on English football at the time: 'He changed it with diet, the way he treated and spoke to the players. He made us stretch before games, after games, after and before every training session. English football has so much to thank him for, he really did change the face of so many things – training, preparation and the way the game was played. It was incredible.'

Players embrace change a lot easier when you can see results on the pitch. But Wenger recalls those difficult early days with amusement. He felt everything was against him – there was scepticism among the players, fans and the media – and, rather like most managers, he enjoyed proving people wrong. 'People were asking who I was. I was a complete unknown. And there was no history of a foreign manager succeeding in England. So I was in a situation where no one knew me and history was against me.

'There were some amusing details. I changed a few habits [of the players], which isn't easy in a team where the average age is thirty years. At the first match the players were chanting, "We want our Mars bars back!" So there were some fun things. At half-time in the first game I asked my phsyio Gary Lewin: "Nobody is talking, what's wrong with them?", and he replied: "They're hungry." I hadn't given them their chocolate before the game. It was funny.'

Wenger's first game in charge was at Blackburn Rovers and the squad stayed in a hotel near Ewood Park. He sent round a message to all the players to assemble in the hotel's ballroom, but it still came as a shock to them when he tried to introduce some yoga, basic pilates moves and stretches. This was 1996 and, for at least another five years, it was still deemed a story in the newspapers if a player was brave enough to admit using yoga to help their movement. It received a mixed response from the players: David Platt, in particular, hated it while Steve Bould credits the stretching with prolonging his playing career by another two years.

Winterburn remembers that first stretching session in the ballroom at Blackburn.

He did it wherever he could. Wherever there was a spare room, we just went in. It didn't matter what sort of room it was. Sometimes it was a massively open place, sometimes quite cramped, and you'd not have a lot of room to manoeuvre. He didn't mind where it was, it was just part of the warm-up ritual that he'd like to do. We would do it every single game without fail.

We used to get up on a match day, go for a walk. We used to go into a room, do the different sorts of stretches, do some pilates-style stretches, legs up the wall and so on. I think the idea was to stretch the body back out again ... I didn't see any reason why that wouldn't help me and the rest of the team, so you go along and you do that ... I'm assuming they probably still do it. The morning of the game, there was a set time to meet; we would meet, walk – a quick walk just for ten or fifteen minutes – go back into a room, do these stretches and then have our pre-match meal. That was pretty much the same routine during the time I was there.

Hughes recalls how the English players in particular struggled to take it seriously at first: 'The stretching was the weirdest thing in the world. When we all first walked in, it was legs up on the wall. All the English lads were farting and burping and the gaffer didn't like all that. He saw it as a time to get your mind right; it took a while ... and then it became sort of normal.'

Wenger also wanted to bring in stretches at 8 a.m. on the morning of an evening game. It took Tony Adams, the club captain and unofficial shop steward, to lead a protest and it was then altered to a pre-match walk on the morning of the game.

That first game was at Blackburn on 12 October 1996. Arsenal didn't play particularly well. In fact, Ian Wright scored early on, but Blackburn went on to be the better team and were unlucky to still be behind at half time. The Arsenal players went into the dressing room, expecting the worst. They feared Wenger would immediately tear into them. The opposite happened.

According to one of the players in the dressing room, it was a full eight minutes before Wenger spoke. Even Rice, by all accounts, found Wenger's silence unnerving, but it had a calming effect. Arsenal went out for the second half, Wright got another goal shortly after the restart and Arsenal won the game 2-0. The Wenger legend, the Wenger effect and the Wenger story had begun.

Hartson, who played in that first game, recalls:

It's funny because he never really got involved that much. He was on the team bus, he sat in the crowd; it felt like he popped his head into the dressing room more than giving a big team talk.

It was a great day for me – I absolutely smashed Henning Berg all over the pitch! I remember winning a header for the first, Wrighty scored both goals. I think I made the first one ... I was aggressive. I was 21 years of age and he probably thought I was fiery, red-haired, a bit raw, and I think he quite liked that. Throughout his career, he's always enjoyed playing with a big man up front.

He came in after the game. He told us it was a great performance and that he was looking forward to working with us all. Then he really went to work with us on the training ground from the following Monday. I really enjoyed that first game and the training.

Still today, Wenger often says nothing even after the heaviest or most demoralising of defeats. He would rather sit back, digest, collect his thoughts, and then have a debrief at the training ground. Dressing-room etiquette is something that Wenger clearly thinks deeply about and, in particular, a manager's conduct, his behaviour towards the players, how best to motivate or lift them.

'I have been aggressive at half-time, yes, but you have to adapt to the culture of your team,' said Wenger. 'When you go to Japan, you have to be cautious, because what looks normal in an English dressing room suddenly looks completely shocking in a Japanese dressing room.'

There have been countless stories of dressing-room bust-ups over the years, when a manager has let rip. Probably the most famous incident of all was when Sir Alex Ferguson kicked a boot in anger and it hit David Beckham on the head, requiring stitches. You could never imagine that from Wenger, no matter how angry he was.

Wenger did adapt to a different culture in England and, slowly, the dressing room adapted to him as well as recognising the change in the way the manager treated them. He preserved some traditions – allowing the players to keep their music blaring out in the dressing room before games when everything else concerning the inner sanctum was about calmness and serenity – and modified other routines.

Wenger's lack of rollickings can even unnerve players. Real dressing-room shouting matches can probably be counted on the fingers of one hand. That is how Wenger is: in the main, calm and collected. It's his way, his method and his philosophy. He has lost his temper in press conferences, but not often. He's lost it with staff in front of the media on occasion – mostly after a defeat away from home in Europe when he's rushing to get away from the stadium and on to the bus to catch the plane home. He gets most uptight and stressed about travel arrangements, and has even been known to chase Paul Johnson, the club's long-serving employee now in charge of first-team travel, off a team bus to try to sort out a roadblock that was obstructing Arsenal's route to the train station to get home. Wenger could be seen banging the desk in anger while Johnson desperately tried – and eventually succeeded – to clear a traffic jam on a bridge. Wenger's early days at Arsenal certainly proved he was very different as a manager.

His style, ideas and methods – so different from anything that had gone before – were ushering in a new era. Arsenal's philosophy was being revolutionised in training, on the pitch and in the dressing room.

CHAPTER 2

FRENCH REVOLUTION

'I THOUGHT AT FIRST: "What does this Frenchman know about football?" He wears glasses, does he even speak English?' These were the cutting words of Tony Adams, Arsenal's legendary captain. He was highly sceptical of Arsene Wenger when he first took over. Adams was a brilliant but very English centre half, set in his ways, loud and strong-willed. He was also seen as the shop steward of the dressing room. Adams had often been sent in to see the manager to try to renegotiate contracts for the squad during the George Graham years.

Graham was perceived as being notoriously tight on contracts during his reign, to such a point that Martin Keown, who grew up at Highbury, left for Aston Villa in 1986 in a dispute over £50 a week. Arsenal ended up having to buy him back, via Everton, in 1993 for £2 million. It made no economic sense but that was typical of Graham: he'd haggle over every penny.

The joke among the players was that Adams would go in to see Graham, promising to stand firm and to get them all pay rises. Then he'd emerge from the manager's office soon after with a healthy rise for himself but not as much for everyone else. While much of it was just dressing-room banter, there was a genuine feeling at the club that the players were hard done by and were not being paid the going rate. Adams tried and failed to convince Graham to give the squad better contracts.

So, the first and perhaps best thing that Wenger did to get the players onside was to improve their contracts immediately. In fact, some members of Arsenal's famous back four even had their pay doubled overnight. Wenger was genuinely shocked at the pay level some of the mainstays of his team were on. He went through the contracts and straightaway insisted to David Dein, the club's vice-chairman who had brought him to Highbury, that the players' pay must be brought up to speed.

Just imagine how the squad must have reacted. One day they're feeling hard done by, under-appreciated despite winning trophies for the club, and the next the new manager has changed it all. If there was one quick and easy way to get the players onside then Wenger had found it. In fact, in the feel-good mood about the place, some players got better deals than they could ever have hoped for. Dennis Bergkamp and Tony Adams were called in to be given new deals after everyone else had been sorted out. When word got round that the two top earners – and arguably the most important players – at the club had been given new pay rises, a delegation of players went back to see Wenger to ask for another rise as they were already well behind their team-mates. Nigel Winterburn recalls:

I think the contracts changed very quickly. To be fair, they changed radically under Bruce Rioch. Bruce was only there for a year so you don't know if that progression is going to continue. But, under Arsene, he assessed very, very quickly that the wages weren't good enough for what he was trying to achieve for the team. They changed very, very quickly. It's always the same. You never really know but I was always under the impression that there was an A, B and C level for the players. He tried to keep a realistic gap between the three.

The older players – myself, Lee Dixon and Steve Bould – used to get one-year contracts. We'd negotiated with him that he would tell us in February [if our contract would be renewed]. We had great belief that, with the team we had, we would still be playing in the team, and come February if we were challenging for a title or going for a cup then he'd be unlikely to tell you at that stage of the season they weren't going to give you a new contract ...

He was a man of his word. I remember one year, we'd gone in and he'd given us all new contracts, because he said he wanted to bring us up closer to the top players like Tony Adams, Patrick Vieira, Dennis Bergkamp ... Then Tony came in a week later and said: 'I've signed a new contract.' Bouldy, myself and Lee said that put us back where we were last week.

I said to the other lads: 'Shall I go and see him?' I went in and said: 'I'm obviously happy with the new contract, but you've just put all the other players' contracts up so we're back where we were.' He then said to leave it with him. I went back out to Lee and Bouldy and told them that I thought I'd been fobbed off there. But a couple of days later, he came back and said that they'd have to ratify it with the league but promised to give us exactly the same amount of rise that he'd given us the previous week at the end of the season. But he said he'd have to give us it as a lump sum.

It was absolutely incredible. I've never known anything like it. I would trust him because he's a man of his word. We had nothing written down on a piece of paper, we had our official contracts from the week before but then, come May or June, in one of those pay packets we got the extra money which was attached with a signed form which was ratified by the league. That was absolutely amazing. He's a man of his word, that's for sure. I think that's how and why he kept the unity within the team and among the players.

Despite the perception that Wenger is cautious when it comes to transfers, he always endeavours to look after and reward players because he recognises that if he looks after the players financially they would look after him. Former Arsenal striker John Hartson said: 'He gave the players great contracts, gave them new deals, gave them extensions, more money, and they did the business for him. They won him titles. They were loyal to him and they repaid his faith. He is very loyal to players. Players respond to that. He wants to reward them. It's a real big part of his philosophy.'

Wenger compares his philosophy to a 'socialist model', which provoked laughter from several reporters when he said it in a press conference. Millionaire footballers are hardly associated with socialist principles. But the point is that Wenger tried to keep every player within a similar pay bracket, so as to avoid resentment in the dressing room. If one player in a team were paid ten times more than a team-mate, that, Wenger argued, would create tension and destroy dressing-room spirit.

'We pay well. We pay very well,' Wenger said. 'I've spent all my life making sure people who work for us are paid well and I believe if you can do it, you do it. [We should look] to pay something that makes sense and is defendable in front of every single player. We make exceptions sometimes but they are not maybe so high. If you want to keep making profit you have to respect that.

I don't know how it works at other [clubs]. But it's not only me; it's in co-operation with the board. When we want to go "far", I ask for the authorisation of the board. But we have a more socialist model.'

Wenger has a love of politics, but claims that neither communism nor capitalism works in society, let alone football. But he justifies paying high salaries because 'exceptional talent' should be rewarded. Maybe he squares this off with his own salary, which has always been among the best in the Premier League.

'Politically, I am for efficiency. Economically first. Until the 1980s the world was divided into two – people were either communist or capitalist. The communist model does not work economically, we all realised that, but the capitalist model in the modern world also looks to be unsustainable. You cannot ignore individual interests, but I believe the world evolves slowly. The last 30 years have brought a minimum amount of money for everybody in the West; the next step, politically, would be a maximum amount of money earned by everybody.'

Winterburn appreciated how he was treated but also believes that Wenger's loyalty to the players and keeping his promises can sometimes end up undermining the overall strength of the squad:

When I left in 2000, I had been offered a new deal. I spoke with David Dein in his office with Arsene. When Arsene left me out of the team in the December of the previous season, he said to me after a couple of weeks: 'I know you're unhappy, you've played your career playing every week, but I want you to be part of the squad.' But I got to the end of that season and decided my performance was dropping a little and it was a case of leave or retire, really.

I thought I might get another year, but I felt if I was playing only once every four or five weeks then that wouldn't be good for me. I wanted to push myself to my limit so I told him I wanted to leave and I had a discussion with David Dein. David actually offered me a new contract which was for more money than I was on. But I told David it wasn't about money, I just wanted to play football and when I left the meeting, Arsene Wenger put his arm around me and said: 'Don't worry, I'll make sure it happens for you.'

I know he's done that with not just me, but with Ray Parlour who he helped in his move to Middlesbrough, and it was almost the same with the Thomas Vermaelen move [in the summer of 2014] and he's been criticised for that. If you don't let players go then you can kill their careers, and some players need to play regularly whereas others can come in and out of the team, and Vermaelen is a player who needed to play regularly. With injuries and not playing regularly, he wasn't performing anywhere near to the level of performance when he first came.

[Wenger] did leave himself short but he's a man of his word and if he tells you that you can go, usually he lets you go ... He gets pelters for that at times, when people say he's left himself short. But I also think he feels he owes players because they've played for the club, given their all for him and been loyal to him as well.

Former Arsenal midfielder Stephen Hughes explains just how well Wenger tries to look after his players:

He has a special bond with players. If a player comes over from Spain, he really looks out for them. I think he thinks: 'He's moved, brought his family over and has given everything for the club.' It means he's really loyal to the players. You'd do well to find anyone who really doesn't like him. Even if you're not play-ing, you still fully respect him. You can always ring him, he's a lovely man. He's as good as gold.

I haven't spoken to him for a little while, but if I needed some help or advice and I rang him then I'm sure he'd be abso-lutely fine. As long as it wasn't a ridiculous thing then he would help you. He is that kind of guy. He'd know that players would give everything. I've got a lot of time for him and he doesn't forget. Some people do; you walk out of the door and you're forgotten. But he's never like that.

It was not just contracts that tested Wenger early on. Two signifi-cant things happened. First, the training ground building at London Colney burned down. Wenger didn't know whether to laugh or cry. He hated the outdated facilities there and demanded a better training ground be built elsewhere. The second was the emergence of horrendous and completely false rumours about his private life, which are still used in nasty terrace songs to this day. Wenger, anxious to show he was in charge, addressed both issues head-on.

The Colney training ground had been rented from University College London, and if players hung around long enough they would run into students in the afternoons. Legend has it that a youth-team player ended up burning the training ground building down after a mishap with a tumble drier, which exploded and caused a fire.

Wenger pushed hard to get a new state-of-the-art training ground built in its place. In fact, he made it a point of principle: 'Without an assurance of that freedom and control, I would not have stayed,' he later said. It was built at a cost of £12 million and paid for out of the funds raised by Nicolas Anelka's sale to Real Madrid.

Wenger, naturally, took a personal interest in the development, even choosing the cutlery in the canteen and the chairs. There are no locks on locker doors, as Wenger believes it will stop communication among players because the doors will stop them seeing each other and conversation. Shoe covers must be worn at all times, while the building was designed to ensure there is always natural light. Displaying his customary eye for detail, Wenger insisted on ordering custom-made benches for the training ground dressing rooms, so that they would be the right height for short and tall players.

The training facility was an important matter for Wenger, and the first team spent nearly two years being shuttled by coach between the training pitches at London Colney and the nearby Sopwell House hotel. At the hotel they would change, eat and be very well looked after. John Hartson recalls: 'After we went to Sopwell House, it was like going to a health spa every day. Massages, a rest down area, spa – it was so spot-on.'

By contrast, the youths and reserves would change in Portakabins in the car park at the training ground and feel very isolated from the first team. It created resentment, which was vexing for Wenger, especially when training times were changed and the youths, reserves and first teamers went weeks without seeing each other. The training ground remains Wenger's base. His office is there; he gets in early, leaves late, and that is where negotiations and meetings take place and transfers are done.

The second early test of Wenger's reign was the disgusting and false rumours about Wenger's private life. They began to circulate – driven by gossip in the City of London – and gathered so much momentum that radio and TV stations were alluding to them and the press camped out on the steps at Highbury. It came to a head on the day that Arsenal were playing a reserve game, when it would have been easy for Wenger to hide away and not address the issue.

He had flown back to London that day from France and was in a taxi on his way across town from the airport to Highbury. When the taxi stopped outside Highbury, Wenger, oblivious to the gathering storm, remembered the driver giving him a strange look. He stepped out of the taxi and was immediately confronted with radio, TV and newspaper reporters anxious to talk to him about the rumours. Still completely in the dark about what was going on, Wenger was incredibly courteous and, apologising, said he'd be back once he'd dropped his baggage off in his office.

On his way there, Arsenal's newly appointed press officer Clare Tomlinson, who had just joined from the Football Association, saw him and intercepted him. Hers was the unenviable task of telling him why the reporters were there and what he was being accused of. Tomlinson, who went on to work for Sky, recalls that awful day:

I was sitting on the floor of my office – I'd just started and they still hadn't delivered the furniture – and I saw him go past ... So I ran into his office and shut the door. I really can't tell you what I said; I've blanked it out of my head. His English was brilliant, but I had no idea if he knew what the word paedophile meant. Then what do you say? How on earth do you put it?

All I remember is his reaction. I remember him going very still, very white. He was so furious. It wasn't like a Fergie red mist – he went white cold, just disgust, and I often wonder how close he was to just going outside, getting in a taxi and going back to Heathrow and giving up. To accuse a man of rape is bad enough but to accuse a man of raping children is absolutely disgraceful.

I found myself almost barricading the door. I told him I needed to talk to him about the legalities and said: 'Arsene, there are cameras out there – what you do now will last forever because it will be on tape. Nobody believes this; you have to handle it but you will be on record.'

I'm not a lawyer but I've got vague ideas of what slander is. I told him to get them to say it. 'If they say: "What do you make of the allegations?" make them say it, make them say it in front of witnesses. That's the only way.' This man's world has just fallen in. He stood and he listened, took it all in and I can't tell you the amount of admiration I have for him. My whole life with him is based on that day, the way he handled it – he was amazing. He handled it so well, didn't lose his cool …

After he'd finished talking to them, Wenger said: 'Well, if you haven't got anything more to ask me then I will go inside and watch a reserve match.' Tomlinson remembers apologising for her country, but also recalls what happened the next day:

I was back at the FA and, of course, the papers had run something which would have gone past all their lawyers in terms of what they could get away with in terms of libel. I remember he phoned me at the FA the next day – which is very unusual for him because I worked for him for two years and I can count the number of times he phoned me on two hands – and he was so angry. He was saying: 'I've spoken to the lawyers, the board and you seem to be the only one who is taking this seriously. Why can't I sue? Why are all these papers printing this? In France it is completely different. Why can they print all this?' He was just so crestfallen …

He was getting calls from friends in Japan, Germany, from France, and they were all asking: 'What's going on?' The story had travelled around the world. Everything that he had worked for was reduced to such a horrible, scurrilous and baseless accusation. It was disgusting and he was disgusted. But the way he handled it was a mark of how he handled everything afterwards. He was remarkable.

That day, Wenger adopted a very deliberate policy of putting himself in the public eye. He sat in the directors' box and all of the press cameras were trained on him rather than the game. The reserve players all went into the game aware of the unfolding scandal. They didn't want to believe it, but some had heard the story on the radio coming into the game and struggled to comprehend what was going on. But Wenger's decision to take to the steps at Highbury and confront the issue head-on highlighted his strength of character and showed that he never backs down from any situation.

To this day, Wenger has never spoken about it to the players. He remains appalled by the chants of opposing fans – which, sadly, are still heard on the terraces – as police, stewards and the authorities seem reluctant or unable to punish the offenders. Even Sir Alex Ferguson made a personal appeal to Manchester United fans, asking them not to sing it at games.

Football writer Henry Winter recalls of that day: 'Arsene was absolutely brilliant in the way he handled it. He was fuming and was saying that they don't have that intrusion in France. The way they are in France, certainly until the last couple of years, private life is private life. Arsene was shocked by the intrusion into his private life and the scurrilous rumours that came out. But he called it on with the journalists and brought out Clare Tomlinson, his press officer at the time, to stand by him. It was a strong image of Wenger with this glamorous woman by his side.'

Those vile chants based on false and malicious rumours are perhaps the thing Wenger likes least about English football. He loves the atmosphere at grounds, the crowds and the passion. But those taunts haven't gone away and you'd have to be very thick-skinned to be able to shut them out completely, no matter how many years have now gone by.

It was undoubtedly a distraction and an annoyance, but it didn't stop Wenger from carrying on with his Arsenal revolution. Having taken over in October, Wenger led Arsenal to third place at the end of the 1996/97 season. So his first pre-season was in the summer of 1997 and that was a startling insight into some of the old-school traditions at Arsenal. It was in pre-season when many of the Arsenal players had enjoyed their big drinking sessions. It was an approach that was alien to the foreign players and something Wenger clamped down on.

Arsenal switched from Scandinavia, where previous tours had taken place, to a spa town in Austria called Bad Waltersdorf. It was a tiny place with two small hotels and a village football pitch, but the thin air and high altitude made it ideal. Typically, Wenger knew all about it and began taking his players there each summer.

It also signalled the end of the big drinking nights that had astounded Dennis Bergkamp.

It was something I just couldn't understand. Pre-season, we went to a training camp in Sweden and trained twice a day. In the evening I went for a walk with my wife and saw all the Arsenal players sitting outside a pub. I thought it was unbeliev-able. The funny thing is you never noticed it in training because they were so strong and they always gave 100 per cent. I didn't drink, and they respected me. They did, and I thought: 'It's part of England, so you've got to respect that.'

The next year, Arsene came and it all changed. Later, we were successful because of our English defenders. They put the spirit in the team, which the Europeans lacked. They would say,

'Get stuck in!' and all sorts of other phrases. I loved it, especially: 'How much do you want it?' I thought about it. It stuck
with me. Do you really want it more than the opponent? How
much are you prepared to give? How much time do you want to
put in to become better? It's the English warrior tradition; a
moral code. We go out together and we're going to give 100 per
cent.

Changing the drinking culture was perhaps the biggest element
of Wenger's French revolution. The infamous Tuesday Club was
indicative of the hard drinking that was rife before. A contributing factor was that most Wednesdays were a day off, because the
university wanted to use the training ground then. It's not hard
to imagine the look on Wenger's face when he was told about
that.

'I'll always remember the first pre-season tour with Arsene
Wenger,' said former Arsenal midfielder Ray Parlour. 'New French
lads had come into the team, like Patrick Vieira, Emmanuel Petit
and Gilles Grimandi. We worked our socks off and, at the end of
the trip, Wenger said we could all go out. We went straight down
to the pub and the French lads went to the coffee shop.

'I'll always remember the moment Steve Bould went up to the
bar and ordered 35 pints for five of us. After we left the bar, we
spotted all the French lads in the coffee shop and they were sitting
around smoking. I thought, "How are we going to win the league
this year? We're all drunk and they're all smoking." We ended up
winning the Double.'

When Parlour's recollections were put to Wenger, the Arsenal
manager smiled fondly and recalled: 'You can trust him [Parlour]
on that! The physical constraints have massively changed. The
players 20 years ago were as much winners as today. They had
more freedom than today because the physical demands are much

higher, and because the spying facilities of society have increased. Therefore, it is much more difficult today to be anonymous. On that front the pressure on the players is much bigger than it was during Ray Parlour's time.'

Wenger did not ban boozing the moment he arrived, but he definitely changed the boundaries. For example, back in the Graham and Rioch eras, there were beers, pizzas and roast dinners with wine, all served on the luxury team coach. The food remained into the Wenger days, but the booze was outlawed as Wenger insisted the players 'refuel' properly, while the squad also stopped having alcohol in the players' lounge at Highbury out of respect for Tony Adams, following his public admission of being an alcoholic.

The 'back seat brigade' was made up of characters like Ray Parlour, Steve Bould and young midfielder Stephen Hughes, to name but three. It was just like being back at school when the loud, funny and popular gang sat on the back seat of the bus. One particular journey home from a long away trip in those early days produced an amusing story – and resulted in a rollicking from the up until then mild-mannered Wenger, who made it clear when the players overstepped the mark.

By then, Arsenal had Marks & Spencer food on the bus, with everything from sandwiches to salads and desserts. The players on the back seat grabbed the desserts – ranging from tiramisu to Black Forest gateau – and had a bet among themselves as to who could eat the most puddings. All the losers would have to pay the winner £100 each, but the matter of dressing-room pride was more important than the cash.

Hughes recalls: 'We didn't think he had clocked it, but he had and was fuming. I think Ray won it in the end because he went to a fifth pudding! We all piled off the coach, feeling sick, stomachs hurting, and we were all giggling as we got in the cars. But we all got pulled in the morning and told: "That can never happen again."'

Wenger was a very serious man; there were fewer laughs, he could even be quite moody, although few have ever heard him shout when at the training ground. But he does like a laugh, has a good sense of humour and certainly enjoyed that particular era.

Wenger definitely didn't want to be laughed at, but often joined in with the fun. His clumsiness caused much amusement in the dressing room. In fact, it became a notorious trait, particularly as it is sometimes hard to imagine such a serious, intelligent man doing things which are a bit, well, silly.

One of the first training sessions saw Wenger carry out a huge net containing footballs. He put the net down on the pitch and looked for the hole to get out the balls. He couldn't find it and slowly got tangled up so badly that he tripped up. Over rushed Pat Rice, his loyal assistant, to try and untangle him, making the whole farcical scene even more amusing.

Then, the night before an away trip to Aston Villa, the players were staying in a hotel where the food was served but the dessert (apple pie) was on a buffet trolley. Wenger, who was sitting at a table with the coaching staff, finished his main course and went over to pick up a piece of apple pie with a cake slice and put it on his plate. As he turned round to put the cake slice back, the pie slid off and Wenger, completely unaware, walked back to the table with an empty plate. The eyes of all the players in the room had descended on Wenger as he sat down, picked up his fork and then realised there was no pie. He began looking around, completely bewildered, while the players tried to stifle their giggles.

Another famous moment of accident proneness happened during one of the first pre-seasons, when they were staying in Bad Waltersdorf. A friend of Wenger's had come to see him at their hotel, which had huge windows at the front, and the players were looking out as they ate their lunch. Wenger saw his friend and went over to the window, beckoning him to come in and join them. But the friend, the players could see, didn't understand and cupped his ear as if to show he couldn't hear. Wenger tried to open the window but turned the handle the wrong way and, rather than opening it sideways, he opened it lengthways and brought the huge great window crashing down on his forehead. The players were in stitches and, to make matters worse, when he went to sit back down he then hit his head on the light hanging over the table.

'Are they laughing at me, Gary,' Wenger asked physio Gary Lewin.

'Er, yes, boss, I think so.'

Some of the players were hiding under the tables they were laughing so much. Winterburn remembers how it was:

He has got a good sense of humour. He will have a little chuckle at himself when things like him tripping over the nets to try and get the balls open or if he can't do up his zip on his coat ... So many things that seemed to happen to a man who is so, so clever. But he does stuff, silly things that make you go: 'Surely this guy is not for real!' But you realise when you work with him why he is so liked by the players and that's the most important thing. You are never going to get results if the players don't like you. That's what he does so well.

When he opened a window on himself, the thing about it was that we were in pre-season; we were working really hard, physically and mentally you are pushing yourself to the limit to get to your peak for the first game. Those little things might not be that funny afterwards but, at that period of time, it was just a relief, it really made us laugh. We were saying: 'I don't believe he's just done that!' It was incredible. The amazing thing was that he always seemed to carry on as if nothing had happened. It was just so bizarre.

But Wenger's willingness to share a joke and have a laugh with the players really endeared him to them – even if he failed to see the funny side when Ian Wright bought himself a pair of roller skates.

'He loved the jokes. He would either get involved or you could always see him look over, giggling and trying to listen in because he really enjoyed it. Ray Parlour was always trying to get him involved and he nearly always found it funny,' said Stephen Hughes.

'Of course, there were times when he didn't find it funny. I remember pulling Wrighty down the Marble Halls with him on roller skates. I remember Wrighty going: "Come on, Hughesy, pull me!" Just as he got there, the gaffer's head popped round the door and he saw me pulling him down on roller skates. I was thinking: "Oh no." He wouldn't find that funny at all whereas Wrighty was like a kid with his new roller skates.'

Wenger could dish out a rollicking – and when he did so, the players would really notice. Once, when travelling home after an away game up north, Danish striker Nicklas Bendtner, renowned for being a character, was having a bit of banter with a couple of team-mates as they filed through airport security. They had been talking about *The X Factor* and Bendtner launched into an impromptu impression of an *X Factor* contestant. Wenger saw it, looked on in disgust, rushed over and shouted at him: 'Do you think losing is funny?' Although relatively easy-going, Wenger has a temper and, when it snaps, he will shout and his good humour and good nature quickly disappear.

Wenger's methods were also taking shape on the pitch in the

1997/98 season. Long-standing players, the no-nonsense defenders like Tony Adams, Steve Bould, Martin Keown and fullbacks Lee Dixon and Nigel Winterburn, were passing the ball better; they were being stretched technically and were building play up from the back rather than hitting it long down the channels.

Wenger was, in addition, making full use of his French connections. Not only did he know the French league inside out, but he also championed the French African market, bringing in players from far and wide thanks to the contacts he'd made while at Monaco. Through agents in France and Africa alike, Wenger was picking up bargains, signing future World Cup winners and the heroes of France's 1998 triumph for tiny fees in comparison to English players, who, in a general and broad comparison, cost twice as much.

It took time, as Wenger arrived on 30 September 1996 and had to wait until the following summer to bring in key signings. But, a month before he arrived and knowing that he was going to take charge, Wenger recommended that Arsenal sign Patrick Vieira and Remi Garde. The French revolution had begun.

Vieira, 6ft 4in, a bustling, powerful and skilful midfielder, was plucked from Milan's reserves for just £3.5 million. He was to become one of Arsenal's all-time great players. Again, Wenger's knowledge of the French youth set-up meant that he knew Vieira not just as a player but as a person and, although he was only 20, recognised him to be a great natural leader. He heralded a new-look Arsenal. Garde, recently the manager of Lyon, was also signed in a way that gave rise to questions about who was actually recommending the players, let alone doing the deals. Clearly, Wenger was giving advice on players even before he was installed.

In the dressing room, there was scepticism about the new signings. Tony Adams, uncertain about Wenger and whether the players would fit in, said to his team-mates: 'He's signed this Remi Garde, Patrick Vieira – never even heard of them.'

Vieira immediately made an impression on the pitch, even if he spoke little English when he first arrived. He was quick, powerful and strong. He stood out in his first reserve game and got better and better. Garde was not in the same class and, as his career went on, was regarded with some suspicion among the players. While Garde was a nice guy and popular, the players always felt he was brought in to be Wenger's eyes and ears in the dressing room, as he was very close to the manager and certainly had a different relationship with him. Maybe it was even a smart move on Wenger's part.

Suddenly, Wenger was bringing in players from abroad and – strange though it may seem now – Arsenal were a largely British team until that point. This reflected a broader trend: in 1995/96, the year before Wenger arrived, 101 foreign players made at least one appearance for one of the 92 league teams, by 1997/98 that figure had increased to 176. In Wenger's first game in charge, the 2-0 win at Blackburn in October 1996, Vieira was the only non-British player involved. The line-up was: David Seaman, Lee Dixon, Nigel Winterburn, Patrick Vieira, Steve Bould, Tony Adams, Martin Keown, David Platt, Ian Wright, Paul Merson, John Hartson. Ray Parlour came on as a late substitute.

The foreign invasion was about to begin and, while supporters of other clubs moaned, the Arsenal fans were not bothered: they saw the arrival of top-quality players who began to raise the bar in terms of talent, technique and style. The foreign players also provided a breath of fresh air, a new oxygen after the boring and dull philosophy of the tail end of George Graham's reign which his immediate successor, Bruce Rioch, struggled to transform beyond a few tweaks.

But it's often forgotten that, in Wenger's first season, he went with the defence that Rioch had introduced: three centre halves – most regularly Adams, Bould and Keown – with wing backs. Adams, in particular, liked the system and Wenger didn't want to upset the old guard, so stuck with it.

But, in the summer of 1997, Wenger pressed ahead with his own revolution, overhauling the squad. He switched to a 4-4-2 and brought in new players. In came Gilles Grimandi, Emmanuel Petit, Nicolas Anelka and Marc Overmars.

Grimandi was a valuable squad player and is now Arsenal's scout in France. He could occupy several positions in defence and also worked in midfield. Petit was close to joining Glasgow Rangers and Tottenham before Arsenal signed him. He had been in discussions with the then Tottenham chairman Sir Alan Sugar and when Arsenal got wind of this, a message was sent to him not to sign for Spurs until he had heard what Wenger had to say. Petit told Sugar that he wanted time to think and that he was going back to his hotel. Spurs even paid for the taxi, but, instead of going to his hotel, Petit went to meet Wenger and Dein. Unwittingly, Spurs had paid for the cab for Petit to go and join Arsenal. Instantly recognisable because of his blond ponytail, Petit formed a strong central midfield partnership with his fellow countryman, Vieira.

Overmars nearly joined Arsenal during Graham's era, but decided to stay and sign a new contract at Ajax. Later, the Dutch winger sustained a serious knee injury and it was seen as something of a gamble on Arsenal's part when they picked him up for £7 million, on a contract worth around £18,000 a week.

Suddenly, the dressing room was changing, becoming more multicultural. Ray Parlour remembers that Wenger was clever in the way that he managed to maintain the dynamic among the players, so that they all stayed united and did not lose their team spirit.

Parlour said: 'I remember Manu Petit at first. He'd walk straight past us, ignore us and we'd think: "That's a bit rude." But we had the sort of dressing room where you could say something to him, tell him to say good morning – and if he didn't we'd cut his pony-tail off!'

Stephen Hughes reflects on that period of change:

The English lads who were already there were big characters. It was a really strong dressing room. It does make me laugh now to hear and read players saying how great they were and I'm thinking: 'Hang on, they hated each other!' But it didn't really matter because I look at a big picture of the 1998 Double-winning team in my house and I think … the group was so strong, full of personalities.

It was mad because it was always policed from inside – if it got too silly or too mad, then people would sort it out. Wrighty was a big character; Dennis was great for me, such a character with a brilliant sense of humour, so dry and so funny. Without a doubt, Dennis was one of the funniest guys I've ever come across … Marc had a stupid sense of humour which I liked. Dennis would wind Martin up constantly. I used to sit there and laugh, and Martin was the pantomime villain. We loved each other's company. Dennis was a lovely guy, but hilariously funny.

It was a weird dynamic because you had the French lads on one table, the cool English lads on another table and I used to call us the misfits because it was me, Martin, Marc and Dennis. Martin wasn't cool enough to go with the English gang, I was the geeky one who roomed with Martin because I got bullied into it and the Dutch boys loved Martin and me.

The most interesting and perhaps least known of the new players was Nicolas Anelka, a teenager plucked from Paris Saint-Germain, with Arsenal having to pay just £500,000 in compensation. Within two years, Anelka went to Real Madrid for £22.5 million – a bitter and ugly departure as Anelka's gratitude to Arsenal and Wenger was to threaten to go on strike. He was called 'Le Sulk' in the press and yet, for two amazing seasons at Arsenal, he was sensational.

Anelka, it could be said, typified everything about Wenger – his faith in young players, pace, power and skill. Anelka had it all and, as well as winning trophies for Arsenal, he improved as a player under Wenger because he was thrust into the first team and he made the club a healthy profit. Throughout Wenger's reign, there are numerous examples of such players, who have come in on the cheap and gone on to fetch huge transfer fees. Emmanuel Adebayor made Arsenal nearly £20 million, Kolo Toure made them about £18 million and Robin van Persie brought in a £20 million profit.

This record is a testament to Wenger's ability to spot raw talent, realise the potential in that talent by improving the player and giving them a chance, and then selling them on at the right time. In any other walk of life, Wenger would be hailed as a genius salesman and businessman – indeed, he has always been interested in the similarities between management in football and business. In football, when players are sold even for a large profit, the selling club is branded unambitious and the selling manager is often painted as betraying the fans.

But those days were yet to arrive. In that first season, Arsenal finishing third behind Newcastle on goal difference meant they qualified for the UEFA Cup rather than the Champions League. If anything, though, it was seen as something of a success. Wenger had not been in charge for the first two months; taking over someone else's players midway through a season is always seen as difficult, and the jury would sit in judgement only at the end of his first full season.

Wenger was exceptionally busy in the summer of 1997. Out

went Paul Merson, John Hartson, Eddie McGoldrick, David Hillier, Andy Linighan and Paul Dickov, as the club brought in more than £10 million in transfer fees. Another player who was allowed to go that summer was Adrian Clarke, who was on his way to becoming a regular under Rioch but was hardly given a chance under Wenger.

But Clarke remembers Wenger as a very good man manager who treated the players with respect. After initially training with the first team, Clarke was relegated back down to the reserves in Wenger's early days. Clarke asked to see the manager.

In the meeting he said something along the lines of: Tell me about yourself.' He wanted to know my family background, what I liked doing away from football, et cetera. I also told him I was doing A-levels in my spare time and he was very interested in that. Having a good education was something he regarded as important. We ended up talking about lots of stuff which wasn't football-related. He could really hold a conversation, and we spoke for about half an hour about anything but football.

When it came to our football chat I said to him: 'The reason I came to see you was that I'm frustrated. I trained with the first team every week last season, and played seven games, yet this year I'm with the reserves every day.' He looked very embarrassed and said: 'You played? I am really sorry I didn't know that.' It was a bit of a surreal moment, and whether it was true or not it did make me feel like I had a fresh chance.

He promised to watch me more closely. But unfortunately for me, the good games that I had he wasn't at and I didn't do especially well whenever he came. I was being used as a wing back at the time, and was like a fish out of water defending! I didn't impress. So it all came to nothing and within weeks I moved elsewhere on loan. I left the meeting feeling ten feet tall though, and that's because he took a real interest in me as a person.

After a season of being farmed out on loan to Southend, Clarke was summoned to see Wenger in the summer of 1997 and, despite being released, he speaks well of his former manager. Now working as a journalist, Clarke continues:

My contract was up so I had more than an inkling that it wouldn't be renewed when I was summoned to Sopwell House to meet the boss. After 12 years at the club, it was just me and him sat on two chairs around a table in the empty dining room of the hotel.

To be honest, Arsene Wenger was so fair in the way he explained the situation that I couldn't be angry or upset with him. He explained how players of a certain age – I was 22 at the time – needed to be playing first-team football and that he couldn't guarantee that I'd be in his squad the following season.

Southend had been in touch, I'd been on loan there, and they wanted me to stay permanently. Arsenal had initially wanted a fee, which was a sticking point, but he said that he'd waive the fee, so as not to put any obstacles in my way. I remember saying to him: 'I can't argue with that, I haven't been quite up to scratch since you arrived, and it's up to me to prove you wrong.' He said he hoped that I would, but it didn't happen that way, obviously. He said he'd heard I'd done well at Southend but that he wouldn't stand in the way of my moving on.

It was only a five-minute chat, but there was no point in prolonging it! It was quite an emotional moment in my life, but I couldn't be upset with him personally. I'd been there 12 years, he'd just let me go – and I even ended up thanking him! He put it across in such a way that I could have no argument, and it felt like it was for my benefit to leave the club. It was strange thanking him for being fair and honest with me, but that's how he'd made me feel in the meeting. It was a bit like Lord Sugar when he's just sacked a candidate on *The Apprentice*, and they thank him for the opportunity!

When I came outside, I saw Matthew Upson waiting there to sign and it felt like it was out with the old, in with the new. It was almost symbolic. Here was this younger guy, who I knew from reserve football, and he was coming in and I was going out. I got to my car and then it hit me. I started to cry! Knowing I had to phone people and say what happened, and knowing I'd never play for Arsenal again, choked me up big time.

It was a similar story for John Hartson. Wenger and vice-chairman David Dein offered him a four-year contract to stay, but West Ham boss Harry Redknapp was offering more regular football. Hartson said: 'I left Arsenal in 1997; they went on to win the Double in 1998. That still rankles with me a little bit. I left before such a great era. Arsene Wenger offered me a four-year contract to stay; he liked me as a person and as a player.

'I was very young at Arsenal; I broke the record as the most expensive teenager in the country. I had some difficult times. I had a big decision to make when Harry Redknapp came in for me but, if I'm honest, if I had my time again then I would have stayed at Arsenal. But I was very set in my ways, very stubborn. I had a good career with West Ham, Wimbledon, Celtic and Wales. But, with hindsight, I wish I'd let Wenger get hold of me because I could have become an Arsenal legend, I could have been there for ten years.'

The softer, caring side of Wenger – and his loyalty – to former players was highlighted in 2009. Hartson was in a critical condition in hospital, having undergone emergency surgery after testicular cancer spread to his brain and lungs. He recalls that Wenger gave him a huge lift when he was fighting for his life. 'He organised a big card with a picture of me on the front in my Arsenal kit with about 50 or 60 messages inside. The main one at the top was from Arsene Wenger saying: "John, it was an honour to work with you, I really hope you can pull through." It was so touching because I was at my lowest at that point. All the staff signed it, the girls who wash the kit, the chef, the kit man, everybody.'

After Hartson's departure, in came not just Upson, Anelka, Petit, Grimandi and Overmars, but a raft of squad players, including Alex Manninger and Luis Boa Morte. Wenger, with the signing of and instant impact made by Anelka, quickly gained a reputation for being able to pluck an unknown and turn him into a star.

English football fans back in 1997 were far more insular than they are today. Even French internationals were relatively unknown, except to real students of the game, but Wenger quickly made French players household names in England. He tapped into a market for relative bargains and was able to pick up players whom he knew would fit his style and system.

Arsenal made a good start to the 1997/98 season. They did it with their new-look line-up, which also included a familiar hero. Ian Wright broke the club's goalscoring record on 13 September in a 4-1 win against Bolton. It was an incredible time: Arsenal were scoring goals aplenty, beating early leaders Manchester United at Highbury 3-2, and the signs looked very promising. They did not lose a game in the Premier League until 1 November – a painful 3-0 defeat at Derby County.

But what followed turned Arsenal's promising start into something of a crisis, especially as three defeats in their next four games left them ten points adrift of leaders Manchester United and languishing in fifth place. The early promise had faltered and Arsenal looked as if they had blown the title already.

Ray Parlour remembers that time and, in particular, Arsenal's November curse. They always seemed to slip up in November. 'A lot of teams have bad patches. We used to have a bad patch in November. Even in the 1998 season we had a bad patch. It always seemed to be November, no idea why.'

After the 3-1 home defeat to Blackburn on 13 December, there came a turning point, a defining moment which would resurrect their season and put them back on the road to success. It also represented what has become a familiar and recurrent theme throughout Wenger's reign. When a crisis strikes, there is often a players' meeting. Down the years, it's happened so regularly that it must be something Wenger encourages. It only occurs about once a season, usually after a big defeat or major disappointment, when the players get together and air a few home truths.

Wenger does not like confrontation. Some players say that he struggles with it so much that he rarely looks them in the eye, especially if they are not in the team. Instead, he often leaves the players to police themselves.

Stephen Hughes recalls: 'You'd get more stick from the kit man. Vic Akers clocked everything. I remember coming in after a game, we'd drawn or lost and no one would say anything. It was calm. I remember when I first got in the first team it was like World War Three, with people trying to fight everyone. But it was all quiet and no one would say anything ... and Vic came over and said: "Had one today, son, didn't you?" All I wanted was a cuddle, and he said it again: "Fucking had one, didn't you?" I was absolutely gutted.'

After that Blackburn game, the players took it upon themselves to call a meeting. Sometimes it's the players, sometimes it's Wenger who will call the meeting. Little was said immediately after the Blackburn defeat, but a couple of days later the players held their meeting at Sopwell House hotel, when the real inquest took place and, with it, a line was drawn and a turning point for that season was established. Home truths were spoken, fingers pointed, players were geed up.

The defence – David Seaman, Tony Adams, Steve Bould, Lee Dixon, Martin Keown and Nigel Winterburn – sat down with Emmanuel Petit and Patrick Vieira and told them: 'You haven't got a clue what your job is – we need some protection. We're not getting any cover from you.' That is when Petit and Vieira changed their game totally, and the team went on a long unbeaten run lasting the rest of the season and ending in the league and FA Cup Double.

The Petit and Vieira midfield axis went on from there to establish one of the best pairings in Premier League history as they defended, attacked and created in equal measure. They won almost every midfield battle they took part in. And, tellingly, the Petit and Vieira double act was fully established after that players' meeting. Wenger had the foresight to sign them both, bring them together, and yet it was their team-mates who told them how they should play.

It was a familiar theme under Wenger, who preferred calm discussions in the dressing room and was happy for the players to intervene and almost manage themselves.

'To be honest, he was never a manager who'd go mad straight after the game,' said Ray Parlour. 'It's always much better, in my opinion, to do it afterwards. You can calm down, take it in and think about it. Sometimes if you do it straight after a game then you get it totally wrong. He always seemed to look back at the videos, he'd watch them two or three times over the weekend and then we'd come in on the Monday morning and we'd have a meeting and he'd say: "What went wrong?"'

'He'd always want your feedback. He'd say he thought one element went wrong and then he'd want the players to have their say. Then we'd try and solve it as players. He'd give advice. But he would want your personal opinions about what happened in the game. He was always that sort of manager.'

Marc Overmars and Nicolas Anelka also showed their true potential in the second half of the 1997/98 season. Anelka was described as a 'miserable sod' in the dressing room and struggled to fit in with the other players, but on the pitch it was a different story. From his first reserve game to shining in the second half of the Double-winning season, it was very clear that Anelka was a special talent, full of power, pace and goals.

The proof was plain to see as Arsenal went on a remarkable run, forcing their way back into the title race as Manchester United lost some momentum, with defeats away at Southampton and at home to Leicester.

Arsenal were a long way behind, but they found form and consistency; and, even though some bookies had paid out on Manchester United, Wenger refused to give up. Going into March, United were 11 points clear, 12 points ahead of Arsenal, who had games in hand. You could sense in Wenger's smile that he was not just paying lip service – he truly believed it was possible.

Before Arsenal went to Old Trafford for what would be the biggest game of the season, Wenger claimed that United had a 'responsibility' to make the league 'interesting'. The press, TV and radio were all warming to Wenger and his soundbites. He was the calm, cheeky and charming foreign antidote to Alex Ferguson, who gave the media little apart from some angry outbursts.

On 14 March 1998 came the game that really signalled a shift in power. Arsenal went to Old Trafford and won, thanks to Marc Overmars' brilliantly taken goal. Parlour recalls: 'I think that was probably Marc Overmars' best game for the club. It was definitely his most important goal.'

United had been sloppy, had thrown away games, and yet one thing that Ferguson was particularly good at was keeping his nerve in the big games. The fact that Arsenal had gone to Old Trafford and won sent a strong message, and Ferguson began to crack.

The headline on the back page of the *Mail on Sunday* the following day read: 'Wenger: Now Do You Believe Me?' That summed it up. Cynics, fans, journalists and the whole football world, until that point, had been sceptical about Wenger, Arsenal and their new challenge. That victory on a Saturday lunchtime changed everything. Wenger said after the game: 'It makes it exciting for everybody. I've always believed, but the players will start to believe again.'

Interestingly, Wenger, looking healthy, happy and vibrant, never bit on Ferguson's attempt at mind games, as the United manager claimed the pressure was now on Arsenal, they would drop points. Ferguson said: 'They've never been under pressure – let's see what happens now.'

Wenger's response was simply to state that United still had the advantage as the points were on the board, while his players responded by going on a record-breaking run that would take them to the title. Meanwhile, Christopher Wreh – who celebrated his goal with an overhead flip – helped them beat Wolves to reach the FA Cup final. Arsenal were in the groove. By 10 April, after United dropped points against Liverpool, Arsenal were seven points behind but had three games in hand. Even Ferguson admitted: 'The balance of power is in Arsenal's hands. They can only throw it away really.'

Arsenal were determined not to throw it away. Their title-clinching win over Everton made it ten in a row, which was a Premier League best, and they ended up as champions with games to spare. Fittingly, Adams and Bould, two members of the famous Arsenal back four now playing with Wenger's inspired continental flair, were pivotal in the victory over Everton on Sunday 3 May, as Wenger won his first title at Highbury. Adams' 89th-minute goal after a through-ball by Bould also set up one of the most iconic pieces of commentary in Premier League history.

Sky commentator Martin Tyler's words are now famous, and are actually on display on one of the walls at the Emirates. 'And it's Tony Adams put through by Steve Bould ... Would you believe it? That sums it all up!' It was a magical, unforgettable moment of proof that Wenger could get anyone to play the beautiful game with a bit of practice and belief.

Tyler recalls that goal as one of the most memorable not only of his career but also in the Premier League era.

Most of the commentaries I've ever spoken about are down to the fact that I've been lucky enough to be at one of these iconic football moments. Sergio Aguero was the most recent one. You are very much a person of fortune to be there. You don't go there with some sort of Shakespearean line in your mind, knowing that something amazing is going to happen. You just have a fraction of a second to know that it's going to happen. That's football's sixth sense, or call it what you will.

When Tony set off, I thought this is incredible because Wenger has this reputation of revolutionising Arsenal and you had these two centre halves he inherited as bastions of the back line – he'd freed up the spirit so much that Tony set off, Bouldy found him and it was simple really: it summed up what Arsene Wenger had brought to Arsenal since he arrived.

The fact it turned out to be the last goal on such a big

occasion was fortuitous, I guess. It pressed a button in my head at the time and all these years later we're still talking about it.

Tony Adams and Steve Bould were so in tune – not just in tune at stopping the opposition before Arsene came, but Arsene had brought this new belief into their game and they had the ability to back it. It was an amazing moment. I remember moments when Tony Adams pushed up front to try and nick a point, but I can't remember many others apart from that. It was the liberation of the moment. It was very much what I thought Arsene had brought to Arsenal and English football.

And there was more to come: Arsenal won the FA Cup, beating Newcastle at Wembley. Overmars and Anelka were both on target in a very one-sided final.

Perhaps the biggest compliment you could pay to that 1998 team was the view from the opposition. Of the title rivals, Manchester United battled Arsenal from 1998 to 2004 and perhaps the odd season after that. But of all those thrilling title races, there is no doubt that the players at United felt that the best team of all – even including the 2004 Invincibles – was the 1998 Double-winning side.

Manchester United winger Ryan Giggs, who won the title 13 times, said: 'The toughest Arsenal team for me personally was the 1997/98 Double-winning team. They just had a bit of everything really. Quality with Bergkamp, pace with Anelka and Overmars, the experience of the back four, and then the toughness of Vieira and Petit in midfield.'

Arsenal had all the ingredients of a great team and, again, the view from inside the dressing room from someone who played in all three title-winning teams was that the 1998 era was the most fun. Patrick Vieira said: '[My greatest time] was the 1998 Double with Arsenal. I remember the atmosphere at the stadium at every single game we went to, and the way the home and away fans responded.

'The stadiums were packed. The response from the fans was unbelievable and that is why I enjoyed every single game I have played in this country. It was really special because we had a fantastic team. That was the first time for me to be at a really high level and winning things. This is the time when I really fell in love with the English game.'

Wenger, of course, built three title-winning teams – in 1998, 2002 and 2004 – and Winterburn, who played for the club from 1987 until 2000, believes the first would definitely have given the other two a run for their money.

They were all pretty strong teams. In my time at Arsenal, the 1998 team was the best team I played in. Luckily enough, the players we had and the players he brought in seemed to complement each other terrifically well and obviously that came to fruition very, very quickly with the Double team.

It had everything. It had pace up front, it had goals, Overmars out wide, power in midfield – it was unbelievable. It could dig a result from nowhere. Obviously we lost, you take it for granted that you will lose occasionally. It could play football but scrap it out as well. That's the best way to describe that team. It's very difficult to rate it against 2002 and 2004.

That team in 2004 went unbeaten. But I'd probably say that those three teams would give a hell of a game to each other, if that makes sense, and I wouldn't like to pick a winner. They are so different. Thierry Henry came in during my final season and got better and better. He was in his pomp in 2004; I only had one year with him when he was still finding his way. They were all slightly different for different reasons. I'd fancy the team that I was in to dig out the results the most. But in terms of flowing forward football, the 2004 team had the most. In 2002, Arsene changed it, changed the back four. Each team would be capable of beating each other on any given day. They were so close.

Arsenal had set the standard, the gamble had paid off. Wenger had transformed Arsenal in terms of training methods, changed the culture of the dressing room, turned them into a cosmopolitan line-up full of flair, entertainers and, more than anything else, had made them winners. They had regained their standing in the game – and done it in style. Wenger had become the first foreign manager to win the league title in England, following the success of Chelsea's Ruud Gullit as the first foreign manager to win the FA Cup, in 1997, and Gianluca Vialli winning the League Cup earlier in the season.

But Wenger's title success set him apart. Winning the title, being the best team over the course of the entire season, is the ultimate gauge of success and Wenger had done it with great style. He had become hugely popular with the fans and it's no wonder that he became something of a trendsetter. From there, the move towards appointing foreign managers instead of going British really began as they increasingly became the norm.

It was proof that Arsenal had made the right choice and a vindication of David Dein's efforts to bring in the unknown Frenchman. Dein adds: 'People often ask me how I knew Arsene was the right man for the club. My reply is, winning the Double in his first full season was a pretty good clue!'

With a strong squad, big-name internationals, a new forward-thinking manager and success under their belts, Arsenal had entered a brave new world.

CHAPTER 3

ADOPTED ENGLISHMAN

A RSENE WENGER HAD BECOME the first foreign manager to win the Premier League. It set him apart as a trailblazer and this, together with a fascination for his style of play, his amusing soundbites and cutting remarks, suddenly made him the new king of the back page. His regular jousts with Alex Ferguson were entertaining and brutal, and the press were lapping them up. For the neutral as well as the dyed-in-the-wool fan, Arsenal represented a refreshing change from Manchester United's dominance.

The other appeal of Arsenal under Wenger was their dramatic change in style. They had gone from being 'boring, boring Arsenal' to the most entertaining and attractive team in the Premier League. It's easy to forget now, but it should be remembered that Wenger was, in his early days, a revolutionary. Wenger set up his team to be attractive and brought in spectacular players like Thierry Henry, Robert Pires and Nicolas Anelka. Wenger had inherited Dennis Bergkamp and enjoyed building his new team around the strengths of the Dutch forward, one of the best players to have ever graced the Premier League and who will be remembered as an all-time great at Arsenal. Supporters of other teams would be loath to admit it, but they were developing an admiration for Arsenal, rather like neutrals now applaud Ronald Koeman's Southampton.

Back then, Wenger was a 4-4-2 man, believing his style of play would simply go out and beat opponents. He was not overly worried about stopping them because he believed the opposition could not stop his team, which meant he was cavalier in his approach. Alex Ferguson had won trophies with flair at Manchester United, proving it could be done. However, Arsenal's success under George Graham in the late 1980s and early 1990s had been gained with a safety-first approach. Graham always railed against his team being called boring, holding up the likes of David Rocastle, Anders Limpar and Ian Wright as flair players. But there was a formulaic approach to Graham's style. They defended first, won second.

The magic formula of management must be the elusive balance of being able to entertain and win at the same time. Some managers, like Jose Mourinho, will set up a team to win at all costs and then add in the flair later. Managers like Wenger begin their philosophy with entertainment and then figure out how to win later. They build from a base of scoring goals, creating chances and skill. He is one of the few managers who put winning and style on the same level of importance.

Wenger, detailing his philosophy, said: 'We are in a job where you have to win. But the truth is that the ambition of every great club must be to win and to win with style, and to think of the people who pay a lot of money to come to watch the matches. You always have to have it in your mind that you want people to wake up in the morning with a love of going to the stadium and for them to go home having enjoyed themselves. In fact, the real goal of professional football entails not just winning but also enabling people to discover the pleasure of watching something beautiful.'

The Arsenal fans had lapped up the mix of success and attractive football in the 1997/98 Double-winning season, when they overhauled Manchester United to win the Premier League title and then completed the job by winning the 1998 FA Cup final by beating Newcastle 2-0 at Wembley. But it is always difficult to emulate success. The following season Arsenal came desperately close to repeating their 1998 Double – but finished the campaign empty-handed.

Football fans are by their very nature impatient because they always demand more. Just six months after the Double, Arsenal fans were already getting restless. After a disappointing 1-1 draw at home to Middlesbrough in November 1998, there were a few rumblings of discontent and frustration among the supporters. In his post-match press conference, Wenger came up with a typically brilliant response: 'If you eat caviar every day, it's difficult to return to sausages.'

Football is always about fine margins and they shared an FA Cup semi-final classic against Manchester United on 14 April 1999. They ended up losing to Ryan Giggs' incredible solo goal in extra time, but this was after Dennis Bergkamp had wasted a glorious chance to win the tie, only to see his penalty saved by Peter Schmeichel in injury time.

If that wasn't bad enough, Arsenal blew the title (eventually finishing as runners-up to Manchester United by a single point) after losing their penultimate game at Leeds following a mistake by Argentinian defender Nelson Vivas, on as a substitute for Nigel Winterburn, who failed to pick up Jimmy Floyd Hasselbaink and stop the Dutchman scoring the winner. Wenger rarely criticises players publicly, but he made an exception in Vivas's case, allowing his frustrations to spill over, and the Argentinian's Arsenal career never recovered.

But Wenger believed that semi-final replay defeat at Villa Park was the turning point in Arsenal's season and felt its aftermath continued for a lot longer, even perhaps in their next two or three seasons. After the match, Wenger was as angry, frustrated and downbeat – in the tunnel, on the coach home and over the next few days – as some regular observers had ever seen him. And, in fact, some believe it is still the angriest he has ever been.

The reason is simple: United gained momentum from that victory in a title race that was neck and neck between the two clubs. Alex Ferguson also acknowledged the importance of that semi-final replay and the way it shaped the rest of the season. He said: 'In actual fact, we should have already been through. Roy Keane scored a perfectly good goal, pulled back from the by-line, scored and the linesman gave it offside. But that replay, from my point of view, was the game which had the galvanising effect on that season. There were supporters on the pitch when Ryan scored the goal, the dressing room was unbelievable. The atmosphere was incredible.

'The fans couldn't wait to get home to tell their kids, wife or whoever. The dressing room was incredible, the players going mad, jumping around. It was amazing to see. From that moment, I thought to myself: "We've got a great chance here." We were galvanised by beating Arsenal, I've no doubt about that.'

United went on to win the Treble in 1999, cleaning up with the Premier League, FA Cup and the Champions League, while Arsenal won nothing. Wenger was right about the 1999 semi-final being a game-changer – it set in the rot, at least as Wenger saw it, for the next three seasons when they failed to win anything.

Ray Parlour believes the defeat was the key moment of that season and admits it handed the momentum to Alex Ferguson:

We were definitely the best team that year. Bergkamp puts the penalty away, Schmeichel doesn't save it then we were guaranteed to go on and win the league and get another Double.

Manchester United were 1-0 down with ten to go in the Champions League final and came back to win 2-1. It's so close in football, always. I suppose you flip it round and Ruud van Nistelrooy hits the bar in the Invincibles season and we go unbeaten and it's very, very similar. That was the battle at the time – us and Manchester United, it was so close, the rivalry so tight.

But it wasn't a lull after 1999. We were one kick away from reaching the final of the FA Cup. Dennis Bergkamp missed a penalty. We were one minute away from winning the league when Hasselbaink scored up at Leeds United. I wouldn't say it was a lull. It was one of those seasons. We were so close to winning the Double again. Sometimes it's such fine lines in football.

But in 1999 it was very, very close. Schmeichel saves the penalty kick, Ryan Giggs with a wonder goal; Nigel Winterburn gets injured and Nelson Vivas comes on, switches off for a split second and then Leeds win and we've lost the league as well. From there, United kicked on, had the momentum and we had two or three years without winning. But it definitely started with that semi-final.

Winterburn adds: 'When you look at it you realise how close we were. Bergkamp missing the penalty, the defeat at Leeds – I didn't even know the result of that game until a couple of days later because I went straight into hospital for an operation. You could say: "What if?" We could have won the cup, the title and United wouldn't have won the Treble. It was so close.'

Sky commentator Martin Tyler remembers that night at Villa Park as a turning point for Wenger and Arsenal:

He's the worst loser I've ever seen – worse than Fergie. And I mean that as a compliment. After the 1999 FA Cup semi-final, he was absolutely furious. They missed a penalty and, at that time, they were on a good run of results against Manchester United. He felt that semi-final let United back in and, of course, he was right. The next two or three years was theirs until Arsenal got going.

That's the worst I've seen him. There's been times when Arsenal have been embarrassed, like the 8-2 or the 6-1 at Manchester United, he's been sent to the stands, or the pushing and shoving with Jose Mourinho. But I happened to see him after the game at Villa Park and I realised there and then what a competitor he was. It was only 1999, he hadn't been around for long, and he was absolutely steaming. As it turned out, he was probably right to be. He smelt the danger … It put United on the trail again; they won the Treble and Arsenal had to wait for their next trophy.

Arsenal finished the 1998/99 campaign downbeat and down-hearted. But while some managers then change their philosophy, Wenger was forced into rebuilding his team over the next couple of summers. In the 1999 close season, Nicolas Anelka made it clear he wanted to leave. It turned into a protracted transfer saga, the blow softened by the huge profit the club made in selling him to Real Madrid. They further softened the blow by replacing him with Thierry Henry.

The Anelka transfer remains one of Wenger's biggest regrets because he could see talent and potential, and he wanted him to stay and be part of his team. Whether Arsenal would have bought Henry if Anelka had not been sold is an interesting question.

Anelka and his brother Claude, who acted as his agent, met with

Wenger and David Dein at Sopwell House in St Albans. The player told them he wanted to leave and made it clear that if he was not allowed to go then he would simply not report back. Wenger was visibly upset and disappointed. He had put so much time and effort into making him a big star, having taken him from relative obscurity and turned him into one of the most exciting talents in Europe, but Wenger knew that Arsenal had no choice but to sell. Their only challenge was to get as much money for him as they could.

When Anelka finally got up to leave, an emotional Wenger tapped him on the shoulder and said: 'Nicolas, I hope one day that you may think that I improved your career just a little bit. Goodbye.' The fact that Wenger nearly re-signed Anelka in 2007 shows that he was not a man to bear a grudge.

But, as great as Henry was to become, even he admitted it took him a while to adapt at Arsenal. Wenger converted him from winger to an out-and-out centre forward and his shooting ability became increasingly accurate. I remember covering Arsenal's win at Southampton when Henry broke his duck in mid-September 1999 in his ninth game. Typically for how his career would develop, it was a spectacular goal, Henry cutting in from the flank before unleashing a thunderbolt into the far corner to secure a 1-0 win. I went down the tunnel to speak to Henry, who was less confident in his English than he is now and, despite being a World Cup winner, he was down to earth and humble. As the goals flowed (he ended up scoring 26 that season) the confidence followed and he went on to become a global superstar.

Over the next couple of years, as the defence he had inherited began to age, Wenger sought to strengthen, delving into the transfer market and bringing in lesser-known players such as Igors Stepanovs, Moritz Volz, Guy Demel and Niccolo Galli. While he had an eye for a forward, his attempts at signing defenders were less successful, which perhaps tells you something about where Wenger's priorities lie. He even jokes about his fullbacks, wanting them to be more like wingers.

The accusation levelled over and over at Wenger was that he merely inherited Arsenal's famous back four, the defence of Dixon, Bould, Adams and Winterburn, and that he has never been able to build a solid defence, such is his obsession with the attacking side of the game.

Before then, Wenger went to great lengths to try to extend the careers of some of his senior players. While Tony Adams struggled with a long-running back injury, Wenger urged his medical staff to look hard for alternative solutions. For far too long the image of a physio with a wet sponge running on to the pitch had been used to illustrate football's idea of treating injuries. But with rapid advances in science and sports medicine – and with Wenger's different approach plus some of the best professionals around (Gary Lewin would later become England's physio) – Arsenal were eager to embrace new theories, however bizarre they seemed.

Adams flew to France to see unorthodox French fitness expert Tibruce Darrou, and had his wisdom teeth removed as Darrou believed they were the root of some back problems as they would provoke muscle spasms and affect balance, posture and his whole back. In later years, Robert Pires travelled to the South of France to see Darrou as well, after his cruciate knee ligament injury. Wenger is very receptive when it comes to new medical, physical and psychological thinking and reads extensively in this area.

After the near miss of 1999 came more frustration in 2000 as they finished the season empty-handed yet again. Runners-up to Manchester United in the Premier League once more, though this time they trailed them by 18 points, they lost the UEFA Cup final to Galatasaray in Copenhagen on penalties after playing poorly.

The game was also marred by ugly scenes of crowd violence between supporters in the Danish capital, making for an unsavoury, unsatisfactory end in every respect.

Wenger is notorious for being a ditherer when it comes to transfers and his indecision has arguably let many potential signings slip away. Conversely, his stance with players has always been that if they wanted to leave Arsenal then generally he wouldn't stand in their way. There were a few exceptions, of course. Year after year, Arsenal fought to keep Patrick Vieira, even when his behaviour drew widespread criticism (he spat at Neil Ruddock in one fiery London derby at West Ham when Arsenal's frustrations got the better of them again). It almost became an annual saga, as he was sought after by a string of top clubs, often headed up by Real Madrid. Then, in later years, they also battled to keep Cesc Fabregas.

But, in the summer of 2000, Wenger made more substantial changes. Up until then, it had been little tweaks each year. This time, Arsenal evolved into the second team of Wenger's reign. It happened largely because they decided to sell Emmanuel Petit and Marc Overmars to Barcelona in a huge double deal. The negotiations lasted for weeks as Barcelona publicly declared their interest and then haggled over the price.

Petit's midfield partnership with Vieira was one of the most powerful in the Premier League. But over the course of the previous two seasons, Petit had grown increasingly frustrated with English football, insisting he was often picked upon.

Petit wrote a regular column in the *Daily Mirror*, one of his last spilling over into a rant about referees and officialdom. Having been sent off four times in 17 months at Arsenal, he complained bitterly in his column, saying: 'I've just had enough. And I won't change my mind. I'm totally fed up with what has been happening. If I'm going to be shown the yellow card every time I open my mouth or make a mistake on the pitch – while others are getting away with much worse – I'm wasting my time here.'

For all of Petit's frustrations with English football, that didn't stop him returning to the Premier League with Chelsea after just a year in Spain. Petit, like a few players who left, was never the force he had been in those early days alongside Vieira, when they had been one of the best midfield double acts in Premier League history: brutal, brilliant and dominant. They did get themselves into trouble and it is amusing now to think of Wenger complaining about his teams receiving rough treatment when, back in the early days of his reign, his side were often the ones getting stuck in.

There was a time when reporters would go to every Arsenal game with the number of red cards totted up. It seemed that a landmark of red cards was passed on a weekly basis. 'That's the fortieth red card of Wenger's reign' someone would helpfully shout across the press box. Then Wenger would be asked about it afterwards and, famously, it became a standing joke as he would insist: 'I did not see it.'

In the summer of 2000, having sold Petit and Overmars, Arsenal spent big as they raided the French market again for two internationals. They broke the club record transfer to sign Sylvain Wiltord for £12 million and they paid £10 million for Robert Pires. Wiltord was a versatile forward who could play wide, off the striker or through the middle and had pace to burn.

Pires, meanwhile, was an attacking midfielder, who took time to settle in the Premier League. He had an odd-looking running style, appearing flat-footed, and he seemed intimidated by the physical nature of English football. It took him a season to find his feet. One memory burns brightly of a north London derby at Tottenham when he struggled to make an impact at all, seemed reluctant to go near to the wide areas and looked visibly shaken when he was on the receiving end of a torrent of abuse when he went to get the ball back from the home fans in a far corner of the ground.

Despite the recruits, Arsenal's new era took time to bed in and the 2000/01 season saw some unpredictable and shocking results, the 6-1 defeat at Manchester United being the worst of all. In that game, Igors Stepanovs was horribly exposed as United ran riot; Wenger lost his temper in the dressing room at half-time (with the score 5-1) and it was clear that Arsenal were a team in transition. They had gone from being 1998 Double winners, to the nearly men of '99 and then empty-handed in 2000 and 2001, although they finished second in the Premier League three years in a row and were runners-up in the UEFA Cup in 2000 and the FA Cup in 2001 (losing 2-1 to Liverpool). They were going close and yet desperately needed the missing ingredients to rule again.

Pires made his debut at Sunderland in the opening game of the 2000/01 season, starting from the bench during the second half. It was after the final whistle that the match descended into all-out war, when Wenger's temper was exposed again after Vieira had been sent off in the last minute. He was involved in a furious tunnel bust-up with fourth official Paul Taylor and Sunderland boss Peter Reid, as he remonstrated angrily near the dressing rooms.

In front of TV crews and radio interviewers in the tunnel at the Stadium of Light, Wenger blew his top and completely lost it with Reid, who was blaming Vieira. One witness said: 'He lost his temper that day with Reidy. It was reasonably comical. It was Patrick again. Patrick got sent off and Reidy was going absolutely nuts about the challenge. Arsene thought Patrick had been fouled as much as he'd been fouling.

'Up the tunnel, full time, Peter was swearing fluently as he does. Arsene was shouting: "No, fuck you! No, no, no, fuck you!" The players were going: "Oh my God." Bearing in mind this is Arsene Wenger, the man everyone thought was incredibly studious and calm. Then, as calm as you like, he went into the press conference and was in complete control.'

Taylor and Sunderland's Darren Williams were both called as witnesses and the FA hit Wenger with a 12-game touchline ban after finding him guilty. Wenger insisted it was a 'minor' incident, appealed and claimed he was just trying to separate players.

It was, however, a reminder that Wenger – as well as being serious and thoughtful – had a fierce temper. It was also a welcome to English football that Pires would never forget. Wenger said with a smile: 'I remember before his first game at Sunderland, I said to Pires, "Today you don't start – you sit next to me." After half an hour, he said to me, "Is it always like that?" And I said, "It can get worse!" Sometimes the players, at the start, have a shock. But, when I arrived [in 1996], it was much more violent than today.'

Pires was already an established French international, making his full debut in 1996 and playing regularly during a time when France dominated on both the world and European stage. So there was no shortage of clubs wanting to sign him when Marseille decided they would sell in 2000. Real Madrid was one such club and that was a big temptation because, as a child, he grew up wearing the white shirt of Madrid.

But Pires admitted it was Wenger who persuaded him to join Arsenal and helped him become a world-class player. 'In 2000, Madrid wanted me. But Arsenal wanted me too and I chose London because of Wenger. I spoke to him lots of times. I knew what he wanted and I knew that I would play. Madrid is a great club, of course, but it's a club with little stability. Everyone thought I was on my way to Madrid but I didn't want that.

'It was an honour to work with Arsene Wenger every day. He was such a great teacher, Le Professeur. He always taught you something, tactically or technically. Without doubt, the best years of my career were with him at Arsenal between 2000 and 2006.'

But that period – as new players took time to settle in – represented what was seen as a highly inconsistent spell. In both 2000 and 2001 they came very close to success, just as they had in 1999, epitomised perhaps by the 2001 FA Cup final defeat when they dominated the game but ended up losing after conceding two late goals to Liverpool. But in the league, Arsenal lacked the consistency needed to overhaul Manchester United, their nearest and most fierce rivals. As close as the margin was in 1999, United won by 18 points in 2000 and ten points in 2001.

Parlour puts much of it down to Wenger's efforts to overhaul Arsenal's famous back four, as the defence at least was going through a period of transition. 'It was a period of time where the back four was getting a bit older, a few were leaving and Wenger was changing the side really. He changed the back four. Lauren came in at right back, Ashley Cole came in for Nigel Winterburn, Kolo Toure came in and there was a lot of change at the club and sometimes it takes time.'

For a top club, Wenger took on a large number of trialists; added to which, the doors were always thrown open for former players to come and train. It caused some disquiet behind the scenes because the training ground was becoming a bit like an old boys' club. But Wenger, avoiding confrontation at all costs, did not like to say no. Be it David Beckham, Pires or Thierry Henry, at various times they could all come to London Colney and train.

It was the same for trialists. Stepanovs, a lanky Latvian international, was welcomed in after a recommendation from an agent. He really struggled, and he became a bit of a joke among the players, who loved to tease Martin Keown who was easy to wind up and therefore a regular target for the dressing-room jokers like Dennis

Bergkamp and Ray Parlour. They had already kidded Keown that a delivery man to the training ground was in fact a new central defender and fooled him to such an extent that he went to see Wenger for reassurances.

Then, a few began to pass comments when Wenger and Keown were within earshot, saying what a good player Stepanovs was, just to goad their Arsenal team-mate, even though they never believed the big Latvian would be signed. Even in a friendly game, sitting behind the bench, a few of the jokers clapped every time Stepanovs touched the ball, said what a good game he was having and tried to wind up Keown. Who knows whether it really made up Wenger's mind? But there were a few looks of astonishment when Stepanovs was signed a few weeks later.

Stepanovs had four years at Arsenal, starting just 17 league games, but the lowest point came at Old Trafford when Arsenal lost 6-1 and Wenger lost his temper at half-time in the dressing room as badly as he has ever done during his time in charge at Arsenal. To this day, those close to him insist it is the worst they have ever seen him lose his cool during half-time. The Frenchman appeared to be physically shaking as he made his way up the tunnel to the Old Trafford dressing room. Parlour recalls what happened:

> He went crazy at half-time at Manchester United when we lost 6-1. The back four that day were Oleg Luzhny, Igors Stepanovs, Gilles Grimandi and Ashley Cole. We were 5-1 down at half-time and David Seaman had a blinder – he was tipping them over the bar. It could have been 10-1.
>
> I will always remember seeing Arsene Wenger. We weren't used to this, he was so calm. But then you had him starting swearing, he was swearing in English – but sounded like a Frenchman! I wanted to laugh really because it sounded so

strange; no one could look at each other otherwise we'd start laughing and we'd start each other off. You could imagine George Graham or Sir Alex Ferguson swearing, but it didn't feel right with Arsene Wenger. That's the only time he really properly lost it. I've never seen him lose it like that before or since. It was a really poor performance, to play like that and be 5-1 down at half-time, you can't do that ... [He] and Ferguson were having some mind games and he felt it really bad.

If you were 1-0 or 2-0 down at half-time then he would keep his calm and his cool. He knew the characters he could gee up a little bit more and the ones he couldn't.

After the result itself, the Monday meeting was most important. We spoke about it, then the Tuesday and Wednesday was all about bouncing back. You can't play well all the time. The meeting after that Man United game, or any heavy defeat, was always important going forward.

I remember another game at Highbury, we were 2-0 down to Villa. People were pulling out of tackles. You could see Pat Rice absolutely fuming. He came into the dressing room, he started tearing into the players. Then Wenger came into the dressing room and said: 'Shut up, Pat.'

His theory was that if you had a go at certain players then they would go into their shell and not want the ball, someone like Robert Pires. We got the early goal; we ended up winning the game. He saw every player as different, a different individual, and they all needed different management.

Winterburn, who had left before the 6-1 thrashing at Old Trafford, added:

In the four years that I did with him, never once did he raise his voice, let alone lose his temper. It was a weird feeling because at times you thought he was going to give it to the team, or if you'd not done well then you thought you might get a dressing-down. But there was nothing. He just talked about how to rectify the situation. It was something I'd never experienced before or afterwards in my whole career.

He didn't like anybody – particularly staff – shouting at the players, full stop. There was one game, against Aston Villa, where Pat Rice was bawling at the players. Arsene came in and he gave Pat a bollocking for it!

It was so different. George Graham was so different in every way. He did a lot of team work; he made very clear boundaries which told us: 'I'm the manager, you're the players.' Tony Adams was the medium between the two. I had many an argument with George, during a game or at half-time. It's something that happens but, like everything else, you just forget about it and move on to the next game . . .

[During Wenger's time] if there was a disagreement at half-time or full time, the players would argue. He didn't step in. He just let it go. He was there listening, then all of a sudden would step in: 'Right, this is what we're going to do.' It was almost as if he was taking notes; he took on board what was said and assessed what needed to happen. I think that happens with a lot of managers, but it's about how the players react as well and he was quite clever at that: letting the players have words and then taking what he needed out of what they said.

During games, at half-time or whatever, he would make his points – like the tempo is too slow, need to be quicker on the counterattack, more disciplined defensively. He would try to make you calm and make you focus on his beliefs as to how you would win a game. I don't think that's changed too much now, from what I hear.

That day, Arsenal were given the run-around at Old Trafford by United's pace as Dwight Yorke scored a hat-trick, and Ole Gunnar Solskjaer, Teddy Sheringham and Roy Keane all scored in the rout. It was humiliation at the hands of their biggest rivals, led by Wenger's biggest managerial rival in Sir Alex Ferguson, at a time when Arsenal were supposed to be the closest team to Manchester United. Wenger's pride was hurt.

After the disappointments of 2000 and 2001, Wenger now had a clear idea of what was needed: he was about to address the issue in his defence and begin the rebuild of Arsenal's back four as they embarked on a new era of success.

CHAPTER 4

THE GLORY GAME

THE SUMMER OF 2001 undoubtedly laid the foundations for a new era of success at Arsenal under Arsene Wenger. And yet, curiously, they had a very mixed – but expensive – time in the transfer market, which was telling in many ways. They bought Francis Jeffers for £8 million, Richard Wright for £6 million, Giovanni van Bronckhorst for £8.5 million and, the most eye-catching deal of all, Sol Campbell on a Bosman-style free transfer.

Campbell arrived from Tottenham – the ultimate transfer coup by Wenger, capturing their bitter rivals' best player and captain, and persuading him to join Arsenal ahead of Inter Milan, Manchester United and Barcelona. It was a stunning transfer, a statement of intent, a signal that Arsenal were determined to get back to the top after three barren years.

Wenger, without question, also wanted to spend big to send a very clear message to some disaffected players. Henry was frustrated after the 2001 FA Cup final defeat. Perhaps even more telling in retrospect was Patrick Vieira's angry outburst in April

2001 after Arsenal lost at Valencia in the Champions League and once again went out of Europe.

He could barely contain his annoyance after the game in Spain, and insisted he would not discuss or answer any more questions on his future at Arsenal, casting doubt over whether he was about to leave the club. The message was clear. Vieira, one of the most sought-after midfielders in Europe, was telling Wenger and Arsenal to improve the squad and make themselves competitive again. That summer, as much as in any year of the first half of Wenger's reign, they really went for it in the transfer market.

When Campbell was unveiled to the press at the club's training ground, there was a collective gasp of amazement when he walked through the door. It was a deal that stunned the English game and Campbell's impact should not be underestimated. During his time at the club, Arsenal won the league and FA Cup Double, the FA Cup a further two times and the league title in the 2003/04 Invincibles season, as well as reaching the Champions League final in 2006.

In Campbell, they signed a giant who was as important during that era as any player, including Thierry Henry, Dennis Bergkamp, Patrick Vieira and Robert Pires. By contrast, the other deals were not successful. Van Bronckhorst suffered a cruciate knee ligament injury, which held him back, and he was sold without ever really establishing himself as an Arsenal regular.

Wright, a promising keeper who was capped by England and was briefly heralded as a potential successor to David Seaman, was signed from Ipswich, having played a blinder against Arsenal at Highbury, but he never fulfilled his potential at the club.

The other English signing was promising young striker Jeffers, whose career was hampered by injury and who was often blamed for putting Wenger off from signing English and British players for years to come. It's difficult to blame a player when his career is dogged by injury. But a picture of the 2002 title-winning celebrations, which still takes pride of place at London Colney, has Jeffers – who played only six games in that campaign – at the front wearing a huge pair of joke sunglasses.

Funnily enough, though, Jeffers will never be forgotten because he was always saddled with the expectation of being the answer to Arsenal's goalscoring problems and their search for a prolific striker. He was expected to be a goal poacher, the sort of clinical finisher Arsenal lacked among their spectacular strikers.

Jeffers was christened Arsenal's 'fox in the box', after the phrase was coined following the 2001 FA Cup final. Arsenal dominated the game and should have had a penalty when Liverpool defender Stephane Henchoz handballed on the line. Arsenal went ahead late on through Freddie Ljungberg, only for Michael Owen to score twice in the last seven minutes to win the trophy.

Afterwards, in the mixed zone at the Millennium Stadium – where the players conduct media interviews – it was difficult to get any Arsenal player to say anything of note, such was their frustration. The best line was delivered by Thierry Henry to the French media: he said Arsenal needed a '*renard sur le terrain*' – literally, fox on the pitch – which became 'fox in the box'. In fact, Henry even adopted the saying himself, using the English version in interviews for years afterwards. Jeffers was signed to be the fox in the box, but it never worked out and, just over two years later, he rejoined Everton on loan.

But while Arsenal were struggling to find extra quality in the opposing box, they had signed a colossus in their own penalty area. Campbell was strong, powerful and typified the sort of physical specimen that Wenger was looking for in his team. Arsenal's key men, like Campbell, Vieira and Henry, all fitted the new prototype of powerful athletes.

It was, though, a daring deal on Arsenal's part. Campbell

remembers that period so well. Arsenal's vice-chairman David Dein was the key negotiator, convincing him to leave a club where he was captain and to join their biggest rivals. Tellingly, Campbell believes the chemistry between Wenger and Dein made them a perfect double act in the transfer market. Wenger would identify the player; Dein would charm the player and get the deal done.

Weeks and months went into recruiting Campbell from arch rivals Tottenham. Campbell had become disaffected and frustrated at White Hart Lane. Arsenal were ready to seize their opportunity as he was a free agent. Moving abroad would have been the easy option. But Dein was determined to convince Campbell that the hard option would be more rewarding – even if it threatened to widen the north London divide.

Campbell's negotiations with Arsenal were held in secret at Dein's house, where they would talk and talk. Campbell would insist on going to Dein's house in the middle of the night because he was so obsessed with the press finding out. They would walk around Dein's garden in the darkness, discussing the possible transfer.

Campbell is a deep thinker. Getting him onside and convincing him the time was right to leave Spurs was a huge challenge. It was Dein who finally persuaded Campbell to move to Arsenal in one of the most controversial deals in Premier League history. Campbell will be remembered by Arsenal supporters as a legend for, as they see it, doing the dirty on their fiercest rivals.

Campbell provides a fascinating insight into the dynamic of the Dein–Wenger relationship when it came to transfers, as Campbell recalls:

I didn't see so much of Arsene, it was more David Dein. He was an excellent communicator. He knows how football runs. He can talk to chairmen, directors, managers, even canteen ladies. He's got the human side as well. That was a big plus for me. Together, the two of them were so successful as a pair. David was like a sounding board for Arsene. They were so good together . . .

At Tottenham, I was running around covering for about three or four players, doing my own job as well and it's great when you have got that trust, self-belief, belief in others and it spreads throughout the team. It involves the keeper as well. It's not telepathic but you read certain positions. It comes with chemistry, understanding and a bunch of lads for whom it worked. It was great to be involved in an amazing team which was great both offensively and defensively.

The sad thing about Tottenham was that I had a lot of managers, far too many managers. At one stage, at the end, I was just running on talent. There was no structure, no philosophy in place. Someone else comes in and there's a new philosophy in play. It was just like a revolving door. There was no persistent forward thinking . . .

One reason I went to Arsenal was the structure. There was a philosophy in play, a stable environment, but also a way of playing football as well. I fitted in really nicely and that's the key. If you fit into a place with your type of mentality and playing style then you're not going to have a problem. It suits you. Yes, it does help to have fantastic players, world-class players. I was part of that cog, you all fit together and make an amazing machine and that's what we were: part of a machine. An organic machine, you know.

For me on a personal level, it had to work. I had no option. I had to win something. Massive move, lot of pressure, half of north London probably wishing it all goes horribly wrong. It had to work. I came in injured. I had to get over that, get into the team, and there were a lot of hurdles to get over. Ultimately, though, I was saying to myself: 'It has to work; if it's not your day, then you have to make it your day.'

The eyes inevitably turned to Campbell that season when Arsenal played Tottenham and, in particular, the ex-Spurs captain went back to White Hart Lane for the first time in November 2001. The Arsenal team bus had bricks thrown at it as it drove in and out of White Hart Lane – with home supporters hiding in an adjacent pub's beer garden to throw their missiles – and the level of abuse towards Campbell was horrendous. Tottenham fans have never forgiven Campbell for what they see as his betrayal.

It was an unforgettable game that Campbell remembers with a mixture of pride and dread. He also recalls that Wenger was ada-mant that he should play, and there was never any question of him missing it with a diplomatic groin strain.

It's funny, you see the hate in the people's eyes. You see women, children, whoever, almost frothing at the mouth. They were burning effigies of me outside of the ground. I knew it was going to happen, but it went beyond a level that I could have imagined. It was so tight coming into the ground, then the car park opens up. I walked into the ground – and then went into the wrong dressing room! It was so funny. It was just a habit.

Everyone was looking at me. I made a point of warming up, and going to every corner of the ground. It was vile, it was dis-gusting, but I had to get on with it. Once I got changed, I ran to all four corners to adjust to what was going to happen to me, to hear everything that was going to be said to me. I went to all the edges to take it all in ... I had a game plan. I was ready for it. But one thing that really stands out in my mind was the banners. But it was a tough game for me – not football-wise, but emotionally it was tough.

Arsenal drew at Tottenham that day, Pires' late opener being cancelled out by Gus Poyet's last-gasp leveller.

Campbell also has an interesting insight into Wenger's football philosophy. With Lauren and Ashley Cole at full back, and a combination of Adams, Keown and Campbell in the centre, Arsenal had a rock-solid back four again and a wealth of brilliant attacking talent. But Campbell makes it clear that Wenger expected the players themselves to take a lot of responsibility for tactics. He felt he had enough quality, with players such as Pires, Bergkamp, Henry, Wiltord and Ljungberg, to be good enough to beat any opponent. Therefore, they didn't need to rely so heavily on tactics or an inspirational substitution to change or a win a game. Basically, Wenger was of the opinion that it didn't matter what the opposing team could do – Arsenal could do better. He adds:

[Wenger] puts a lot of onus on players to change the game. He believes in that. There is a structure within that. He wants to play a certain way. But he wants certain players – especially in the last third – to be able to produce it and give something different.

He's looking for that magic. Everyone's looking for that magic, but if you have three, four or five players going forward who have got that magic, then it's great. It's fantastic. It just keeps other teams on their toes; they don't know whether they're coming or going. They always know they're going to be in a game because if ... you've got two players heavily marked, then you've still got another two players free. That's what you want: whoever you are playing against, they can't lock you down and shut you out completely.

Wenger had once again found a team with a perfect rhythm: strong in defence, powerful and creative in midfield, and with wonderful attacking flair. Quietly and in an understated way, Wenger had built another Arsenal team and one which, as Campbell alluded to, had enough leaders in the ranks to ensure that the manager's wishes and instructions were adhered to on the pitch. Wenger had also achieved it without radical change, as Campbell was the only significant signing from the summer of 2001 to really make a major impact on the team.

The players signed in 2000, the likes of Pires and Wiltord, had taken time to adapt and produce their best form, but they really kicked on in the 2001/02 season. Wiltord will always be remembered for scoring the winner at Old Trafford when Arsenal clinched the Premier League title. That was perhaps the best revenge possible for Arsenal losing the FA Cup semi-final to United in 1999 but, more than that, proof that Arsenal had reclaimed their place at the head of the English game.

It came after an impressive title run-in, in which Swedish midfielder Freddie Ljungberg was often the key figure as the team won their last 13 league games. He enjoyed a prolific spell, scoring seven goals in as many games on the way to the title, and he also scored in the FA Cup final win over Chelsea in May 2002.

Ljungberg remembers the period fondly: 'It was the best time of my career, definitely. The most enjoyable, the time when I felt the best and the manager would give you a lot of confidence. Winning trophies are always highlights for every player. Also, the connection I have with Arsenal fans. That was something special for me. On a personal note, I won the Premier League Player of the Year award [in 2001/02]. That hasn't happened to other Swedish players and was nice for me.'

At this time, Wembley was being rebuilt, and so trips to the Millennium Stadium for cup finals became a regular pilgrimage, with the lengthy traffic delays over the Severn Bridge living as long in the memory as the cup games themselves.

The FA Cup final of 2002 was particularly memorable because Arsenal beat Chelsea on a gloriously sunny Saturday – and then had a title decider at Old Trafford the following Wednesday when they knew victory over Manchester United would win them the Double. Wenger knew that a cup final win – no matter how much such an occasion took out of his players' legs and minds – would be the key. He certainly didn't want a repeat of 1999 and that demoralising FA Cup semi-final defeat.

It was a tight, tense final as Chelsea, still in the pre-Roman Abramovich era, had big players like Marcel Desailly, Frank Lampard and William Gallas. But Arsenal's line-up that day looked formidable and highlighted their strength: Seaman; Lauren, Adams, Campbell, Cole; Wiltord, Parlour, Vieira, Ljungberg; Henry, Bergkamp. Arsenal were easily the best team in the country that season.

However, they still only managed to edge it with late goals, Ray Parlour breaking the deadlock after 70 minutes with one of the best goals of his career – a curling 25-yard shot into the top corner – and then Ljungberg continued his prolific run with a second ten minutes later. Parlour has vivid memories of the occasion:

That was probably the most important goal of my career. It was a really tough game against Chelsea. They were buying good players.

It was a weird week ... To be honest, the lads were getting a bit tired, feeling a bit of fatigue. You never get tired when you're playing in an FA Cup final. But we knew if we lost, that would make us feel tired.

I remember as a kid watching every cup final. Then to play in my first FA Cup final was a real honour; then to score in one was a dream to come true. I remember making a run. Thierry

Henry made a great run, he took two defenders away from me, and then it was me and Desailly and all I really did was get the opportunity to bend it round him and hope for the best.

I used to score loads of them in the training! But not many in a game like that. It was so good to see it curl into the top corner. That was a great week for myself and a great week for Arsene Wenger as the manager. Roman Abramovich came in, put the money into Chelsea and that became a different battle. But they were such a good team even in that final and to beat them, then go to Old Trafford and win the league with one of our best performances away from home, was fantastic.

After that FA Cup final, Arsenal were buzzing. I remember getting the train from Euston up to Manchester for the game at Old Trafford on Wednesday 8 May 2002. Rarely do you go to a game at Manchester United with such a strong feeling that the away team will win. Arsenal were that strong, that dominant and that good. It didn't seem in doubt. Victory looked inevitable.

Arsenal had to make changes, with Thierry Henry, Tony Adams and Dennis Bergkamp dropping out, but they were able to bring in Martin Keown, Edu and Kanu. United were fired up, and Paul Scholes, Phil Neville and Roy Keane were all lucky not to see red in a frantic opening 45 minutes. Sir Alex Ferguson was determined that United would not roll over. But Parlour recalls that night at Old Trafford as one of the best experiences of his career as Sylvain Wiltord scored the 55th-minute winner, pouncing on a rebound after Fabien Barthez saved from Ljungberg. Parlour said: 'United were desperate, absolutely desperate, to beat us. We played so well. It was one of the best weeks of my career because I got Man of the Match at Old Trafford. I scored in the cup final then got Man of the Match on the Wednesday when we won the league. It meant we won the Double, so you can't get much of a better week than that.'

Arsenal went into 2002/03 as Double winners and full of confidence, playing with a style and swagger which saw them make a sensational start to the season. It was such a good start that one of the journalists who regularly covers Arsenal, the *Daily Star*'s David Woods, went as far as to ask Wenger whether he thought they could go through an entire season unbeaten.

Woods recalls: 'You could tell Wenger was not sure whether to go for it, but after a slight hesitation he gave the answer we did not expect. Yes, he insisted, it could be done and that other top managers, including Sir Alex Ferguson, felt the same but were too scared to say so. He said it with the usual half-smile on his face, and pointed out AC Milan had already done it.

'But we all know that what managers think and what they actually say are two very different things, and you can imagine some of the players were as surprised to read what their manager had said as we were to actually hear him say it.'

Wenger made two memorable signings in the summer of 2002 with very different results. In came French defender Pascal Cygan for £2 million from Lille, while Gilberto Silva was bought from Brazilian club Atletico Mineiro, fresh from winning the World Cup with the Brazilian national team.

Gilberto is a softly spoken, charming man who flourished at Arsenal in the role of midfield general, as part of the two anchormen in front of the back four. He was often an unsung hero in Arsenal's midfield while, in contrast, Cygan became yet another of Wenger's defensive signings who never lived up to expectations.

Gilberto spent some time with Wenger during the summer of 2014 at the World Cup in Brazil and also met up with David Dein, the man who brokered the deal. He recalls how he came to move to Arsenal:

I had a few options but it was funny looking back. David Dein was in Brazil in the summer for the World Cup and he told me the story of how he brought me to Arsenal. He saw me together with Arsene during the World Cup in Japan in 2002 and at some point Arsene said: 'He's a good player.' David asked him if he wanted the player and Arsene said: 'Yes, OK.' David just told him to leave it up to him. He flew to Brazil, flew home with me, and was joking that he put me in a box to make sure I couldn't get away!

I didn't speak the language and it took me a while to settle in to the country. What was important was the way I adapted to life in England. I'd just finished winning the World Cup with Brazil. I could have gone there thinking: 'I'm a world champion, I'm the best in that position.' There was one very important thing for me and that was to make sure I started from zero. In England, I was nobody.

I didn't know much about the culture or the football. I needed to learn the whole thing. Even though everything was new for me, I was very open to learn things and that solved everything. For me, in the club, Edu was very important. He would take care of me in training, outside of the club as well, he really took care of me.

Gilberto believes Wenger was very clever in the way he combined a mix of nationalities, different characters and mentalities, to slowly build a dressing room which would quickly go on to reach new heights.

The combination of players was really important. Even though we had the French guys, the English guys and me and Edu, the two Brazilians, some other foreigners, the combination was really important because everyone thought in the same way to win games, to win competitions. We had a great mentality. We wanted to win.

We'd want to win games, even in training against each other. We put all this effort in every game. That's why we could win the league unbeaten. Because we had this mentality, we went into games and inside our minds we knew we could win the game. We worked hard to win games; we worked so hard to win competitions.

Wenger, despite thumping Leeds away from home and comprehensively beating the likes of West Brom, Charlton and Birmingham, was put back in his place when Arsenal surrendered their unbeaten start, losing 2-1 at Everton in mid-October. They went down to a 90th-minute winner from a certain Wayne Rooney, who was just 17 at the time.

Wenger would, of course, revisit that target of finishing a season unbeaten the following year. But Arsenal struggled with consistency in the 2002/03 season and the unbeaten target lasted all of nine games.

They faced a reinvigorated Manchester United, boosted by the record signing of Rio Ferdinand, who went unbeaten in the league after Boxing Day. A 1-1 draw at Highbury on 16 April wasn't enough. In May 2003, Arsenal lost 3-2 at home to Leeds (having also dropped points at Bolton in the previous game) and the title had returned to Manchester. As with many managers, victories that don't mean anything only leave them wondering what might have been. So when Arsenal thrashed Southampton 6-1 in the next match – including a hat-trick by youngster Jermaine Pennant – Wenger was full of regret rather than enjoyment.

Little did Wenger know at the time but Pennant had enjoyed a huge night out before the game, as he was not expecting to play. But hangover or not, he still scored three goals.

Two weeks later, Arsenal played Southampton in the 2003 FA Cup final at the Millennium Stadium. Pires scored the first-half winner in a rather forgettable final, one of the most memorable aspects of which was that veteran keeper David Seaman captained the team in what was his last and farewell game for the club.

Interestingly, Arsenal didn't have an open-top bus parade through the streets of Islington as they hadn't won the league, but they did have a club party on that Saturday night in a hotel in Marble Arch. Those who were there remember it as anything but a celebration of winning a trophy. It was more of an inquest into what had gone wrong that season. That is an indication of how far Arsenal had come, the level of expectation and also the desire to win within the squad.

Senior players even rallied among themselves, ramming home the message that it wasn't enough, they were going to come back stronger and have a better season next year. It was a sombre affair full of frustration. The party had been overtaken by a group of big characters like Henry, Campbell and Pires, who wanted more each season.

It had been Gilberto Silva's first season at the club and, despite winning the FA Cup, it is obvious that was seen very much as a consolation prize:

The FA Cup was a great feeling. The feeling was amazing because when you are at a great club, a big club, you have to work hard to win titles because it's what they expect from you. The only way we could compensate our sacrifice during the season, to pay a tribute to the fans, because we lost the league, was winning the FA Cup, even though we wanted the Double ...

But a strong group with a winning mentality becomes even more determined when you have a disappointment. You want to work even harder. You want to improve from the year before.

Don't let anything pass you by. And that season was a bit of a disappointment [because] we let the opportunity to win the league pass in front of us ...

We learned a lot from that season. For me, the way I started at Arsenal and what the club achieved was fantastic. In my first year in Europe, I think I started in a very good way. There were many good players, good guys who supported me from the outside. But the biggest thing in that group was the characters, the determination and the desire to win.

Wenger had seen a remarkable mentality and character develop throughout the squad. But even with some big promises and lofty ambitions, surely the following season must have been beyond their wildest dreams.

CHAPTER 5

THE INVINCIBLES

A PICTURE HANGS in the entrance hall of Arsenal's training ground which serves as a reminder of the greatest season in the club's history. Sol Campbell and Patrick Vieira are pictured together, their arms locked. That encapsulates the reason why the Invincibles were able to win the Premier League title, going the whole season unbeaten. Played 38, won 26, drawn 12 and lost none.

Campbell started what became a tradition among the players in 2003/04. They would gather together in a huddle on the pitch before kick-off, lock arms and Campbell would shout: 'Together!' It epitomised a phenomenal and unbreakable team spirit. They had a couple of incredible let-offs: Ruud van Nistelrooy memorably crashed a late penalty against the crossbar near the start of the season, when Arsenal shared a goalless draw with Manchester United. Then there was Robert Pires' dive – which even his own manager admitted – to win a penalty against Portsmouth, which Thierry Henry converted to earn them a draw.

But over the course of the season, to go unbeaten was a remarkable first in Premier League history and is the biggest testament – and tribute – to Wenger's reign as Arsenal manager. They were solid defensively, creative in midfield and had the most lethal striker in the world. That season, Thierry Henry was unstoppable.

They got lucky early on but grew stronger and stronger. They were determined enough to survive when the going got really tough over the Easter period, and that is why Wenger believes the Invincibles will go down as his best ever team, even if it wasn't necessarily his hardest season.

When asked, Wenger said: 'The easy answer will be 2004 because we are the only team who has won the championship without losing a game. But the best years are not necessarily the hardest years. The hardest years are when ... for example, like in 2013, when we had no room for any mistake and sometimes the work of a manager is more difficult in the years when you struggle a bit. But certainly the best team was 2004.'

It is a view backed up by two members of the Invincibles who played in previous title-winning teams. Dennis Bergkamp said: 'I'd have to say the Invincibles! We had games where I had the feeling: "It will be 3-0 or 4-0 today", without making an effort.'

Robert Pires admits Arsenal always believed they would win every game – and with style. 'It wasn't a question of whether we'd win games in the Invincibles season – it was by how much. What I would say is that it's not arrogance, but we felt so strong and so sure of ourselves that we said to each other: "Today, we are practically unbeatable." And that is why we went a whole season undefeated ... A very great time and a very great era.'

Arsenal were unstoppable that season: they had used the frustrations of 2003 as a motivational force, built on the Double-winning team of 2002 (their only significant signing in the summer of 2003 was Jens Lehmann from Borussia Dortmund) and formed a remarkable unit. They had evolved as a group. Cameroon international Lauren had made the transition from midfield to right back, Kolo Toure had found his home in central defence and elsewhere you had a blend of talent and physical power – Patrick Vieira, Thierry Henry and Robert Pires. It was a wonderful mix.

Wenger insists the defence – Lehmann in goal, Lauren, Toure, Campbell and Ashley Cole – does not get the credit it deserves. The old and rather lazy criticism of Wenger is that he inherited the famous defence of Dixon, Adams, Bould and Winterburn. That's true enough, but he also built his own. He brought in Lehmann, converted Lauren and Toure from midfield to defence, signed Campbell from Arsenal's biggest rivals and helped bring Cole through the youth ranks. And Toure, let's not forget, was brought in as an unknown trialist in 2002 and signed for just £150,000 from Ivory Coast club ASEC Mimosas.

It was almost the perfect combination for Wenger – home-grown talent, discovering an unknown, nicking a free transfer from your biggest rivals and coaching a midfielder to become a defender. Building a team from those ingredients is far more satisfying to Wenger than assembling one from record signings.

But the memory of Toure's trial at the club still causes much amusement, as Ray Parlour remembers well:

Kolo Toure came into training one day. [Wenger] would put on games for trialists. He'd put Martin Keown in games for centre forwards – he'd be a good marker; he'd kick players and you'd find out about the player.

I remember you had Kolo Toure and Martin Keown. Against them, you had Dennis Bergkamp and Thierry Henry. I was playing on the right. Arsene would sit there; it was more for pattern play really. But I remember the ball was rolled into Thierry Henry and Kolo Toure, from nowhere, smashed him from behind. It was a terrible tackle, a red card in a normal game, and our best player was rolling around.

Wenger was shouting: 'Kolo, what are you doing? Don't tackle!' The next minute, the ball was into Dennis Bergkamp and Kolo did exactly the same. We were thinking: 'We're trying to win the league and a trialist has taken out our two best players.' Anyway, Wenger said: 'No more tackling.'

We went again, this time Kolo made a great tackle, the ball went up in the air and landed right at Arsene Wenger's feet. He was on the pitch, watching training. So next thing you know, Kolo Toure took him out with a two-footed tackle! All you could hear was Wenger screaming. He had to go back to the medical room, and the trialist had taken out Henry, Bergkamp and the manager!

Kolo was nearly in tears, his big day ruined. I went into the medical room and there was Arsene with an ice pack on his ankle. I said: 'I don't think he meant it.' He told me there and then: 'We're signing him tomorrow. I like his desire.' He knew he could get the best out of him and he went on to being a great player for the club.

Toure switched to central defence alongside Campbell and they became the first-choice partnership in the summer of 2003. It was a great pairing, with Campbell's size, strength and power in the air and Toure's pace, tenacity and incredible will to win. And you had that perfect combination all over the pitch, with Vieira partnering Gilberto Silva in central midfield, Freddie Ljungberg, Pires and Parlour often being the wide players and the irresistible talent of Thierry Henry up front, supported by the guile of Bergkamp. Sylvain Wiltord gave them options, as did Jose Antonio Reyes, whose January signing is often wrongly dismissed as a mistake when, in reality, his pace and goals gave them a lift after he joined midway through the season.

This was Wenger's ultimate team, coming together with pace, power, experience and youth, and the spirit within the camp gave them an unbelievable never-say-die determination. Of all the teams that Parlour played in, in a career spanning 1991 to 2004, he believes the Invincibles were the best.

The Invincibles team was fantastic. It was a team which never knew when it was beaten. A team which was very solid. We had a bit of everything, a bit of flair. The 1998 team was a brilliant team, a much smaller squad to pick from ... In 2004, we had a bigger squad, Wenger had more to pick from, the chance to change it when needed because you always have a few bad games but you had characters on the pitch. They were born winners. They never knew when they were beaten. There were occasions when we should have lost after going [behind], and still came back to draw the game or even win ...

It's hard to compare the squads and say that is definitely the best. On paper, the team which went unbeaten has to be the best. But I still think the 1998 team was a great team. It was different because we only had United against us. But in 2004, we had Chelsea coming through, United, more competition ..., but I think the Invincibles had a bit of everything.

Lauren, the midfielder-turned-right-back, was a warrior and remains so. He's still a keen amateur boxer, mixing fitness and sport with a blossoming career as a football agent. But in everything he has done in his life and in his career, nothing compares to being part of the Invincibles team. And he still refers affectionately to Arsenal as 'we' and regards Wenger as a 'father figure'. 'None of us were thinking about being Invincibles or winning the league without losing a game,' admitted Lauren.

We went game by game. We were focused only on the next game ... being unbeaten or being Invincible never crossed our minds at the start. It was a big, big achievement and no one has repeated it since or before. It's such a hard thing to do. We managed to do it because we had winning players, everyone was focused on the same thing. There were big characters in that dressing room.

In football, there are no guarantees. In football, four plus four doesn't necessarily make eight. When I arrived, the team had just won the Double in 1998. The transition from 1998 to 2001, the team didn't win anything. Wenger managed to build a team with good players, strong characters and the ambition to win things.

We had big characters in that Invincibles [season]. It wasn't just the 11, but we had ... 20 big players. Everyone wanted to win, everyone wanted to play, and we all had the motivation and ambition to win. You could feel that. It didn't matter who was in the team. You could see it in the players. You could see it in training, in the dressing room; you could see the desire to win and to do something.

He said to us the previous season that we could do it [win the title unbeaten]. We didn't do it. But he kept that belief. He always had that in the back of his mind. In the run-in, even after we'd won the league, he kept saying to us, to everyone: 'We have the chance to do something very important – keep the concentration high, this could be a very special achievement.'

Sol Campbell, the defensive kingpin in the Arsenal team, added:

It was fantastic playing with those guys. Ashley Cole was growing in stature, Lauren was accomplished and Kolo, surprisingly, was willing to learn. For me, it was a dream to be on a team – especially with that back line – that was enthusiastic, were fighting for each other. We had an excellent team. You only dream of being in that position. It doesn't really happen a lot that you get the chance to be part of such a great team.

There's guys who are very good but never get the chance to be part of a defence like that, or be in a good midfield, be in a front line where they get a good partner. It's very hard to get there unless you move. Some players are lucky – you've got Ryan Giggs, and I'm sure he'd have moved if Manchester United hadn't been the best for so long. As a player, you have to be lucky to get a team like that and if it doesn't happen then you're going to move.

We were a real tough side, men, really strong physically and good experience as well. I think even now [Wenger] should go back to proven players; there's time to groom and develop players, but go back to signing experienced players. They did something like that with Davor Suker before I came and it can work. You need experience and big characters and that's what we had in that team.

For Lauren, it is easy to understand his determination and loyalty towards Wenger, because the Arsenal manager developed him as a player and as a personality. From day one, Wenger told Lauren that he saw him in the long term as a right back rather than a midfielder because of his positional sense, athleticism and tenacity. Throughout the team there were big characters in every department and Lauren believes that, while there was an element of luck that they all came together at the same time, Wenger was very clever with his man management and nurturing of players. When

I spoke to Lauren, it was obvious he still has immense respect for Wenger:

He was like a father to me, the biggest and best influence on my career. You could talk to him about anything, he's a great man. I still call him boss! Mainly, he was a coach, who at the training ground had a very clear idea about tactics, football, but was also very clever on other things ...

One day, if I want to become a manager, then I would like to be like him. He took care of everything. If you needed to talk to him about anything, then he would always listen. Not just about football, but if you had a doubt about your position in the game or if you're playing 4-4-2 and you've got this problem and you don't understand that, then you can talk to him and he will give you the best advice.

In your own lives, if you had any problem or whatever, then you can say: 'Boss, I want to talk to you about this,' then he will listen to you carefully. He is a manager who listens to the players.

He wants players with personality. He won't tell you to go home and study something about an opponent. He won't tell you to go and look at something tactically. He wants you to go and do whatever you want. He wants you to express yourself.

He had this idea. He had it in his mind from when I came from Mallorca. When I first arrived, I wanted to play in midfield or right midfield because it was the position I knew. But in his mind, he saw me as a right back. He thought I had the conditioning and fitness to get up and down; he wanted players who could come inside and wanted players who were good on the ball. He wanted players to link up with the midfield. It was always in the back of his mind.

I don't think he built the team because of characters – but the characters fell into place. You can go to watch players, scout them, but you don't know about their characters until you work with them day by day. I don't think he signs players because of characters. Of course he wants good characters. And you try to look into their characters. But, in my view, it was a coincidence of that generation ...

You can sign five or six players and they won't always have the character and the ambition as well as the motivation to win things. They won't always have those qualities, and that's why we had been three or four years without winning things. We suddenly became successful again during our time.

To be honest, I haven't stayed much in contact with the boss. I would like to be more. I have been to games with him, no problem at all, and he's always so friendly, as if we were still working together. He used to see everything. He would take care of every small detail. Sometimes as a player you cannot see that at the time. He was good at that, looked after everything.

It is a view echoed by Parlour, who says Wenger's strengths were his man management, treating players as adults and instilling a never-say-die winning spirit even in training.

You've got to have that as a player. Character is so important. You can lose games and be disappointed but you always have to have that belief. Before the season starts, you have to believe you can win something.

We used to have meetings before the start of the season and set targets. We used to set our standards of trying to win everything every single season. You have to do that. We'd done that the year before the Invincibles and not done it. A few thought: 'What's he doing?' But it was designed to push us as much as possible. He was very clever at that, setting targets for the players. It's the same at every club. For some teams it'll be about staying up, but we had enough quality to win Doubles ...

His worst time of the week was in training on a Friday afternoon when we played eight versus eight. The tackles were flying in – how we got away with it I'll never know. We were so pumped up, so competitive, we were all trying to win. That was the desire and [the] winning formula, so he'd let some tackles go because it showed desire and quality and what you needed to win games. You put those 16 players together against someone else and you always had a chance of winning every game. And he knew that.

We concentrated and worked hard, but we'd also have a little bit of fun before the training sessions. That's really down to a good team spirit. Make sure that everyone knows their jobs but have a bit of fun off the field.

The way he conducted himself, the way he worked day to day, the way he kept you in the frame, assuring you that you could be back in the frame sooner or later. That made sure that when you came to leave the club you left on good terms. He was brilliant at that. Every single player who left that club – going back to Ian Wright and players like that – would have good words to say about Arsene Wenger.

I certainly had a good relationship with him. I was a bit of a muck-about person. He knew that but he also knew the other guys would respond to that as well. So he let me get away with a bit more. But I knew when I had to work, then I'd work and really concentrate so I did both and he knew that.

After finishing second behind Manchester United at the end of 2002/03, when some players such as Martin Keown believed the talk of going unbeaten had created too much pressure, Wenger's sights were set on reclaiming the title. Former Arsenal captain

Gilberto Silva, a central figure in the Invincibles team, remembers the belief growing within the camp and the elements of the squad that made them truly special:

It was a healthy pressure that the manager created and put on the players. When we lost the season before, with lots of points of difference from Manchester United, we went into a new season with more determination. We knew we could have won the season before. It was a big disappointment for us.

The players were winners, they wanted to win things, they were there to do the job. We started slowly, slowly. As the season went by, game by game, we became very strong. After about ten games without losing, we looked deep into ourselves and said: 'It's great, we feel good, we can keep going.' We put pressure on ourselves, kept working hard, and the winning mentality made such a difference because we were there to win, do whatever we could to win the game and if we couldn't win then it became important for us not to lose.

Gilberto believes Arsenal's strength in depth was the biggest factor in their Invincibles season, and he says that is also a tribute to Wenger's man management and being able to keep all the players happy:

We had so much quality. The hardest job is how to make all the guys play and how to control the guys with lots of quality on the bench. If you are a good manager, a good manager knows how to control all the players. He controls the guy who plays normally in the first team, but he also controls the other guys and ... still keeps the balance of the team.

Every player played some games during the season, either in the league, the FA Cup or Europe, or the other competitions. It's important because it means that it kept everyone fresh; they were all ready to come in whenever needed and we had big international players on the bench. But whatever team played, there was always quality. That was probably the most important thing of all – the whole squad had quality and a great mentality. No one was feeling down or not part of it. It was an incredible team spirit.

At some point, you always need the squad. It's important. We had so many international players and when there was an international break, a lot of the players would go and play for their countries. For example, I travelled to South America to play. When I came back to England, I was tired from the games and all the travel. Most of the time, I didn't play the first game after the international break because he put in another player and, for the team, that was good because he could put someone in with good quality and we were always fresh, with lots of energy. If you put in everyone who is tired then the results would not be very good. For sure, we would suffer a lot.

Thierry was fantastic. He was amazing that year. It was important because he made the difference up front. But of course he got support from the rest of the team. He always expected us to support him from the back. But every position we were so strong, from the defenders to the midfield. You couldn't see any difference even when we made a substitution. Sometimes I played with Edu, sometimes with Ray Parlour, sometimes I was out of the team. Patrick [Vieira] played with somebody else. But the balance of the team was the same ...

When you have that, you have the big guys who normally played in the first XI, but you also had guys on the bench who you could put on the field to make a difference. The support all over the pitch for Thierry was so important; we helped him a lot, but he was so important for us. We also had such great quality with players like Pires, Bergkamp, Freddie. It was an incredible team.

After those early escapes at Old Trafford and against Portsmouth, Arsenal grew stronger and stronger. And, as the belief grew, the results became more and more impressive: they smashed Leeds 4-1 at Elland Road and thrashed Inter Milan 5-1 in the San Siro.

But, just when it seemed to be running so smoothly, the wheels nearly fell off within the space of six days at the start of April. Not only were they unbeaten in the league, but they had reached the FA Cup semi-final and the Champions League quarter-final. On 3 April, they lost to Manchester United at Villa Park in the FA Cup. Surely they weren't about to suffer the same fate as in 1999, when an FA Cup semi-final defeat at Villa Park to United brought their season crashing down?

Then, having drawn at Chelsea in the Champions League and failed to win the first leg despite dominating the game, they lost to a last-gasp Wayne Bridge goal at Highbury. Their European dream had gone as well.

Lauren remembers that, even throughout the sticky spells, Wenger was a manager who always kept his cool and his familiar habit of rarely talking at half-time:

People question him on tactics or his methods, but he knows exactly what is going on at half-time. He will not confront the players or start to shout, throw things or lose his temper. He doesn't need that … He would say nothing, let you calm down, then he would start to speak. He would go straight to the key points. He would see the gap of the opponent: 'You must do this, do that, do this movement and you will succeed.' We would go back on to the pitch and it would happen exactly like he had told us.

Of course, you have to have the players who are able to extrapolate what the manager had in his mind. But if the manager doesn't have it in his brain then you can't do it. The communication between the manager's brain, and for the players to understand what is going on, was a real gift. It was perfect. We understood perfectly.

I've never come across like that before or since. I played under another big manager, Hector Cuper, who managed at Inter Milan, but it was not the same. Not at all. Wenger was so calming, such a good influence and always with a lot of knowledge. It was something amazing.

They needed that calmness mixed with determination on Good Friday 2004. Just three days after being knocked out of Europe – and with it went perhaps their best ever chance of winning the Champions League – they faced Liverpool at Highbury. Arsenal were flat, they had suffered two body blows, and at half-time they trailed Liverpool 2-1. The whole crowd held its breath, wondering whether Wenger's entire season was about to implode. But during that half-time interval Arsenal lifted themselves again. Martin Keown, a substitute that day, tried to rouse the players with a speech calling on their spirit and character to turn things around.

'I can't remember his speech! Martin? Nah,' says Parlour, enjoying a laugh at the expense of his former team-mate and number one target for ribbing. He adds:

I will always remember that nightmare week when we lost in the Champions League, went out of the FA Cup and suddenly we had to beat Liverpool. We were trailing them and that's when

Thierry Henry really turned up – scored a hat-trick, turned it round and got us back in the mix.

Everybody knew that Liverpool was a big game. We'd suffered two big blows and could have been out of everything in a week. That's how bad it gets in football. If you had a defeat then you'd have to try and get back to winning ways as quickly as possible, to have someone in the dressing room to gee up the players. You have to bounce back.

Arsene Wenger gave us a bit of extra mentality. The English lads had that anyway from George Graham's era. George was a winner. That back four knew how to win games. Then the players Wenger brought in, like Vieira, Petit and so on. They were winners as well. Sometimes when you're having a bad time, to get things back on track takes big characters and that's what people don't see ... The players would have to say: 'We've got to sort ourselves out here. If we don't sort it then we'll be out of the league and playing for nothing. We need to sort it.'

A lot of it was down to the characters in the dressing room and that was a big part of the success. I suppose that's also down to the manager to build the dressing room. But also often he'd let us get on with it ourselves and talk to each other, try and get things right to get the best out of us.

Gilberto agrees that the second-half fightback in that Liverpool game – when Henry scored twice to complete a hat trick and Pires also scored in the 4-2 win – was testament to the spirit in the group. 'We had two big setbacks in the week before. The results went against us. But we wanted to turn the situation in our favour and that showed the character of the team. The other teams became more and more difficult because as the season went by they became more and more motivated to become the first team to beat us. But we refused to lose. It became a symbol for us. It

Arsene Wenger cut his managerial teeth at Monaco (above) and Grampus Eight (below), moving to Japan after he became disillusioned with match-fixing allegations in France. (*Mirrorpix/Action Images*)

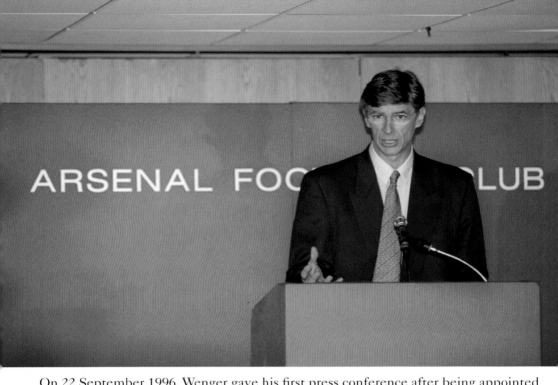

On 22 September 1996, Wenger gave his first press conference after being appointed manager of Arsenal. (*Getty Images*)

Wenger has Pat Rice and physio Gary Lewin by his side as Arsenal take on Blackburn Rovers in his first game in charge of the club. (*Getty Images*)

On Wenger's arrival, the training routines completely changed, and everything was timed. (*Mirrorpix*)

However, the players weren't immediately impressed by his ability on the ball. (*Mirrorpix*)

But his advice on stretching was quickly taken up by the players, as Ian Wright demonstrates. (*Getty Images*)

Even before Wenger had formally joined the club, he had advised Arsenal to sign Patrick Vieira from AC Milan's reserves. The young French midfielder quickly impressed his team-mates, and showed that the new manager had plenty to offer. (*Getty Images*)

Wenger went back to France to sign striker Nicolas Anelka, who was soon in prolific form. Here the two men celebrate during their 3-2 win over Manchester United in November 1997. (*PA*)

Wenger's first full season ended in a glorious Double, as the Gunners overhauled Manchester United to take the Premier League (above), beat Newcastle at Wembley in the FA Cup final with Marc Overmars scoring the first (right), followed by a victory parade that ended at Islington Town Hall (below).

(Getty Images/Getty Images/PA)

Tony Adams makes a desperate lunge but can't stop Ryan Giggs from scoring the winner in the 1999 FA Cup semi-final replay, a result that Wenger felt the club took a couple of years to recover from. (*PA*)

A lethal pairing: new recruit Thierry Henry celebrates with Dennis Bergkamp in November 1999. The Frenchman would go on to be Arsenal's most prolific goal scorer of all time. (*Getty Images*)

A dejected Wenger heads for the dressing room at half-time after Arsenal went 5-1 down by the interval against Manchester United in February 2001. It was a rare occasion when the players saw him lose his temper. (*Getty Images*)

One of Wenger's best defensive signings – Sol Campbell arrived on a free transfer from local rivals Tottenham. (*Getty Images*)

Back on top! Wenger celebrates a 2-0 victory over Chelsea in the 2002 FA Cup final to complete a second Double in four years. (*Getty Images*)

Wenger and Sir Alex Ferguson argue on the touchline at Highbury in March 2004 – the pair's long-standing rivalry eventually gave way to something more amicable. (*Getty Images*)

While the children held a fake trophy, Wenger soon had his hands on the real thing as the Invincibles crowned one of the most impressive managerial feats of all time. (*Getty Images/PA*)

became our motivation, especially after we had a setback in Europe and in the FA Cup.'

After the Liverpool game, Arsenal had seven games left: they drew four of them and won three. They clinched the title at the home of their greatest rivals, Tottenham, but they did it feeling disappointed. They blew a two-goal lead and Jens Lehmann's temper gifted Tottenham a last-minute penalty when he pushed Robbie Keane, who had trodden on his toes to wind him up.

But Arsenal's 2-2 draw was still enough to win the title and Lauren remembers it as one of their 'lucky escapes' that season, when the unbeaten record nearly went:

There were many key games. It wasn't only that one at Manchester United. We beat Chelsea away from home, we beat Tottenham at home and drew away. When you win big games it sends a message. Suddenly opponents think: 'Be careful with these guys – they're winning the big games.' They get a bit concerned, they get a bit scared. This Arsenal team managed to beat United, Chelsea, Liverpool, and before the game they were always a bit concerned, a bit scared of us. That's my impression.

In the tunnel, you could see the fear in the opponents' eyes. We would look at the other players and you could see they were thinking: 'We're not sure what's going to happen, I think they're going to beat us today.' You can feel that. We had the winning mentality. That made the difference and that counts for a lot.

Few had a winning mentality as strong as the Arsenal captain's. Patrick Vieira and his midfield battles were a key part of Wenger's success from the 1998 Double right up until the final kick of his Arsenal career, when he scored the winning penalty in the shootout with Manchester United to win the 2005 FA Cup final. But none of his other successes are, according to Vieira, quite as memorable as the Invincibles season of 2003/04:

> I remember everything about it because I think one day that record will get beaten. Records are out there for teams to beat. I think a team will do better than that, but how long it will take we don't know. I remember every single thing about it because I'm still in contact with some of the players. We achieved that record because we were quite close [off the pitch] and we were a strong team on it.
>
> And when you have quality in the team like Dennis Bergkamp and Thierry Henry, it gives you more chance to achieve this kind of [record]. We had Thierry at his best. We always knew he was going to score and Dennis was going to create something. We had our togetherness. We had a really strong bond. We knew if we went 1-0 down we would score, because we had the players to do so.
>
> That team had everything. Physically we were really strong, we had players who were fantastic on the ball, and we had players who could score. So we had everything in that generation. It was the complete team.

Arsenal met Manchester United – their fiercest challengers – four times that season: twice in the Premier League, once in the Community Shield and then in the FA Cup semi-final. They shared three draws and United won the FA Cup tie, and each time Vieira went head-to-head with Roy Keane. Their rivalry was such a feature of that season, particularly in their first meeting at Old Trafford in September when Vieira was sent off. The respect between them – as highlighted in the TV documentary *Keane and Vieira: Best of Enemies* – was obvious.

'If there was a fight, it would take a long time to beat him and I would end up with a few cuts,' smiled Vieira, reflecting upon the rivalry with Keane ten years on from the 2003/04 season. 'I don't think he would give up easily! He is not the kind of person to go halfway – he's either everything or nothing. We had similar qualities as players. We were both determined, we wanted to win, and we were both leaders of our teams. We challenged ourselves, we battled, but we always retained respect for each other. At that time, Arsenal were building up a great team to challenge United, who were up there already. Maybe United and Roy weren't used to that kind of challenge.'

As Vieira's memories illustrate, United and Arsenal were extremely close that season – their two draws in the Premier League testify to that. But the determination, spirit and battling qualities of Wenger's men saw them through tough games like those United encounters. And although United ended Arsenal's FA Cup run that season, it was Chelsea who delivered the bigger blow in the Champions League.

'I will always have that in my mind,' said Lauren. 'We beat Chelsea in the Premier League, the FA Cup and then in the most important game we failed. But it's football. I guarantee if you take that team in 15 years, 17 years, like Arsene Wenger has now, if you take that same team with more experience in the Champions League, then I think we would have won the Champions League.'

The Invincibles season surely remains Wenger's greatest achievement and the fact that no one has been able to emulate it – despite Chelsea and Manchester United both dominating the league – only goes to show how impressive a feat it was. Looking back, Wenger still feels an immense sense of pride at the achievement of going 38 league games unbeaten. 'At the time when you do it, it just looks normal and natural. When I look back at the photos today and I see the quality of each player, I think that's where you realise that it was an exceptional team. Not only those who played regularly, but also those who were on the bench.

'It had never been done in the Premier League until then and I can't remember anybody winning the championship without losing a game. I'm very proud of that because there's not a lot of room to do better. Apart from that, the quality of the players I had was absolutely exceptional.'

Arsenal had been unstoppable, but when the unbeaten run – a record-breaking 49 games – finally came to an end in October 2004, the hangover seemed to result in the break-up of the team. But the sense of anger still lingers. The prelude to the now infamous 'pizzagate' tunnel bust-up at Old Trafford was a 2-0 defeat by Manchester United. The all-important first goal came from a Ruud van Nistelrooy penalty after referee Mike Riley judged that Sol Campbell had tripped Wayne Rooney.

'It was a dive,' said Campbell. 'If I left my foot there, but I moved my foot away, rather like a matador with the red cape ... I didn't shake his hand after the game.'

Having reached such heights and feeling unbeatable, the sense of disappointment was overwhelming. Campbell's refusal to shake the hand of an England team-mate spoke volumes for the bitterness and rivalry. The setback was perhaps almost too much to bear for that generation and they never quite recovered. Furthermore, there was now a new rival to consider, as Arsenal and Manchester United, the two titans of the last few years, were soon struggling to keep up with Roman Abramovich and Jose Mourinho's Chelsea.

CHAPTER 6

EUROPEAN MELTDOWN

THE BIGGEST REGRET of Arsene Wenger's reign is, without question, his failure so far to win a European trophy. His biggest chance came and went with the 2006 Champions League final against Barcelona and, rather like when the Invincibles' unbeaten run ended, defeat marked the end of an era for Arsenal.

Wenger's team struggled to recover after losing at Manchester United in October 2004. The devastating blow of defeat and the end of their record-breaking 49-game unbeaten run had far bigger ramifications than anyone could have imagined. From feeling unassailable, they became vulnerable and, slowly but surely, Arsenal went into decline.

Only later can you look back and see the reasons why. The break-up of the team, together with the financing of a new stadium, impacted on the calibre of players who were signed as replacements and Chelsea's new-found wealth meant the whole landscape was changing in English football.

Perhaps the most notable departure during that spell was

Patrick Vieira, not just in terms in football ability but stature, what he represented as Arsenal's captain, their leader and midfield powerhouse. Throughout Wenger's glorious early years, Vieira was arguably the best midfielder of his type in the world. It was perhaps fitting that his last kick for Arsenal was to score the winning penalty in a shoot-out with Manchester United in the 2005 FA Cup final at the Millennium Stadium.

Vieira's departure was also something of an irony. The French midfielder had for so many years appeared to flirt with Real Madrid, complained that Arsenal had not made enough signings to keep themselves competitive and then eventually committed himself to Arsenal. Some thought he seemed to enjoy being the centre of attention almost as much as he enjoyed being in the centre of Arsenal's midfield. But the one time that he wasn't caught up in transfer speculation was the year that Arsenal sold him.

He stood in the mixed zone at the Millennium Stadium after lifting the FA Cup and joked that this summer his future was not an issue. In fact, Vieira even laughed when I asked him about his future. 'Ha ha, not this year,' he smiled. Then he talked warmly about wanting to finish his career at Arsenal and stay beyond his current contract, which was due to expire in 2007. 'My contract with Arsenal is still running and I don't want to leave,' said Vieira.

Within weeks, everything had changed. David Dein informed Vieira of Juventus's interest. Vieira says he asked whether he was still wanted at Arsenal. In *Vieira: My Autobiography*, he claims Dein said to him: 'We are neutral. We are giving you the choice of deciding what you want to do.'

He reported that he was 'angry, surprised and upset' after being with the club for nine years. He knew that 'if Arsenal really wanted to keep a player they fought tooth and nail'. He concluded that 'the word that swung the decision for me was "neutral"' and it was no longer about what was on offer elsewhere.

Wenger had come to the decision that Vieira's statistics – in terms of distance, speed and tackling – showed that, at 29, he was slowing down. That is why he decided to sell.

In later years, despite Arsenal fans pointing to the decision to sell Vieira as a huge mistake and a turning point for the club, Wenger not only claimed that he had no regrets about selling him to Juventus, but also none about not re-signing him when he briefly flirted with Arsenal – and Tottenham of all clubs – before joining Manchester City for one last hurrah in 2010.

Wenger, talking in 2011, said: 'Patrick is a great player but it's difficult to know what would have happened. The team has accumulated a lot of experience despite their age. They are 23 on average, but football-wise they are 26 or 27. I gave them a chance to play at a young age and I don't regret that. Maybe I could have got some more experienced players but it is too easy to say that.'

Back in the earlier days of his Arsenal career, Vieira often cited their failings in Europe as the reason why he wanted to leave and move to a more established European super club. The closest he came to doing so was in the summer of 2004, when only a last-minute change of heart and an emotionally charged meeting with Wenger and Dein convinced him to stay.

I can remember Thierry Henry making one of his what were becoming fairly regular phone calls to me in the 2004 close season. There was a hint that some of the players were getting fed up with Vieira and his dalliance with other clubs, as well as rumours of fallings-out within the national set-up, and Henry was unhappy with those suggestions. Henry, to his eternal credit, would often ring journalists if he disagreed with a story or did not like something that had been written. This time, he rang the day after Vieira had met Wenger and Dein the previous evening. Most papers had run with back-page reports of Vieira being about to leave. After denying the stories of disharmony, Henry laughed: 'You'll see.' He knew Vieira was staying and a few hours later the rest of the world found out, too, as word spread.

Vieira, rather like Wenger, craved European success. He vented his frustration after Arsenal's defeat at Valencia in April 2001, which put them out of the Champions League. David Woods from the *Daily Star* and I stopped Vieira in the mixed zone and he was clearly upset and annoyed. He described Arsenal's season as 'average' and insisted he 'would not discuss his future any more'.

'It was a big year for Arsenal and a great opportunity for us to play in the Champions League final,' said Vieira. 'I don't think we'll ever see such an opportunity because you won't see the teams who went out making the same mistakes. That might never happen again.'

Vieira was hot-headed, single-minded and determined. He knew exactly what he was saying; he needed very little prompting. Our only regret as newspaper journalists was that we didn't run the interview that night. Instead, we decided to hold it and that allowed the *Evening Standard*, who were listening in as David Woods and I posed the questions, to run it first the following afternoon. Vieira was duly quizzed about it by the club and asked why he decided to speak out so forcefully. 'Because I meant it,' replied Vieira.

Better times returned for Vieira with two more Premier League titles, and his complaints during the run-in and summer of 2001 were the precursor to Arsenal spending big, with signings of the calibre of Sol Campbell. But how right he was about the Champions League. Vieira was sold in 2005 and Arsenal didn't reach a Champions League final until the following May. His chance had gone, an ambition unfulfilled for one of the best midfield warriors of all time.

Perhaps the biggest indication of Arsenal's decline after 2004 was highlighted by the Premier League table: Arsenal finished fourth in May 2006. Up until that season, they had never finished outside of the top two under Wenger (excluding his first, partial, season of 1996/97, when they ended up in third place).

And Arsenal only sneaked into fourth ahead of their bitter rivals on the final day of the season, when Tottenham lost at West Ham after Martin Jol's team were struck down by a stomach bug, popularly blamed on the lasagne most of the players ate for dinner the night before. As many as ten Tottenham players complained they were ill (Michael Carrick could barely run) and Spurs lost 2-1 at Upton Park, while Arsenal beat Wigan 4-1 to clinch fourth place and a passport into the following season's Champions League.

Everything had changed; Arsenal's dominance had gone as Wenger began to break up the Invincibles team, and started planning for the future at a new stadium. In the Premier League, Chelsea had retained their grip on the title, while Manchester United and Liverpool (who had won the Champions League the year before) battled it out to be their main challenger. Arsenal were 24 points adrift of the Blues.

And yet, despite this disappointment in the league, they had the chance to bring down the curtain on a glorious era with one last trophy. And, for Wenger, in many ways it was the biggest of all: the Champions League.

They were surely the best football team in Europe in the 2003/04 season and yet they lost in the quarter-finals to Chelsea, beaten 2-1 at home after securing a 1-1 draw at Stamford Bridge. Despite Wenger's burning ambition to achieve European recognition and to make Arsenal a true European superpower, they could never seem to replicate their domestic form and performances in the Champions League.

Year after year, every campaign would begin with a press conference in which Wenger would tell us why this could be Arsenal's year – and yet they would always come up short. Former Arsenal defender Lauren, a member of the 2004 Invincibles team, believes the absence of European success is Wenger's biggest single regret, and he puts it down to a lack of experience compared to other big clubs.

> Not to win the Champions League was a big disappointment. But as the manager used to say to us, we were not a team who had played regularly in the Champions League. We had been in it for four or five years and my perception is that teams like Milan, Barcelona, Real Madrid, when it comes to the big games – the quarter-finals, the semi-finals – even if they didn't play well, they have the experience that tells them that they have to perform. They have been playing 20 years, 30 years or 40 years in the Champions League. There's something in there. You don't need to say to … whoever is in the Real Madrid shirt, or Barcelona and Xavi … because there's something in the atmosphere that makes these players perform in the quarter-finals.
>
> In our time, we didn't have more than five or six years playing in the Champions League so we didn't have the experience or the knowledge of playing the Champions League and that's why, I think, we didn't perform well.

Lauren was one of the players missing from the 2006 Champions League final in Paris as he was out injured. But the starting line-up featured the majority of the Invincibles, with eight mainstays of the 2003/04 title-winning team: Jens Lehmann, Sol Campbell, Ashley Cole, Freddie Ljungberg, Gilberto Silva, Robert Pires, Kolo Toure and Thierry Henry. Cesc Fabregas – an emerging talent in 2003/04 – Alexander Hleb and Emmanuel Eboue were the other three. It was a strong team, boosted by Dennis

Bergkamp, Robin van Persie, Mathieu Flamini and Jose Antonio Reyes on the bench.

Barcelona were a good team but their future superstars, Xavi and Andres Iniesta, did not start and were on the bench. This was Arsenal's big chance, especially because of the way they had reached the final. They beat Real Madrid in the first knockout round, Juventus in the quarter-finals and even survived a late penalty drama to knock out Villarreal in the semi-final. The win in Madrid was the best of all, when Henry scored the only goal of the two-legged tie. It must go down as one of the best results of all time by an English team. What is most remarkable is that Arsenal did not concede a single goal in the knockout stages.

Wenger does not believe he gets enough credit for reaching the Champions League final and it clearly irks him that he has never lifted the trophy.

In 2006 we were in the Champions League final. Nobody speaks about it now but it's still an achievement. It's not a trophy but we did it without conceding a goal in the whole [knockout stage] and we only lost a game in the last 13 minutes of the Champions League. Can you say you have failed that season? I don't think so. On top of that, we managed to stay in the top four that season.

We beat Real Madrid with Zidane and Beckham and all these people, but nobody speaks about it. It's like we have done nothing significant at all. Why? Because at the end of the season you don't parade with the trophy.

Had we won the League Cup that season [they were knocked out by Wigan in the semi-finals], people would say: 'Ah, they won the League Cup in 2006.' But as a manager can you really compare winning the League Cup or reaching the Champions League final without losing a game, what is the difference?

You have to take a little bit of distance with that and assess what is difficult and what is a good season. I know that the trophies are important. But it's not like if you haven't won a trophy nothing happened in the whole season and it was disastrous. You still played football and good games and bad games, and in the season when you won trophies you still played bad games. You have to take a little bit of distance from that. Even if it is important.

Wenger has been consistent in reaching the Champions League knockout stages but, despite going so close, has never been able to take the next step, as Liverpool, Chelsea and Manchester United have done during his reign at Arsenal.

Some years later, Wenger could barely hide his frustration when talking about Chelsea becoming the first London club to win the Champions League in 2012, despite finishing sixth in the Premier League. On the one hand, he has spoken of his desire to lift the trophy and what an achievement it would be. But, after both Chelsea and Liverpool (2005) won the trophy, Wenger likened it to a cup competition, and even used the word 'lucky' when describing Chelsea's success. Wenger does not do losing very well at all. This was how he responded at the time:

It was a surprise, yes, but maybe at the end of the season they [Chelsea] took a little bit more focus for the cups, especially the Champions League, and that cost them a few points. You have to consider that as well. In the Champions League you play one big game at a time. In the Premier League you play many big teams and you have to do well against all of them. I still believe the Premier League is the massive test.

If you tell me would you like to win the Champions League I will of course say yes, but it's a cup competition. Not at the start but in the final part of it, it is a real cup competition. You need to go into March and April with your best players available, fit, and that's not easy, especially when you play in the Premier League.

One of the lucks Chelsea had was Didier Drogba in the first part of the season did not play a lot. He came into it in the second half of the season and he made the difference – he was fresh, focused, had a good rest and was still hungry to make it happen, and he had the quality to do it.

It doesn't depend only on Chelsea; it depends on the other teams as well. You will not have every year Lionel Messi who misses a semi-final penalty and hits the bar, so you need a bit of luck, but it's a good inspiration for us, to show the same resilience and hope, because sometimes the luck goes your way when you have that resilience so we have to show that.

It does not bother me [that Chelsea won it]. For me, it's important that I am proud that the Premier League teams win it. What would worry me is that we have no chance in the Premier League. That a Premier League team wins the Champions League is fantastic. You can say to people that the team who finished sixth in the league can win the European Cup. It's absolutely fantastic for the Premier League.

Arsenal could not find the resilience in Paris that night in 2006. Just as it was with Vieira playing his last game for Arsenal in the 2005 FA Cup final, the Champions League final was to be another watershed moment. Sol Campbell and Robert Pires played their last games, and Dennis Bergkamp didn't come off the bench. But the biggest uncertainty of all surrounding that final was whether Thierry Henry would stay on afterwards. Arsenal's Champions League final opponents, Barcelona, had made no secret of their desire to sign him. The most remarkable aspect of that saga was that, despite Barcelona's very public pursuit of Henry, it didn't really dominate the build-up in the press, nor did it affect the ultra-professional Henry's performance (not that it would, as he has a deep passion for Arsenal).

Qualification for the 2006/07 Champions League, having squeezed into fourth on the final day of the season, at least took the pressure off the final for Arsenal. Otherwise, they would have gone into the game against Barcelona knowing that only victory would secure their return to the competition the next season. Wenger was in good spirits, looking calm and enjoying the night before when he faced the media in the Stade de France.

Wenger's key decision in defence was to leave Philippe Senderos and Gael Clichy on the bench, while Campbell and Ashley Cole started. Campbell, talking while promoting his own biography, was reflective and honest as he recognised how lucky he and Cole both were: 'Senderos and Clichy were playing at the time, but they got injured and that's the only reason that me and Ashley Cole were playing. Arsene says in the book that he would have played me. But no chance. No way. It happened because fate fell on my side and he had to play me. But if those two guys had been fit then me and Ash wouldn't have played. No chance.'

But his biggest decision was to make the emotional call and pick Pires to start ahead of Reyes. And yet, after just 18 minutes, Wenger substituted Pires as he had to sacrifice an outfield player to bring on reserve keeper Manuel Almunia after Jens Lehmann was sent off for bringing down Samuel Eto'o. It didn't matter that Ludovic Giuly had put the ball into the net; play was pulled back, a free kick was given and Lehmann dismissed. It left Arsenal with ten men and a seemingly impossible task, though at least the score was still 0-0.

Incredibly, Campbell headed Arsenal into a 37th-minute lead, which they held on to and, indeed, Henry could have extended their advantage but shot straight at Barcelona keeper Victor Valdes when clean through. Barcelona eventually wore Arsenal down and two goals in the last 13 minutes from Eto'o and Juliano Belletti secured victory for the Spanish club. It was only the second time they had become European champions.

Wenger was left with an unhappy Pires and an uncertain Henry, as well as the feeling of sadness and bitter defeat. Pires in particular felt hard done by:

I was very disappointed. When I saw my number on the fourth official's board to be substituted, I couldn't believe it. It was my last game after six years at the club, a Champions League final in front of all my family in Paris where I became World Cup champion and it lasted just 18 minutes. That was very hard to take.

I will never forget that. I knew Villarreal wanted me but I hadn't made a decision, yet what happened in the final left me feeling very bad. That was the end; my mind was made up. I knew a player had to go off after that red card, but I never thought it would be me. When I saw it was my number, it killed me.

The final in Paris was the worst moment in my career. Two days after the final we spoke about two things. I said I was going to sign for Villarreal and I wanted to know why I was substituted. He was sorry but he saw that with me in the team we would play more defensively; it was complicated with only ten men against Barcelona.

Leaving was the most difficult decision of my career. I thought I would end my career there but, I could see in the final against Barcelona, Wenger had lost his confidence in me. The fact that I was only allowed to play 18 minutes in that final remains painful. I'll never agree with him that he made the right decision.

I don't feel angry at Arsene Wenger at all. I want to thank him for the confidence he gave me and the titles we won. It's a little thing which cannot define our relationship. It cannot erase six years when I learned from him. But I've put it behind me. He is a manager I will never forget.

When Arsenal played Villarreal and Pires returned to the Emirates in the 2009 Champions League quarter-final, Wenger even offered his apologies. 'I feel sorry for having done it, sorry for him. But I had to take one offensive player out without taking Henry out because we had to play on the counterattack. You keep your strongest, quickest player in the team on the pitch. Maybe [I regret it], it's very difficult to say. We were left with Hleb and Fabregas, who were offensive, Ljungberg as well – then Gilberto. We had already one defender left in there.'

Gilberto Silva remembers that final with great regret. Rather like Wenger, not winning the Champions League was the biggest disappointment of his career, and losing to Barcelona was the single most painful defeat.

It was very bad for us, the way things happened. We knew that a win against Barcelona wouldn't be easy. But we were full of confidence that we could do it. To lose the way we lost that game was painful, very painful for me. It was one of the games that I've lost in my life that I always remember; I always view with great sadness. It is very sentimental to me when I think about it. It's part of the game. You have to deal with it, deal with the frustration, but it was very hard. I cried afterwards and I've cried since, but we were so close to winning it and achieving the one last trophy we really wanted.

It was a kind of story that you write in your life. I will remember it forever. I think everyone who lost will remember it always.

Even though we lost, the people who watched that game will have a good feeling about it, about what we did, how close we came to winning it.

Back in those days, the press travelled on the team plane along with a few executive fans. We were always hurried from the press conference, mixed zone or our rewrites towards a bus to take us to the airport, where we would board the plane along with the players and management.

This meant that, over the years, we witnessed some unusual sights. For example, there was the time we were rushing to catch a plane only to see Marouane Chamakh – known for his spiky hair – get stopped at security because he had so many cans of hair mousse in his bag. When interviewed years later, even Chamakh laughed at the memory of his embarrassment at the time.

Players would regularly walk down to the back of the plane to have a word or a row. But the flight home after the 2006 final remains probably the most unforgettable because of Henry's speech over the public address system at 35,000 feet.

Straight after the final in the press conference, amid complaints from Henry and Wenger that Eto'o's goal was offside and the referee had been far too lenient in the face of constant fouls, both had been rather evasive on the question of Henry's future. Wenger was insistent that he felt Henry would stay, but he couldn't be absolutely sure. Henry claimed he didn't want to talk about it straight after the game and even walked away from a huddle of journalists when we pursued the line of questioning in the mixed zone.

On the plane home, Henry's voice was cracking with emotion as took up the microphone in midair. 'This is Thierry speaking,' said Henry to the passengers, who then clapped and cheered enthusiastically when he spoke passionately and in determined tones about next season and made it clear that he was staying. 'We have to take it on the chin. We must pick ourselves up and make sure we come back stronger next year.'

His reference to 'coming back stronger next year' was a fair indication that Henry had decided to stay. Many deals are done way in advance, players paying lip service as sagas play out on the back pages while knowing in their heart of hearts whether they are staying or going. Some crave the attention. But with Henry, his future had been genuinely undecided. If Arsenal had won, maybe he would have been more inclined to leave. After losing, Henry clearly felt he had unfinished business.

It became a familiar theme of Arsenal's European trips that Henry made a captain's address to the other 200 or so passengers on board the team plane, made up of team-mates, staff, journalists and a few dozen fans who would pay to go on expensive executive trips. The speeches on the way back from Real Madrid and Juventus were uplifting and victorious, but after the defeat in the final, Henry was brief, full of emotion, dejection – and also hope for the future.

The tradition of giving a speech was always embraced by Patrick Vieira and Henry, but it eventually trailed away when Cesc Fabregas and Robin van Persie took over the armband. Perhaps it was in some way a reflection of the bond between players and the fans slipping away. Henry always had that connection with the club, and it remains the case. The others less so. It was undoubtedly part of the reason why Henry decided to stay at Arsenal – at least for another year.

The flight arrived back in Luton in the small hours and the day was then spent trying to nail down the 'will he or won't he' stay story. Having heard his speech, my instinct was that he would not be leaving, but there followed frantic efforts to get confirmation. And, on the Friday morning, the *Daily Mirror* back page declared that Henry was staying.

The press conference was held at Arsenal's training ground. Henry, Wenger and David Dein sat at the top table as the French striker's remarkable patience – matched by his fondness for long-drawn-out answers while talking at a million miles an hour – saw him speak for the best part of an hour.

With the departures of Bergkamp, Campbell and Pires, keeping Henry was vital, especially as Arsenal were moving to the new stadium, which felt like the start of a new era. How would it have been perceived if they had just sold their best player and one of the best strikers in the world?

Henry, 29, signed a new four-year contract worth £110,000 a week, uncharted territory for Arsenal. They also gave him a substantial signing-on fee as part of the package to persuade him to stay, while Henry pointed to the reaction of the fans on the final day of the 2005/06 season at Highbury, when they chanted his name and pleaded with him not to go.

By this time Arsenal had become real contenders in the Champions League. They should have won it in 2004 when they had their best team; they then lost the final in 2006, lost the 2009 semi-final to Manchester United and in 2008 they lost to Liverpool in the quarter-final. In later years, however, they became also-rans in the competition, going out at the last-16 stage five years running from the 2010/11 season.

Wenger believes it is much harder now to win the competition and says that, if anything, the Champions League has become too predictable:

We would love to win it as it has never been done with this club and we have flirted with it a few times but I feel in recent years we have not been helped by the draw. We have played Barca, Milan, Bayern, so we have had difficult draws. Recently we haven't had the quality to go through.

It's difficult to predict because it's a cup after the group stage.
After Christmas it's about who is available, who is fit and who
isn't, you cannot plan. After two or three years, Barcelona were
above everyone. In October you know if Messi doesn't get
injured they will win it ...

In Europe, we have beaten everybody, which is what people
forget. And we are the only team that has gone into a final without conceding a goal [in the knockout stages], despite the fact
that we have never had a good defensive record.

Of course, it's something I miss that I will try to fight very
hard to fill my CV with. But you play against Barcelona, Bayern,
Real Madrid – every year they are there with a chance. You
always think: 'Let's do it this year – one year it will go for you.'
The competition is higher than ever.

Sol Campbell believes there is an element of luck but also insists
that teams make their own good fortune:

You can say that you're unlucky. The main thing is that you have
to get there. The more times you get there, the more your luck
will change. But if it comes down to a European Cup final once
every ten or 20 years then it's quite hard. The probability goes
down. Some clubs are very lucky in cup finals. Chelsea: you have
to say they deserved it because they won it. But they got a huge
slice of luck ...

When you look back when I was playing a European final for
Arsenal – I scored a goal and we just missed too many chances.
If the other team had had as many chances they would have won
3-0 or 3-1. They were just kind of waiting for that goal to go in.
We just missed too many chances. Thierry had one at the end,
Ljungberg had one, Alex Hleb had a great one ... It just comes
down to putting them away. I know we had ten men for a large

part of the game. We still made chances and we just didn't get that killer goal.

You always have to believe that you can get to the final. Everyone has to believe. It helps we had some really good players as well. It does help, not all the time, but it helps in those big games.

Campbell believes Arsenal have now slipped too far behind; they have regressed since 2006 and need a huge investment to catch up again. He also suggested that Wenger's approach of developing players rather than buying the ready-made article is where Arsenal have gone wrong.

If Arsenal really want to do something on the European stage then they'll have to spend more to compete. You have to frighten teams. You have to get to that stage where you have someone on the wing, someone in midfield, up front, and you need players to unlock opponents. If you've got quality throughout then opponents can't lock down three players. You need options.

The board might have to spend a bit of money, put their head on the block and really go for it. Also, don't be scared – even if you buy a player and it doesn't work out then you still have to go again.

You've got plenty of managers who have made mistakes – big mistakes – in the transfer market and gone again. You've got to get it right. You can't just say: 'I've spent this money, it hasn't worked, we're going back to the old days.' You can't. Those days are gone. If you go back to not really spending money for the right player, then you're going backwards while everyone else is going forward.

If you pick the players, get players through scouting around the world, then great. But ultimately, a lot of these players have to be ready-made. You have to pay top dollar to get them in. I think Arsenal just need some more players who are ready-made and world class.

The summer of 2006 saw some major changes to the squad. Pires (Villarreal) and Campbell (Portsmouth) went; Ashley Cole joined Chelsea after an unsavoury, protracted transfer; and Dennis Bergkamp retired; Lauren was injured and would not play for the club again, eventually moving to Portsmouth in January 2007. Just two years on, few of the Invincibles remained.

Arsenal also moved away from big, physical players and towards smaller, quicker-passing players as, despite his denials, Wenger appeared to look for a completely different style of play and philosophy.

The dramatic shift in Arsenal's finances also played into the change in philosophy as they could no longer afford ready-made stars. Arsenal were suddenly shopping in a different transfer market, looking for players with potential rather than proven talent and pedigree.

They were about to move to their new £350 million stadium, which would alter the entire landscape on and off the pitch and, above all, Wenger's job description. He was about to become accountant as well as football manager, trying to balance the books while keeping the team competitive. By contrast, champions Chelsea were dominant, signing superstars such as Michael Ballack and Andrei Shevchenko, as well as Ashley Cole, John Obi Mikel and Khalid Boulahrouz, while Arsenal were forced to go for younger players. It became men against boys.

Wenger, in one of his many barbs at the spending power of some of his Premier League rivals, claimed he was 'scandalised' by their cavalier attitude to big spending and the huge losses that were recorded as a result.

The Arsenal strategy has since been called 'Project Youth' and Wenger made it clear that he wasn't able, nor did he want to make big signings that would block the path of young players. 'The decision was to go for more youth when we decided to build a new stadium because we are not in a position where we could spend £30 million or £40 million on players.

'In a modern world, people are scandalised when banks lose money but I'm scandalised when football clubs lose money. For me, it's the same process. We have gone with young players and then to put four or five players in front of them is to kill the whole work you have done.'

From going so close to ruling Europe, Arsenal were now a club in transition, about to move to a new stadium and enter the hardest and most difficult period of Wenger's managerial career.

CHAPTER 7

FLIRTING

'FOOTBALL IS AN ART, like dancing is an art – but only when it's well done does it become an art.' One of the many surprising things about Arsene Wenger is that he loves to dance and is very good at it. He is fleet of foot and glides across the room, sweeping his dance partner along with him. At social functions, if he is not dancing with his partner Annie then he is holding court around a table. She is a tall, elegant woman who dresses beautifully, her designer clothes coming from the most exclusive of boutique shops. At a lavish charity event hosted by former Chelsea chairman Ken Bates, he astonished those who attended as he danced the jive with Annie.

At another charity event in one of London's grand ballrooms, an onlooker remembers seeing Wenger at a table surrounded by about 12 women, and he kept them all entertained as they laughed and joked. He is a gregarious individual; he likes meeting people and making contacts. He enjoys female company and even – in another of his famous soundbites – likened the beautiful game to beautiful women: 'A football team is like a beautiful woman. When you do not tell her, she forgets she is beautiful.'

Wenger has given up a lot of his personal time to promote charities, conducting interviews and also attending fundraising functions. At one such event, after Arsenal fan and *X Factor* presenter Dermot O'Leary had bid for and won Arsenal's giant green mascot Gunnersaurus to attend a children's party, Wenger made a sizeable donation towards a sleep monitor machine for Great Ormond Street Hospital. Enough money had been raised on the night for one of these machines, but Wenger made a donation to help buy another. He wasn't interested in acquiring something or bidding in an auction – he just wanted to make a donation.

Although he's often seen socialising during World Cups and European Championships, during the football season he seldom leaves the comfort zone of his day job. On a rare visit to the theatre one night back in September 2002, Wenger went to see a new West End play. 'I don't do this, this is not me, football is too all-consuming. I don't have time for London and what it has to offer,' he complained.

Wenger would far rather be at home than out on the town. He is intensely private, to such a degree that when he moved house in 2011 the new property, just a few doors down from his old place in Totteridge, was gated, less public and far less accessible. That suited him just fine.

His day starts early with a healthy breakfast at home. The drive to the training ground – often in his sponsored Lexus – takes about half an hour and he is generally in his office at the training ground by 9 a.m. After training, he has lunch with the players in the canteen. He will often choose chicken and steamed vegetables. Wenger believes it is important not just to eat healthily but to show the same dedication as his players; he believes he should respect their commitment by following the same habits. It's a key part of his management ethos: he does not believe he can expect from them what he himself is not prepared to give.

He likes to play tennis and keep fit; he runs most days, if not around the fields at the training ground then on a treadmill. A few times he's turned up in a hotel gym on a pre-season tour only to find himself running on a treadmill next to a journalist. He always finds it amusing.

He is one of the last to leave the training ground, often at around 6 p.m., and he will then have a light meal, invariably a salad, in the evening. It's no wonder he looks so fit, trim and healthy even into his mid-60s.

When he's at home he's generally watching a game on television. The satellite dish on the side of his house means he can pick up any game from anywhere in Europe. Keeping track of what is happening elsewhere has become much easier in these days of satellite television.

The press pack enjoy having a little fun with him at the end of press conferences, probably trying to tease out a Wenger quip or a funny one-liner, and no more so than when it's his birthday. Wenger always puts on a mischievous smile and has a cheeky answer for the reporters who suggest he go out to celebrate the occasion.

Football writer Henry Winter recalls one such occasion: 'We were winding him up once. It was a big birthday he was having and we were asking him what he was doing: maybe go to the West End, a party or go wild in a Totteridge wine bar. He said: "No, there's a very important Bundesliga game which I must watch." We told him to live it up for once and have fun. He said: "No, I must watch it – but for you I will put candles on top of the television!"'

Apart from football – and a fascination with Alexander the Great, about whom he has read extensively – his other great passion is politics. Wenger has been to the Houses of Parliament on a number of occasions, talking to the MPs on an All-Party Football Group. But he is very difficult to define with regard to his political allegiance. A close friend insists he's 'more red than blue', but that sits strangely with his rather capitalist attitude to wealth and earnings. 'It never stopped Fergie from being very openly Labour,' the friend added. Wenger enjoys the important debates, admitting he often picks up pointers on how to deal with his own Arsenal press conferences from live televised political discussions.

Wenger likes to stay on top of news and current affairs, and is always fascinated to learn about the countries they visit on Champions League trips. When taking a UEFA car to pre-match press conferences, he will invariably strike up a conversation with the driver. On one such occasion in Ukraine, Wenger quizzed the driver about politics in the country, the economy in Kiev and how many fans were expected for the game.

Although his job is his life and his life is Arsenal, there is no doubt that he has flirted with other football clubs in the past, a few times coming close – even by his own admission – to leaving. Ultimately, though, Wenger has never been able to break the bond. No one can question Arsene Wenger's loyalty to Arsenal. He has turned down offers from Real Madrid, Paris Saint-Germain and England, as well as an approach from Manchester City.

The one time when he did perhaps come close to leaving Arsenal was back in 2007 when his close friend and ally David Dein was ousted in a boardroom coup. The fallout left Wenger questioning whether he could stay without Dein and whether he should resign as an act of support for his friend. Dein insisted that he did not want Wenger to leave as a result of his departure and Wenger remained in charge of the club.

Admirable though his loyalty is, there have been clandestine meetings in hotels, approaches, phone calls and big-money offers. There have even been stories that he received a pre-contract agreement with Real Madrid, though Wenger denied it. The only person who really knows just how close he ever came to leaving is Wenger himself, but some will find it hard to understand why, if there was no chance at all of his going, he even met with other clubs.

Interestingly, Wenger did not deny meeting Sheikh Hamad Al-Thani, the owner of Paris Saint-Germain, in November 2012. On that occasion, he explained that they met because of his work with the Al Jazeera television channel and because he has long-standing links with the sheikh.

Nor did Wenger deny having offers from Real Madrid and Bayern Munich. When Real Madrid president Florentino Perez was reported to have made an approach to appoint Wenger in 2004, the Arsenal manager responded to the stories by saying that he would have to be really desperate to go to the Bernabeu. 'If tomorrow I'm in the streets with no job, I will not turn Madrid down. I have no desire to leave here. I'm happy where I am and I rate what I have. My target is to develop this club and the team and I feel I still have a big job to do here.'

A few newspapers put their own spin on Wenger's remarks. The *Daily Express* mocked up a photo of him dressed as a tramp, claiming he wouldn't leave Arsenal for Real Madrid even if he was on his knees. I remember getting a phone call from an Arsenal press officer insisting that Wenger was really upset about the interpretation some papers – including my own, the *Daily Mirror* – had put on his remarks. A few days later, I saw him in the departure lounge at Luton airport before a European trip. I went up to him – not to apologise for the story but to say sorry if he was offended – and he looked at me as if I was completely mad. He had no idea what I was talking about and even found it rather funny.

You can never tell when Wenger is going to be upset by a story; however one thing that doesn't seem to bother him is being linked with other clubs. It could be argued that interest from other chairmen, chief executives and clubs only helps to increase his market value.

The closest that Wenger has ever come to leaving Arsenal for another club, according to my information, was in 2006. It was a pivotal time for Wenger, as they had just lost the Champions League final and the club was about to move into the Emirates Stadium and enter into a transitional period when finances would be restricted.

Real Madrid again came calling. This time it was one of the presidential candidates, Juan Miguel Villar Mir, who based his whole campaign around appointing Wenger. In May 2006, Wenger met the wealthy industrialist, a lifelong Real Madrid fan, in the famous Hotel de Crillon in Paris, where Villar Mir said a pre-contract agreement was offered.

Villar Mir, whose candidacy had the support of Florentino Perez, later told journalists that Wenger had signed it and the Spanish media reported that Wenger was the coach they wanted. They went into the details of the offer: Wenger had the chance to be general manager, coaching the team as well as choosing players to sign, as was the style in England where a manager takes complete control. In Spain and most of Europe, the coach coaches and works with players who are bought for him by the club, director of football or president. They were prepared to rip up the Real Madrid rule book to get Wenger – and they believed they had him.

But despite the promise of appointing Wenger, Villa Mir lost the election to Ramon Calderon, so we will never know if he might have been tempted to join them. Perhaps Villa Mir's close association with Perez cost him dear: Real Madrid wanted to move away from the Galacticos era as the big stars had not produced success under Perez's reign. Perez, of course, later regained power, but Calderon did bring a new era to the club under Fabio Capello.

Wenger has subsequently spoken about Real Madrid offering

him a job and, while Arsenal publicly denied reports in Spain that any pre-contract agreement had been signed, there is no doubt the offer was a serious one.

Calderon recalls Perez targeting Wenger in 2004 and believes that Wenger, from various conversations over the years, was tempted at other times too:

> I imagine that anyone – be it a coach or a player – at some time in their career is interested in coming to a club like Real Madrid, especially when you have been at a club for fifteen years, or however long, in England ... Anyone working in any other industry would be interested in change. I think it's a good idea to have a coach who has a long-term plan ...
>
> He was talking to me about Real Madrid and, at that time, he was very interested in the club and what was happening. I remember he said: "Are you going to Hollywood again, or to make a football team?" He meant are you going for film star Galacticos or to make a proper football team.
>
> It's something you have in England that is a very good thing. You have it at Arsenal, you had at Manchester United, that the manager could stay at the club for a very long time. It's impossible here. In Spain, Barcelona and Real Madrid, fans and followers only want titles, trophies and championships. In England, it's something they do well – to give the coach confidence and support. Get a good relationship between the club and the coach. Wenger is proof of that.

Calderon has the utmost respect for Wenger and, even though he appointed Fabio Capello after winning the club elections in 2006, he believes Wenger is one of the best coaches of all time. He says Wenger's manner, his philosophy and even his human kindness set him apart:

I'm sure Arsenal appreciate what they have and that they didn't want him to leave because it's not easy when a big coach leaves. You see what happened with Manchester United. They made the change and it didn't work. You look at Wenger and he works with young players, he develops them, develops the team.

He is a good coach; he can be successful at any club in the world. But the trouble here is that even if you build a good team, are a good coach, then if you don't win a title then you get the sack. Look what happened with Pellegrini. He is a very good coach, but he came here, got one year and was sacked. Look at Mourinho. He won one King's Cup and was sacked, also. When I had Capello ... he was successful, but the supporters were not happy with the way the team was playing and we had to sack him ... They also had the problem with Mourinho ... Arsene Wenger is not that kind of coach. His team also tries to play in an attractive way for the spectator and for the people ...

But it's always the same problem. It's difficult to have a coach here for more than three years. They suffer the pressure. The media here is very difficult to cope with. It's a real trouble for a coach if he doesn't win and even if he does, but doesn't play the style of football they like, then it's not enough. Maybe he would have been successful, but if you come here there is so much to overcome.

I imagine that he was really sad that he didn't come because it was an opportunity, a change and a new challenge. But things didn't work out and he has clearly loved his time at Arsenal ...

Wenger ... is respectful. You never see him in arguments. There might be occasions where he complains about referees but not in the way that Mourinho does. He's a very, very kind man. I remember talking to him, just sitting down in a hotel for a cup of coffee, before the Euro 2008 final. He was just enthusiastic about football. He is a wonderful manager, a really nice man and I am so pleased that he has been so successful, but I also think he would have been very good at Madrid. But Madrid is a very difficult club sometimes.

Wenger has been candid about Real Madrid's interest and, despite in recent times being linked more with PSG and the France national job, there is no doubt that the Spanish club have made more overtures to him than any other. In 2009 he outlined why, having been linked again with Real Madrid in a spate of stories in the Spanish press, he continued to turn them down and stay loyal to Arsenal:

What Real want to do is produce what I would call a spectacle of football, a spectacular team. But when it comes to creating a team, there is another dimension that exists. I want to have success by building a team with a style, with a know-how, with a culture of play specific to the club and its fans and with young people. That is what I have chosen in my career and want to ensure I continue here at Arsenal.

I am in a construction project with a young team but my intention is to take that project to the ultimate end. For me, pleasure comes from watching those players showing the football I like to see played. The sums we are talking about with Real can appear shocking. But they are the fruit of a calculation carried out by the investors in the club.

I believe it is necessary to disregard moral judgement and to simply ask whether the operation will be profitable. In my opinion, to recruit more than three players in a transfer window, as Real plan, is taking a technical risk.

More recently, Wenger admitted his feeling of loyalty – even through difficult times – was the reason why he stayed. 'This club gave me a chance. But I think as well, at important periods I have shown loyalty and turned many things down and have accepted to work with restricted potential. And that was knowing that I had to stay at the top. I did that with full commitment.

'Now we can fight with the top clubs financially again. I believe the club is in a very strong position today. I could rate what I have at this club and I think when you come in as a manager you have to adapt to the traditions and values of the club as well as bringing your own style ... The most important thing when you love a job is to wake up every morning and be happy to go in. I also had that here, even when we had the more difficult periods. And that is why I stayed here.'

The players, too, knew of the interest in Wenger from other clubs, as Ray Parlour acknowledged: 'There were times when Real Madrid came in but he'd signed the contract [with Arsenal], wanted to honour it, and he's been very loyal to Arsenal.'

There was another time when Wenger found himself on the back pages because of doubts about his future. In 2000, Kevin Keegan quit as England manager and the Football Association were looking for a replacement.

It was partly because of Wenger's success at Arsenal that the FA were set on hiring a foreign manager who would offer greater tactical nous and a more continental approach, after the Keegan era of 4-4-2, rabble-rousing team talks and betting schools – the big talking point of England's failure at Euro 2000.

Arsenal's vice-chairman David Dein persuaded FA chief executive Adam Crozier to go for Sven-Goran Eriksson instead of Wenger and the potential crisis was averted. 'I saw in Sven a lot of the qualities I saw in Arsene,' recalled Dein at the time. 'They could be distant cousins.'

The theory is that Dein, wanting to keep Wenger for Arsenal, urged the FA to go for Eriksson when others in the FA hierarchy wanted the Frenchman. When I put that to Eriksson, who is a close friend of Wenger and of Dein, the Swede laughs in a charming way. 'I can believe that!' he said. 'David and Arsene are so close. And they built such a great club; they were two extremely important people in the club's history, a new stadium, a new training ground and everything.'

Wenger has always been in demand as a manager but, more recently, there have been times when the Frenchman has considered leaving because he perhaps doubted his own ability. In November 2011, he gave a revealing interview to *L'Equipe*, suggesting he could leave the following summer. That was just three months after Arsenal had been thrashed 8-2 at Manchester United. Quite often, Wenger has stated something in France that gets lost in translation. He subsequently clarified what he meant:

I said the only way I would leave is if I didn't give what was expected. There are many people questioning what I do. If at the end of the season you feel you didn't deliver you have to consider. I'm committed to the club and will respect it to the last day of the contract unless I feel I'm not good enough. I have to honestly rate my performance. Did I take the maximum out of the players? After 15 years I have many questions and have to analyse the situation objectively. It is the club of my life, and will remain so unless I don't do well enough.

I have to wait and see the quality of my work at the end of the season – it is not as simple as top four or else. You want me to say now if we are not in the top four I will quit ... But I won't do that. That I won't say.

After the 8-2 [defeat at Old Trafford] I was determined to put things right, more than ever. I have to analyse the situation in the most honest and objective way. But I don't question my commitment to my contract and I think I've shown that in the past and I will do in the future.

I did an interview with another foreign newspaper after we lost 8-2 ... But it was nothing in my mind especially, just the fact the guy asked: 'Absolutely you will never leave the club?' I said the only way I could leave is that I really feel I am a pain for the club. These things are always in my mind. Every manager thinks that.

The other Wenger statute is that he has never broken a contract in his entire career, although he has been honest enough to confess that he once tried. Wenger's argument is that he cannot renege on a contract and still ask players for loyalty when negotiating or trying to persuade them to stay. It's a principled and honourable stance. But, by his own admission, he did try to walk out on a contract with Monaco when Bayern Munich approached him.

Bayern president Uli Hoeness tells the story:

Even before he went to Japan [in 1995], Franz Beckenbauer and I went to Nice and discussed with him, and everything was clear. But then at the end of the day he decided to go to Japan. We were very surprised. From Japan he went to Arsenal and over the years, whenever we were looking for a new coach, Wenger was always one we considered. He's a very serious person, very strong, and has a very good idea about the game.

There have been a few moments where we have discussed his name over the years. He has always remained loyal to Arsenal, which is fantastic behaviour. But it is true we wanted him at Bayern a few times.

Wenger explained that he did ask Monaco to release him from his contract so that he could go to Bayern:

I can't remember the details because I always said no to every-body. I always had commitments here and I always respected my contract. The first time I said no [to Bayern] was when I was at Monaco. I had one year to go and did not want to extend, so I asked the chairman. They did not let me go so I respected my contract. I said no.

I have no regrets, no, not at all. You do what your gut feeling tells you and you do what you think you are. You believe in the values you have and you do it like that. It is like that in life. You do what you think is right and do not expect anything in return for what you do.

Wenger has always been a manager who does not shy away from talk about his own future, position or being a target for other clubs. His last deal, a three-year contract signed in May 2014, was not just financially rewarding – worth a total of £24 million – but it also ensured he kept his power base. He has laughed many times about how he does not want a director of football to work alongside him, and that is clearly because he wants – and still gets – the final say on transfers and contracts, unlike an increasing number of his Premier League rivals. After all, he has to pick the team week in, week out, so surely he should retain overall control about the players he needs?

Knowing that he is a wanted man not only boosts his ego but also shows that there are other jobs in the offing should the Arsenal board begin to doubt him or want to encroach upon his territory. Perhaps Wenger has got Arsenal over a barrel, but his refusal to work with a director of football is a reminder of who is in charge. He explained his thinking on this point, thus:

I would not work with a director of football because they buy the players and when it does not work you are guilty for not using them well. I am not against having people to help me buy, sell and negotiate because I cannot do it all. But I think the final decision always has to belong to the manager to decide who comes in and who goes out because he is responsible for the style of play and results.

It is like you [journalists] write an article and someone says I will change that and that, and that. You should not accept that. Stand up for what you write! I stand up for the results of a team I have chosen. The manager should be responsible for the players who come in. I have people around me to help, but the final decision has to be down to the manager.

Whatever the case, there is no denying that Wenger is happy in his own world at Arsenal – just as long as he has the chance to remind everyone from time to time who holds the power. And there is no doubting that the interest from clubs like Real Madrid and Paris Saint-Germain is flattering. Every manager has an ego. But despite the occasional opportunity to earn more, to go to a bigger club, to win more, Wenger's heart has always overruled the temptation to leave.

CHAPTER 8

THE BARREN YEARS

DURING ARSENAL'S MOST successful time under Arsene
Wenger, a different story of big finance and political intrigue
was developing in the background.

Arsenal had, from around the mid-1990s, been looking to move
from Highbury, their home since 1913. The introduction of all-
seater stadiums following the Hillsborough disaster in 1989 meant
a reduction in Highbury's huge attendances – record books show
73,295 turned up for a game against Sunderland in March 1935,
and even in the 1970s and 1980s crowds often topped 50,000. But,
despite major redevelopments at the Clock End and North Bank,
by the time Highbury had become an all-seater stadium in the
1990s the capacity had fallen to about 38,500.

Parts of the stadium were listed because of the wonderful art-
deco design, which meant that it could not be redeveloped. The
club's hierarchy realised that, to take the next step, they would
have to move. Arsenal knew they could attract huge crowds, not
least because they negotiated a temporary deal with Wembley to

stage their Champions League games at the national stadium and drew in 73,707 against French club Lens in November 1998.

David Dein, a ground-breaker and one of football's great visionaries, could see a new opportunity and was in favour of a deal with Wembley. But others on the board, particularly Ken Friar and Danny Fiszman, wanted to look for sites closer to home and felt passionately that they should stay in the London borough of Islington. Arsenal's poor results in the Champions League at Wembley, they felt, almost proved their point. Arsenal needed a new home, not lodgings, they argued.

Without question, it caused a split among board members and it was during this testing time, around 2003, that Fiszman and Dein fell out. They had been close, 'peas in a pod' as one former director described them, and they had worked together on the stadium project from 2000 to 2003. Yet suddenly, according to one witness, their relationship 'completely fell apart'. The two men were unable to make up even after the club moved to the Emirates and things were going well.

Two of the most important figures in the history of the club had fallen out, and the Dein–Fiszman feud was a symbol of the ongoing battles in the boardroom that would haunt Arsenal and, in particular, Wenger for the best part of a decade. These were difficult times for Arsenal and they knew that, to make the stadium work, they would have to remain successful and at the top of the game.

But the ambitious project to build a new stadium was not encountering difficulty only in the boardroom. Arsenal also struggled to get the banks to loan them the cash, the stadium even being put on hold in 2003 after one bank pulled out. On the pitch, Arsenal were about to embark on their most remarkable spell – winning the title in the Invincibles season of 2003/04 – but the club was in danger of falling apart around the team.

The concern had reached the dressing room and players

became increasingly worried about whether Arsenal would be able to compete financially, especially with the arrival of Roman Abramovich at Chelsea. The Russian billionaire heralded a new wave of mega-rich owners of football clubs who, in turn, would pose another threat to Wenger's dominance as a footballing force.

Several players went to see Wenger, the directors and other key members of staff, as there were whispers that Arsenal were building a 'white elephant'. They were given assurances that the club was in good hands, even though one director, always committed to the Emirates move, admitted that the new stadium and its funding was a 'pretty reckless escapade'.

We always think of the financial crises that have engulfed other clubs. Leeds United's incredible Champions League gamble saw them go close to the brink after their investment in huge player contracts and transfer fees backfired and nearly crippled them when they dropped out of Europe's elite competition. Abramovich's arrival at Chelsea saved the club from a financial crisis, while Liverpool were allegedly 'one day' away from going into administration before the Fenway Sports Group took over at Anfield. And just look at the way Portsmouth's reckless finances saw them slide from being FA Cup winners and mainstays in the Premier League all the way down to League Two.

But Arsenal were different, known for being conservative. The old Bank of England nickname from the 1930s still had currency, and they were regarded as being wealthy, backed by sensible owners and risk-averse, both on and off the pitch. Incredibly, however, Arsenal went far closer to financial oblivion during the stadium move than perhaps their fans ever realised. In that context, it paints a clearer picture of just how tight money was during the transfer from Highbury to the Emirates.

In 2004, Arsenal were just a week away from not being able to pay their wages until they pulled off a property deal that solved their financial crisis. Just imagine that for a moment. Of course, every member of staff would have been affected, but it's hard to imagine what the fallout might have been had Arsenal not paid their biggest stars, such as Thierry Henry, Patrick Vieira, Sol Campbell and Dennis Bergkamp. It would have been one of the most shocking developments ever in football finance. Not only that, it would almost certainly have led to players' performances suffering badly as a result.

The property deal that saved Arsenal was with housing developer Wilson Connolly, when Arsenal had to sell off land they owned in Lough Road, Holloway, to bail themselves out. At that time, Arsenal's wage bill was nearly £1.5 million a week, making them the third highest payers in the country during the Invincibles season.

It was as close to disaster as Arsenal have ever come. The Emirates Stadium was left on a financial knife edge. The sale of a raft of property in Lough Road – and then later in Drayton Park – kept the project alive. Arsenal were left praying the property market remained stable and interest rates stayed manageable, as they pressed ahead with their plan to build the 60,000-seater stadium at a cost of £390 million.

But word was getting round among the players about just how tight the finances had become, and it remains, in the modern game at least, a miracle not only that the story of the near financial crisis did not get out but also that the players remained focused and motivated throughout this period.

The extent of Wenger's involvement in the planning and development of the stadium often causes some discussion among senior figures at the club, as it was Danny Fiszman, Ken Friar and managing director Keith Edelman who undoubtedly drove the project and secured both the land and the financing. Wenger did have some say in design, most notably when he spotted on the architects' plans that there was a big pillar in the home dressing room. It was very late in the day, building work was well under way, but Wenger insisted that the pillar be removed so that when he gave a team talk all of his players could see him and he could see them.

Wenger has, on more than one occasion, even told supporters' meetings that one bank would not release funds until he signed a new contract, so important did they see his role in ensuring the club reached the Champions League, and the European pot of gold, every season. Clearly Wenger's success and ability to keep Arsenal near the top of the English game was incredibly important to the financial institutions that were loaning the money and, in effect, playing their own game of Fantasy Football. With Wenger picking the team, they felt they would be safe.

Arsenal confirmed funding for the stadium in February 2004 – and Wenger signed a new contract in October 2004. Bearing in mind the financial tussles behind the scenes, it is not surprising that his contract took a lot of negotiating. He has always been one of the highest earners in the Premier League, but his contract reached remarkable levels – thanks in part to Thierry Henry.

The Arsenal board agreed a contract with Wenger which included a clause that meant he earned as much as the club's best-paid player. When Thierry Henry signed a huge five-year contract taking him up to 2007, the thinking was that he probably wouldn't be there in five years' time. Henry was still there, of course, and when Wenger's next contract renegotiation came round, Arsenal not only had to pay him as much as their French superstar striker, but they also tried to buy out the clause. Wenger's lawyer decided to invoke the clause and the Arsenal manager's earnings went through the roof.

But, thankfully from Arsenal's point of view, Wenger also

conceded he could hardly earn much more so allowed the club to buy out the clause. Having reached unprecedented levels – in the words of one source: 'It nearly crippled us' – Wenger's contract remained high, and the deal he signed in 2014 was worth an estimated £8 million a year.

As word got round in managerial circles about how much Wenger was being paid (his previous deal had been worth £7.5 million a year), other managers quickly used Wenger's earnings as a benchmark. Even Sir Alex Ferguson used him as a benchmark, when he told Manchester United chief executive David Gill that he should earn more. United made their enquiries – and discovered it was true. Wenger was paid a fortune and is an incredibly wealthy man. Only Jose Mourinho's return to Chelsea in 2013 saw Wenger toppled as the biggest earner in the Premier League.

But while Wenger's huge earnings serve as another stick for his critics to beat him with, Nigel Winterburn still believes the 'barren years' following the 2005 FA Cup win should be seen as a success because of the extenuating circumstances – namely, the major restriction on finances, largely because of the stadium move.

> I think from 1998 to 2006 and the Champions League final, it was still a fabulous period for Arsenal. People only remember the winners, which is true because you play to win. But Arsenal still challenged every season ... You've given something to the supporters to say: 'We've given it our best shot – but we've come up a bit short.' I think it's important to be there at the end of every season. That gives the supporters that real belief, if you like.
>
> It's difficult to say what would have happened if they hadn't moved [to the Emirates]. Would they have had more money to spend on players? Would they still have been winning titles? I certainly feel during the period of [developing] the training

ground and the new stadium, to me – and obviously I'm no longer on the inside any more – there was not as much money available as had been bandied around.

If the team is not up there challenging, Wenger ... would have definitely realised the need to sign some more players. The players who came in – and he did spend money – were for £5 million and £10 million rather than the £30 million bracket. I have my doubts whether the big money was there for a couple of really big buys. That's how I assess that period.

You can never guarantee you will win things. But there will need to be a serious challenge for the title and maybe another trophy to bring back into the club and then people will say that the club is moving in the right direction again. The stadium was central to that. But now they need to show that they can get back up there.

The two years preceding the 2006/07 season were particularly tight and Wenger did not have much money to spend. Ironically, by the time Arsenal moved into the Emirates Stadium in the summer of 2006, the finances had actually begun to ease, because the really hard times had been weathered. And during that earlier period, Arsenal actually enjoyed some glorious times: the Invincibles season of 2003/04, the FA Cup in 2005 and the Champions League final in 2006.

Wenger did all that against the odds, which were stacked up not just by decreasing finances, but also by the arrival of Roman Abramovich and Jose Mourinho at Chelsea. As we have seen, the west London club were able to channel millions into their pursuit of success and knocked Arsenal off their perch, winning back-to-back Premier League titles in 2005 and 2006.

Just how much that was the case can be shown by the Invincibles season, when Arsenal had the third biggest wage bill in the Premier League – £69.9 million a year, compared with Chelsea on £114.8 million and Manchester United on £76.9 million – and yet finished as champions. In 2010, the *Wall Street Journal* put together a report which claimed that Premier League success is 85 per cent linked to wages. That shows just how much Wenger overachieved in 2003/04. Furthermore, during the 12 years from 2000 to 2012, Arsenal made a net expenditure of £57 million on transfers compared to Chelsea's £570 million.

Arsenal's wage bill has consistently been the third, fourth or even fifth highest in the league, dropping behind Liverpool in the 2009/10 season when Chelsea, Manchester United and Manchester City also spent more. The emergence of both Chelsea and Manchester City has presented Arsenal with a new challenge alongside Wenger's long-running battle with Manchester United for a place at the top of English football.

Wenger is an economist by qualification and that, as much as anything, perhaps influences his thinking on transfers. He tends to remain relatively cautious in his valuation, but in Dein's time there was someone who would take the decision to go the extra distance to get the player the manager wanted. After he left, the club tended to be more cautious in its dealings. Two illuminating stories about his transfer dealings highlight the difference in approach before and after Dein left Arsenal.

Wenger would always have 'transfer meetings' towards the end of each season to set out which players he wanted for the following year. The meetings generally involved Wenger, Dein, Ken Friar and, for much of the period between 2000 and 2008, managing director Keith Edelman. They would discuss targets, the make-up and strategic balance of the squad.

In the summer of 2000, Wenger identified Bordeaux forward Sylvain Wiltord as a player he wanted. He proposed offering

£8 million and insisted they should not pay more. It was pointed out that Bordeaux had turned down £10 million the previous summer and were hardly likely to accept less now, when he had actually improved as a player over the last 12 months. It was left to Dein to go and get the deal done. Sure enough he delivered, and Wiltord cost £12 million.

However, in the summer of 2011, Wenger made an offer of £6 million for Bolton defender Gary Cahill, which Bolton chairman Phil Gartside called 'derisory'. Then Bolton's manager, Owen Coyle, added: 'The word derisory doesn't even cover it.' In January 2012, Cahill – whose contract was running down – joined Chelsea for £7 million and went on to win the Premier League, FA Cup, Champions League and Europa League and become an England regular. If Wenger had been prepared to increase the offer, he might have got his man.

Wenger's views on transfers and, in particular, fees are the cause of much amusement and frustration at the club. He is willing to pay big wages but he will break down his valuations of fees to such a degree that one source compared it to buying a Cartier watch. If the watch cost £2,000 then Wenger would embark on a forensic breakdown of its parts and their value, and insist that it should cost £1,500. But, of course, the jeweller would not sell at a 25 per cent discount. 'He would most likely get into an argument and say: "But that's what it's worth!"' laughed the source.

For two summers running, Wenger's restricted budget meant he probably had only about £15 million to spend, while other clubs were spending £100 million-plus, but that definitely changed in 2006 when the cashflow was eased. Not least because, to secure bonds to help reduce interest payments by between £15 million and £20 million a year, Arsenal secured long-term deals with Nike and Emirates.

The board have since been accused by supporters' groups of

signing undervalued deals, but the truth is that they needed long-term contracts to persuade the banks to lend them money. They had to prioritise longevity over short-term gains; so they took longer deals even if they were worth less year on year, and they have since been renegotiated.

But there remained significant issues for Wenger, even though the club entered a new period of financial health at the Emirates. Not only did Wenger seem to become increasingly reluctant to spend big, but in 2007 he lost his staunch ally David Dein and then underwent years of boardroom turmoil. Many close to him believe this is one of the fundamental reasons why he has struggled to emulate his early success in the second half of his reign.

Financial expert and sports journalist Nick Harris, who runs the Sporting Intelligence website, believes that moving to the Emirates, the emergence of Chelsea and Manchester City and, finally, the loss of Dein have all had a profound effect on Wenger. He says:

The arrival of Roman Abramovich at Chelsea and Sheikh Mansour at Manchester City are the two overwhelming things that have given Arsenal a mountain to climb in terms of competition. In basic crude terms, those two owners have poured in roughly a billion pounds each to turn their clubs from also-rans into champions. In terms of making it harder for Arsenal, it is undoubtedly the money coming into those two clubs.

But, clearly, moving to the Emirates has put extra pressure and restriction on Arsenal spending money and being able to keep up. So, effectively, Arsenal have suffered the double whammy of having two turbo-charged petrol-dollar rivals and also, at the same time, for a large part of that decade have had their own resources redirected into a project which is beneficial in the long term for the club, but it's drawn away from money they could spend on players because they've had to spend it on the stadium and to pay the loans on it.

The reason they've had to do that is because they are sensible. If they were reckless, they would have spent loads on transfers but they are prudent and have made a conscious decision to divert their income into building a fantastic stadium which will bring them benefits in the long term.

The title has undoubtedly become harder to win because Manchester City and Chelsea have poured rivers of money into their clubs. They've given their managers hundreds of millions of pounds to bring in the best players and also pay them top dollar – it's obvious that they are going to be pretty good.

Harris also insists that Wenger has had more money to spend than he has chosen to do so, and also believes he needs more support around him:

It's become almost an annual event now, Arsenal's figures coming out and, if you are a bit of a nerd who likes figures, then the first thing you look at is the annual cash reserve because it's been piling up and up.

It was £200 million one year. It was one hell of a lot of money in the accounts they released in 2014. Theoretically, that money is there to be spent. If you write a story about it then you inevitably get a phone call from the club saying we can't say that. They will say it's there for a contingency for paying off a debt, a contingency for not getting into the Champions League, and it always peaks after the season-ticket money. They will try to convince you that £200 million is actually £40 million. But it's not very convincing because the fact is that Arsenal could have spent a lot more than they did. Not £100 million every summer, but certainly significantly more.

I know they bought Alexis Sanchez for £33 million, Mesut Ozil for £42 million, but there's been more money than they've spent. Why hasn't he spent it? The only person who can answer that question accurately is Wenger himself. We all know that he is an economist by training and he seems to have a genuinely held belief that you should get value in the transfer market. There's a legitimate question to ask as to why he doesn't spend more, and when he does spend, why does he spend it on the same sort of player? The same skilful midfield player.

A few of us went in to see the chief executive, Ivan Gazidis, and he was talking us through the figures, the stadium; the money would be there and everything would come to fruition. I brought up the old chestnut that David Dein's departure had a profound and significant effect on the club. He was clearly a close ally of Wenger and helped bring the best out of Wenger, encouraged him to spend money, and that seems to be lacking.

Wenger probably needs to be encouraged to spend money. Gazidis said it wasn't true and he actually said in that meeting with us all sitting in the boardroom, if he thought David Dein coming back would help the club then he would be on his hands and knees trying to make that happen. But he doesn't believe that to be the case. He said that if you think Wenger needs Dein then you are putting Wenger down and saying he's not his own man.

I'm not saying that. I'm saying that even the best managers tend to have the best support somewhere along the line. Fergie, the best manager the country has ever produced, has always had a strong chief executive and board. They would say yes or no. It's strong support. Rafa Benitez at Liverpool, one of the extremely high-quality managers in the past few years in terms of what he won, was a good manager but needed a strong figure like Rick Parry to curb some of the excesses. The best managers need an ally to help them. It always seemed to me from the outside that Dein was that person for Wenger and they've struggled to replicate that.

Wenger is a smart bloke ... I'd be surprised if he wasn't aware of the relationship between money spent and success. Being an economist, you would think he would be more canny about the way he spends and appreciates money. Maybe that's the reason why he spends it more on wages than transfer fees; maybe he doesn't think excessive transfer fees make sense. He does like to develop players, develop teams from young players, rather than going out and buying big players like Chelsea or Manchester City have done. The Man City or Chelsea model is one that he has never shown any interest in doing. He is an idealist. He has now started buying the odd big signing, but it's still the exception.

You'd never, ever see Wenger doing what Louis van Gaal did and go out and spend £150 million on five players like he did at Manchester United in 2014. Maybe it will work ... But the fact is that Arsenal couldn't do that, go and spend £150 million every summer, because it would endanger everything that Wenger and the club have worked towards. Wenger has gone out and bought small-name players and tried to turn them into big-name players.

But the question remains as to whether this apparent caution is purely down to Wenger or if it is also partly because of those surrounding him. The infighting within the Arsenal boardroom in the past decade could easily provide a script for the most dramatic of political thrillers. Without question, the biggest event for Wenger was the departure of David Dein, the man who brought him to the club and who was the heartbeat of the club for so many years.

When Dein was ousted from the Arsenal boardroom, Wenger had not seen it coming. The tensions had been simmering for some time and yet shortly after it happened, Wenger went into another employee's office and was so shellshocked that he could barely believe his friend had gone. 'He was devastated. Did he think about leaving at that point? I honestly don't know,' said a source.

The day of 18 April 2007 was a turning point in the history of Arsenal. It is rare that a boardroom figure becomes popular among the fans. But David Dein, the club's vice-chairman and a member of the board since 2003, was well known by supporters, instantly recognisable, regarded as a visionary and, above all, the man who brought Wenger to Arsenal. Furthermore, Dein was a fantastic networker, a brilliant negotiator and knew everybody throughout the game. And when it came to transfers, he would use his charm, inside track and those unrivalled relationships to open doors and get deals done. He and Wenger appeared inseparable.

But that day the simmering tensions between Dein and other members of the board, particularly Fiszman, boiled over and Dein was ousted. In fact, as chairman Peter Hill-Wood brutally put it: 'We sacked him.' Dein was marched out of the offices by security, having had his company mobile phone taken from him. It was humiliating, and the board had acted without first checking how the land would lie with Wenger.

The board believed that Dein was trying to set up a takeover with Stan Kroenke, which would see them buy Granada and Lady Nina Bracewell-Smith's shares and his own would also go into the pot. They would then run the club together. Dein denied this to the board, but after he left they did an amazing U-turn on Kroenke – who had been seen as the enemy after Hill-Wood's infamous barb, 'we don't want his sort' – and welcomed the US tycoon into the boardroom rather than Uzbekistan-born billionaire Alisher Usmanov, who also built a substantial stake in the club.

Hill-Wood, in an interview at the time, said: 'Let's be truthful, the rift with David Dein has been festering for some time, although nothing sufficiently as bad as this to make it impossible to continue. We had an idea he was in league with Kroenke and the board did not know what was going on. We put two and two together and came up with the right answer.'

Hill-Wood, talking just two days after Dein's departure, went on: 'Call me old-fashioned but we don't need Kroenke's money and we don't want his sort. Our objective is to keep Arsenal English, albeit with a lot of foreign players. I don't know for certain if Kroenke will mount a hostile takeover for our club but we shall resist it with all our might.

'We are all being seduced that the Americans will ride into town with pots of cash for new players. It simply isn't the case. They only see an opportunity to make money. They know absolutely nothing about our football and we don't want these types involved.'

Dein later sold his shares to Usmanov for around £75 million in August 2007 as they launched their rival takeover attempt. The other remaining Arsenal board members instigated a 'lockdown agreement' among themselves to pledge that they would not sell up, even though share prices were going higher and higher.

Dein, one of the most charming figures in football, always affable and armed with small talk and anecdotes, looked nervous and edgy when he held a very small press gathering at Frederick's restaurant in Islington after he had been ousted. It was there that board members often used to entertain journalists, investors and agents. It was difficult to see Dein, a man with Arsenal and Wenger in his heart, looking in from the outside as the club that he loved so much forced him out.

Dein's message was clear: Arsenal needed new money to compete. 'To provide these financial resources, Arsenal need new investors. I believe the board should welcome non-British involvement. Without new investors, I feel very soon Arsenal might not be able to compete successfully at the very top level, despite the fantastic work of Arsene Wenger.'

He spoke with sincerity but his delivery seemed only half-hearted because he knew, deep down, that he was fighting a losing battle. In fact, in 2008, Dein stood down as chairman of Usmanov's holding company, Red and White, to try to ease hostilities and also improve Usmanov's chances of getting a place on the board. But it was too late for that.

The battle lines in the escalating war in the boardroom had long since been drawn and, with every new development, the remaining directors seemed intent on pushing Dein further away. Almost to illustrate the point, the Arsenal board decided to get back in with the American because Dein had lined up with Usmanov.

The boardroom battle seemed to be as much about Dein versus Fiszman as it was Usmanov versus Kroenke. And if you needed proof of that, Fiszman did a deal on his deathbed in April 2011 to sell his shares to Kroenke, such was his determination to keep Usmanov out. Lady Nina Bracewell-Smith also then sold her 15.9 per cent stake in the club to Kroenke to allow the US tycoon to become majority shareholder in April 2011.

Finally, the cold war was over in the boardroom but some strange dynamics remained, which had also caused problems in the preceding years. Keith Edelman, the club's managing director from 2000 to 2008 and regarded as extremely efficient and good at his job, was ousted after falling out with other members of the board, which didn't seem good enough reason to get rid of a man on the basis of his personality rather than his ability.

Another director, Lord Harris, was criticised by some as too much of a fan and couldn't make the best decisions, but he remained on the board. Richard Carr oversaw, to a large degree, the construction of the club's new training ground at London Colney and also the academy. He was another big miss when he left after yet another boardroom reshuffle, because he was very much regarded as being a 'football man'.

Some managers are very happy to be left to their own devices without boardroom interference. But Wenger had gone from having a very hands-on board, with a lot of support and directors with a strong football background, to a completely new dynamic of an American majority shareholder and a board largely made up of ageing directors. That said, Wenger and Fiszman got on extremely well and were very close, even throughout Fiszman's cold war with Dein.

Notwithstanding all the changes, Arsenal have always remained 'old school' in their approach. Ken Friar, one of the club's greatest ever servants, who worked his way up from tea boy to managing director, had what is amusingly known at the club as a 'bat phone' hidden in his desk to take urgent and very select phone calls on transfers, contracts or board matters. That's the sort of club they are.

Traditionally, everything was secret, deals were done on the quiet, and they took pride in the fact that the club conducted its business behind closed doors without any leaks, as often happened elsewhere. It was notoriously difficult, for example, for journalists to make inroads to find stories or discover the inner workings at Arsenal. That ethos suited Wenger, too, as he regards the dressing room as sacred and he hates stories coming out from his inner sanctum.

Ivan Gazidis, a well-regarded chief executive who has overseen great change in terms of finance and marketing deals, succeeded

Edelman when he took up his post in January 2009. And in September 2009, Arsenal appointed Dick Law to the executive team, although they were very anxious to insist that he was *not* a director of football.

Law is a friendly, charming man and perhaps his greatest successes have been in playing a major role in the signings of Mesut Ozil and, in particular, Alexis Sanchez. It was, without question, Law – who speaks Spanish and Portuguese and has strong links in South America – who had the best links into Sanchez and set up the key meetings with agents during the World Cup, which Wenger attended.

But Wenger likes to have the final say on every deal and maybe that's the best way for any manager to work. Sometimes, though, Wenger takes a lot of pushing to get deals done. Gazidis unquestionably tried to push for a central defender to be signed in the summer of 2014, but none could be found that Wenger wanted. Instead, Wenger took a gamble and left himself short in defence, paying a heavy price. But it's wrong to say that no one was trying to push him, or that he didn't get the support he needed.

Wenger is normally very cautious when talking about boardroom matters, sticking to the script that he is merely an employee. Kroenke rarely talks publicly but also has a deep respect for Wenger and the pair get on very well. However, Wenger snapped when, in November 2014, Usmanov publicly condemned Arsenal – the Uzbeki tycoon claiming they were falling behind, were no longer competitive and Wenger couldn't accept criticism.

Wenger does have a cordial and friendly relationship with Usmanov; they have met on several occasions, Usmanov has been invited into Arsenal's directors' box and the tycoon has his own executive box at the stadium. However, none of that stopped

Wenger rounding on Usmanov, as he accused him of being a virtual outsider and not respecting the club's values. 'First of all, the 18 years I have been here, I have shown that I can take criticism. Everybody has the right to have an opinion. Having said that, we have values at this club. The first one is when we go through a difficult patch, we show solidarity. That is a very important one.

'The second one is that, when you have something to say to each other, we say it face to face. We don't need to go to the newspapers. I don't take it personally at all. It is an opinion that I respect but when you're from this club, you're from this club. You're in or out, you cannot be both.'

Usmanov may have been the club's second largest shareholder, yet the manager felt able to respond in a brutally frank way. It also goes to show how confident Wenger feels in his role as, after all, there are few other clubs, let alone industries, where a manager could so openly attack a major shareholder.

Wenger gave a fascinating insight into his role in March 2014 as he approached his 1,000th game and he looked back on the different and varied challenges of his time in charge. He described being part of the team that decided to build the stadium and the pressure he felt each year to reach the top four to help pay off the debt, and also admitted that he knew it would take its toll on his ability to be successful.

Tellingly, Wenger hoped that maybe one day he will get more credit for the period when the club moved to the Emirates.

I was part of the initial project to build the stadium and push the club to do it ... I felt part of my responsibility was to push the club through that difficult period as well as I could. I knew from the start that our financial viability was linked with us being in the Champions League or not. You can imagine how much I did sweat for years in the last three months [of each season]!

It was an important period. But do you think for the future or the present? You have to make sure the club grows as well. We made that decision knowing that we could suffer a bit financially but what was happening at the same time as that decision was that Man City and Chelsea made huge investments. We had the double effect. We were not only competing with the clubs who were at our level but suddenly two other clubs came in. We did not expect that at that time.

The consistency is the most difficult thing to achieve. If you look at all the clubs that fight at the top, not many are capable to stay in the top four. It was at a period when we had less financial resources. It is not like that, football. When you make a decision you don't say, "OK, we invest in the stadium but we don't want trophies."

It was maybe not the most prolific period on the trophy side, but maybe one day I will look back on it and that will be the period I am most proud of. But it is fast coming out of that period by delivering trophies and winning and competing with everyone again at the same level. You can only show that with trophies. By trophies I mean Premier League, FA Cup and Champions League.

Wenger will get sympathy in some quarters and very little in others. There is no doubt that he is a cautious manager anyway and was extremely circumspect even at a time when Arsenal did have money to spend. As we have seen, in 2014 the club tried to play down the significance of its cash reserves, insisting that much was needed for wages and costs and that, while Wenger did have money to spend, it was more likely to be in the region of £20 million. That was the sum being mentioned by Arsenal's scouts to agents as they looked for players in the next transfer window. Whereas other clubs are happy to be rather more adventurous and reckless and dip deep into the cash reserves, Arsenal's board are, like their manager, careful with how they spend their money.

Sometimes the lines are blurred as to whether it was Wenger who was reluctant to spend or if it was the board being cautious. The truth probably lies somewhere in between and yet both took the blame from the fans in equal measure. Wenger, though, is the more visible public face of the club, so gets the back-page headlines and scrutiny in the media.

Wenger was also fascinating when, in September 2014, he was asked about Tottenham's impending stadium move the day before they played their great north London rivals at the Emirates. He had a knowing grin on his face when he said:

It is massively difficult, if you look at the history of all the English clubs who have built a new stadium and look at where they have finished, then it tells you how difficult it is. The stress is terrible because you feel the future of the club is at stake and you have not a lot of margin [for error]. Every point you lose can be dramatic.

It depends [for Tottenham] on what kind of financial potential they have. It looks like they want to sell the club. If an owner comes in, and says, 'Look, I put £400 million to buy the stadium,' it is easy.

The way we did it is the hardest way, because we had no outside financial help and had to negotiate with the banks just to get the money at the start – and let's not forget we paid £120 million just for the land, we [helped] build a rubbish centre at Islington, we contributed to that, we had a lot of financial problems. In the end we built the stadium for £400 million. Today it would cost £600 million, £650 million or £700 million.

After 2005/06, when for the first time under Wenger Arsenal struggled to get into the top four, they have never subsequently risen higher than third in the table. However, they have always qualified for the Champions League, which was Wenger's barometer for success both in a football sense and from a financial point of view.

Increasingly, however, it was also driving a wedge between the fans and the club as the supporters – paying some of the highest ticket prices in the world – were growing frustrated by a perceived lack of ambition. Furthermore, each year the annual scrap for fourth was becoming harder and harder, the tension around March becoming greater, and it often seemed to come down to the final day to see if they would make it.

At the club's Annual General Meeting in October 2012, Wenger repeated his philosophy that, as far as he was concerned, qualifying for the Champions League was the same as a trophy. Despite the controversy that statement caused during Wenger's reign, it was often the case that he saved the day at the club's AGMs, as he spoke impressively and passionately about football, which was in direct contrast to many other board members who were rather grey by comparison.

'My job is to deliver a team with the resources we have, and I have never complained about that,' Wenger said. 'I want a club to pay players from its own resources, there is no shame in that.

'For me, there are five trophies – the first is to win the Premier League, the second is to win the Champions League, the third is to qualify for the Champions League, the fourth is to win the FA Cup and the fifth is to win the League Cup. I say that because if you want to attract the best players, they do not ask: "Did you win the League Cup?" They ask you: "Do you play in the Champions League?"'

The seemingly never-ending prioritising of a top-four finish, rather than silverware, does tend to result in former players and managers queuing up to give their views. In 2012, ex-Arsenal boss George Graham was particularly cutting when he questioned Wenger's coaching, signings and also standard of defending.

What is remarkable about Wenger is that he manages to keep a very straight face in public while, in private, in the confines of the training ground among his coaching staff or senior players, he will give vent to his feelings. When he was asked about Graham's comments, he replied: 'I fight for what I can master. And I cannot master what people say. It's a waste of energy and of time to speak about people who have opinions. They are entitled to have an opinion, that I respect. But an opinion is just one single person who says something. It does not mean that this person is necessarily right. We live in a world where you have to accept that. I can completely live with that. That is not the most important thing for me.'

That could be his stock answer for so many things. Wenger's best retorts do tend to come when he is spiky and angry, as was the case back in 2012 when the season once again appeared to be falling apart shortly after they crashed out of the League Cup at Bradford. So, predictably, Wenger answered back strongly when asked whether the players were delivering value for money for their contracts:

First of all, you don't know their wages. Secondly, you accuse us of not paying the wages the players want and on the other hand you accuse us of giving them the money they want.

If you are in that situation then it's because we are in the Champions League and we can produce the money. And secondly we are under pressure from Man City, Man United and Chelsea, who pay three times more the highest wages than us, to pay the players these wages.

We live in a competitive world. If they want to sign here – then they can say: 'I can get three times more there.'

Similarly, Wenger was interesting when asked whether he felt he got enough support from the boardroom. 'Yes, of course. The only way to give you support is to let you work and do your job. My job is to be determined and give importance to what is important. What is important is I love football, I love this club and I give my best for this club. The rest, I cannot interfere with that. Believe me, I am highly focused on doing that and all the rest, that doesn't interfere with my thinking at all. I am very determined and very hungry and if I wouldn't be, I wouldn't be sat in front of you.'

There was something of a repeat the following year when, three days after Arsenal's defeat at home to Bayern Munich in February 2013, which saw the end of their last realistic chance of silverware (they did win the return leg but still went out), a few reporters circled around Wenger. As he sat down behind a desk where he conducts his radio and TV interviews, the newspaper journalists towered above him, seemingly pushing and prodding him for answers, as he grew more annoyed with every question.

But Wenger was honest in his replies about money and his reluctance to spend during the stadium move, and he insisted that he was no longer unwilling to spend money:

I'm not reluctant to do so. First of all, we only had money recently. Secondly, in England there is a way of thinking that every problem is sorted out just by spending money but that's not always the case. If it was like that, the same teams would win the Champions League every year. There are two or three clubs in Europe who are richer than everybody else and do not play in the Champions League.

I believe that the problem today is not the money; it's to find the talent that strengthens your team. And, as well, I believe we have to be faithful to what this club is about, which is to give a chance to the young players we educate – that is vital – and therefore to bring in the players only who give us really a plus. If we find tomorrow a player of top, top, top quality, we will take him.

I want to keep everybody happy, you know. I want to win the championship and the Champions League and if we can't do it, we have to question ourselves. But, to do that, first we have to be at that level and, for years, it was vital we were there to pay it back.

When questioned why Arsenal and Wenger were not a bit more up front about not having money to spend while they tried to pay off the stadium, as the fans would have been a bit more understanding if they knew the full picture, he answered:

You cannot come out and say, 'Look, we cannot win the championship.' We were close during this period, you know, we were very close. Because I feel we had the quality. But, I think what angered more our fans is that we lost the players we educated, and that was much more difficult to swallow than all the rest, I believe, and that's what we have to change.

There were many major issues; we were fighting to keep our best players. You can only keep your best players, let's be realistic, by paying the wages of the market. To pay the wages of the market we have to put the ticket prices up. And then the fans turn against you and say, 'But you lose the best players and we pay high prices for tickets,' and they are right. But that was the consequence of the unfair competition that we faced. Having said that, the fans are ready to pay the ticket price if you win the championship, but we didn't.

Talking in the summer of 2013, Wenger said the huge outlay of clubs such as Chelsea and Manchester City had taken some of the romance out of the game:

[Spending] takes a little bit of something out because it doesn't give a chance to somebody who works well in the club and develops, people and players, and focuses on the quality of the game. Because, it's a bit like tomorrow, you start the 100 metres and suddenly somebody buys Usain Bolt and you have to win against him. I don't know how quick you are but it will be a problem for you!

I still believe that even if we are in a stronger financial position then all our values still have to be the same. We must rely on the quality of our work, on the style of our play and the fact we develop our own players. We will only use financial resources to bring in one or two players who will give us something more. It's very important that we keep to our strengths, and to what managed to get us through this period.

That is Wenger's philosophy spelt out and what defines him. Even when he has got more money to spend, he wants to stick to his vision, which is to produce players rather than buy superstars. As he famously said: 'We do not buy superstars. We make them. If I give you a good wine, you will see how it tastes and, after, you ask where it comes from. You can win in different ways, by being more of a team, or by having better individual players. It is the team ethic that interests me, always. The target for every manager is to try to entertain people.'

Wenger is not like every manager, though. He is an idealist; he preaches a philosophy that is based around being able to defy the odds, a long-held belief that money is not the only answer. He believes you can win without breaking the bank. If anything, the stadium move gave him an excuse to try to prove his point.

Although admirable, Wenger's ideals left Arsenal lagging behind and in desperate need of making up ground. One of the most difficult decades in Arsenal's history saw the landscape change beyond all recognition and, while in time history may be kinder to Wenger, the record books will also show the trophies went elsewhere.

CHAPTER 9

DESERTING THE SHIP

DESPITE THE NEW STADIUM costing £390 million, Arsenal maintained that Arsene Wenger was 'never denied funds' when he asked to sign players. Quite simply, that is because Wenger was aware of the finances, the budget and his limitations, so never asked for what he knew wouldn't be realistic. Consequently, he was never denied any funds. But it was a clever statement because it made it sound as if the new stadium didn't affect Wenger's budget at all. And that was far from the truth. Wenger is unlike many managers in that he has one eye on the accounts at all times, so he knew whether a transfer target was realistic or not.

It is interesting that, before the move to the Emirates Stadium was planned, Wenger would simply identify a player and David Dein would go to try to do a deal, telling his manager the club would worry about the cost. That changed even before Dein was ousted from the boardroom because suddenly, due to the construction of the new stadium, Wenger knew he had far less to spend on players, particularly in the two to three years leading up to the move when money was incredibly tight.

Each season, Wenger would sit down with Dein and managing director Keith Edelman and the trio would discuss transfer targets, fees and whether they were available. Up until 2003, Arsenal were able to compete with their Premier League rivals when it came to transfer fees and contracts. Now, suddenly, they were working on a completely different budget.

Wenger became more aware of transfer fees, contracts and costs because he knew exactly what was available. All of a sudden he was working under new financial restrictions and Wenger understood the situation. But for many football fans working within a budget is seen as far worse than being rash with transfer spending.

However, it perhaps helps to explain why Arsenal missed out on the biggest player of all: Cristiano Ronaldo.

In football, every agent, player, journalist and manager seems to have a different take on a transfer. They will always believe their story is right. Wenger believes Arsenal were desperately close to signing Ronaldo before he joined Manchester United in 2003. So close, in fact, that Ronaldo even came to Arsenal's training ground and had a look round, leading Wenger to believe they had got their man.

It was a three-way battle between Arsenal, Manchester United and Real Madrid, who all wanted to sign the Sporting Lisbon teenager. Ultimately, Wenger missed out because, as the interest grew, the price went up and he knew better than to ask for £12 million to spend on a young, unproven, if highly promising, teenager. Arsenal no longer had money to gamble on potential.

Instead, United signed him for £12.24 million. Sir Alex Ferguson laughs off Arsenal's belief that they were close to getting Ronaldo, who went on to become the most expensive player in the world:

We had an arrangement with Sporting Lisbon through Carlos Queiroz. We used to exchange coaches and Jimmy Ryan went over there for a week, came back and said: 'I've seen this player – Ronaldo, plays centre forward, 15 years of age, unbelievable.'

There was no financial arrangement, but it gave us the opportunity to sign him in two years' time. Then they came up with this proposal for us to open their new stadium ... There was this young skinny boy playing outside left against John O'Shea at right back. He twisted him inside out until he bled ...

I'd met Jorge Mendes [Ronaldo's agent] the night before to establish the position, to make sure we were on solid ground. In fairness, he always looked out for the player's best interests and he told me Arsenal and Real Madrid were in for him.

I got the boy down; I told his agent that I wanted him to come back with us. He said: 'I haven't got my passport and I want my mother.' So we hired another plane and brought them over, his sister, his mother, his lawyer, and they all came over and we eventually got it signed.

It was a familiar story for Arsenal and for Wenger. They also had Swedish superstar Zlatan Ibrahimovic at their Hertfordshire training ground and it has now become a standing joke that they wanted him to take a week-long trial when he was a teenager in 2000. Ibrahimovic memorably said of that time: 'Zlatan doesn't do auditions.'

Wenger commented on how the two players had ended up going elsewhere:

[Ibrahimovic] was here at the training ground, and then went somewhere else. That has happened to many players – Ronaldo was here, Ibrahimovic was here. It does not mean they sign for you. The story is true, I wanted to see [Ibrahimovic]. I did not know him – you cannot sign players you have not seen at all because it is not serious. He was 16. I asked him to have some training with the first team. He did not want to do it and I did not sign him.

I have no regrets because I will continue to do that unless our scouts have seen the player and say, 'Look, he is absolutely 100 per cent.' I trust them. But when somebody says he has some quality, you want at least to see, otherwise you would not be serious.

Wenger also tried to sign Lionel Messi and Gerard Pique along with Cesc Fabregas from Barcelona's academy in 2003. He confirmed in November 2014 just how close they had come to getting Messi after a book by Spanish journalist Guillem Balague first made the claim that Arsenal only missed out because they would not buy the Argentinian star's family a flat in London.

Wenger said: 'I think in the end, he was not so keen to move, because it was at a period where Fabregas came, and Fabregas and Messi played together in the same team [at Barcelona's academy]. We wanted to take Fabregas, Messi and Pique. It worked only for Fabregas. It was not completely down to a flat in the end. It was down to the fact that, in the end, Messi was comfortable at Barcelona.'

Ronaldo, Messi, Ibrahimovic and Pique – an incredible roll call. Wenger still trots out the line 'we don't buy superstars – we make them'; sadly for Arsenal and Wenger, they became superstars elsewhere. But Wenger's selling point to any young player was to stress that he would put them into the first team and give them a chance sooner than any other big club. The proof of that came when Fabregas was given his debut by Arsenal at 16, while Messi had to wait for another year to get his debut for Barcelona.

If they are the ones that got away, others also slipped through Wenger's fingers during a painful time when Arsenal struggled to compete financially, both in terms of transfer fees and contracts. Their best players ended up leaving the club: Cesc Fabregas, Robin van Persie, Sol Campbell, Samir Nasri and Thierry Henry all left for various reasons, but the common thread was that they were fed up with not winning. After the Invincibles season of 2003/04, the club was unable to compete either for trophies or when it came to bringing in new talent because of the costs of the new stadium. Suddenly, they were shopping at Primark rather than Selfridges while charging Harrods prices to their own fans for tickets. The quality of the squad went down and the players who stayed became disillusioned.

It didn't always work for those who believed the grass would be greener elsewhere. Alexander Hleb left Arsenal when Barcelona came calling; he barely got a look-in there and pleaded with Arsenal to take him back. They didn't and he ended up back in English football on loan at Birmingham City. And when England defender Campbell appeared to have fallen out of love with Arsenal, they decided to grant him a free transfer in the summer of 2006 after he told them he had a move abroad lined up. Campbell was on a big contract, had become disillusioned and it suited all parties. But his move to Juventus fell through and he ended up at Portsmouth. 'In the way the club was set up, it was like going from a Rolls-Royce to a Fiesta,' smiled Campbell.

Arsenal could offer a state-of-the-art training ground and 21st-century stadium – but after 2005 no trophies until 2014. There was little Wenger could do to stop haemorrhaging talent.

The hardest summer was undoubtedly 2011 when Nasri, Fabregas and Gael Clichy all left. But the most memorable departure came in 2012 when Arsenal sold their best player, van Persie, to their fiercest rivals, Manchester United, in what was – pure and simple – a financial decision.

Of course, the talent drain had begun well before 2011: Patrick Vieira, Henry and Ashley Cole – to name but three – had all gone in the preceding years. Henry's farewell came in 2007; he insisted on delivering a farewell message via the club's TV channel, and made it clear that it was breaking his heart to leave, but he feared for the club over the next few years.

Then, in 2008, a key figure in the Invincibles season, Gilberto Silva, was sold to Panathinaikos. It signalled the departure of yet another holding midfielder – Gilberto had become affectionately known as the 'Invisible Wall' in front of the back four – who, rather like Vieira, was not replaced.

Gilberto had been a mainstay of the Invincibles team, a regular since his arrival in 2002, and in the 2006/07 season he often wore the armband when Thierry Henry, plagued by back problems during his final year, was out injured. When Henry was eventually sold to Barcelona, many assumed Gilberto was the natural choice to be made captain. But he discovered that he had been over-looked for the role in favour of William Gallas only when he read it on the Arsenal website – at the same time as all the fans. This highlighted one of Wenger's faults as a manager: his occasional lack of communication with players. According to many, his fear of confrontation means he dreads having to talk to them directly when there is a difficult decision to impart.

Worse was to come, however, as Gilberto was frozen out in 2007/08 and even complained that Wenger made him feel 'completely useless':

At the time I was very surprised. I spent a lot of the season before as the captain. Then Thierry left and I got a really big surprise when I wasn't made captain any more.

Of course, it was important to be captain, but not the most important thing because I just wanted to play all the games. But then I lost everything – the position as captain of the team, then I lost my place on the team. We won the Copa America with Brazil where I spent most of pre-season before returning to the team. It was really hard for me in the beginning.

I was not so happy in those few months at the club. I was always a very simple person. You only had to talk to me. I believed at the time that he could and should have at least spoken to me about what was his plan. I respect always his decision. But then I asked him in person. We spoke afterwards. But I never had any bad feeling about him even though I was upset and at some point I was angry at the situation. Not with him, but losing my place as captain and place in the team.

But afterwards, I decided to work hard again, go to the training ground and really work hard, do my best as a professional, and I wanted to take the chance when I got to play. It was important to me to stay professional and show your professionalism. You must keep yourself on the right way. That's what I tried to do until my last day at the club.

Then I left because I was not getting a chance; after six months, seven months, I decided I should leave the club. I wanted to play in the 2010 World Cup for Brazil. If I stayed one more season on the bench then I would have no chance. Inside of me, I knew I had the motivation and the quality . . .

It was hard, but the hardest thing was when he called me to his office. I thought we would have a conversation about me staying in the club, I had one more season, but he said to me that if I had any opportunity to leave the club then he would not stop me. It was then that I realised it was time for me to leave. But Arsenal is, for me, the club that I love. It was a big school for me, I learnt so much there.

Even with the situation with me leaving and not playing, I never had any bad feeling about Arsenal or Arsene. It was purely business. I never let it affect the way I thought about him, the respect I had for him, and he is now a friend to me.

Wenger was rebuilding, selling off big players and shaping a new-look squad. Some departures were his choice; others involved players he didn't want to lose. The summer of 2011 was particularly painful because of the scale of the exodus. Wenger has often insisted Gael Clichy was sold to Manchester City that summer because he could see that Kieran Gibbs was breaking through into the first team. Clichy was a terrific player for Arsenal, loyal and a real club man. But his attitude changed in his final season; they believed his head had been turned and it made sense for him to be sold.

While Wenger remains on good terms with most former players, usually sending them a text on their birthdays or on career milestones, he has been known, occasionally, to give even favoured ex-players the cold shoulder. It's fair to say that Wenger doesn't take losing well – and he doesn't take losing players well either. When Arsenal first faced Manchester City after Clichy's £6 million transfer, the French left back approached Wenger in the tunnel, tried to shake his hand and was snubbed. 'I only played for him for seven years,' commented Clichy, as he looked at his former manager in disgust.

Similarly, when Fabregas returned to Arsenal for the first time since joining Chelsea, the Spanish midfielder said that he'd not heard from Wenger since leaving. I joked with Wenger about it and compared Fabregas's complaint about not getting a text from him to Yaya Toure's infamous moan that Manchester City did not get him a cake for his birthday and that when he did eventually get one it was from an airline rather than his own club. Wenger laughed at the thought and said: 'I'm surprised he [Fabregas] mentioned it because I don't remember it. Maybe sometimes you get so many messages that you forget some. You cannot reply to everybody. It happens. If I did forget, I apologise.'

The Nasri and Fabregas transfers were more protracted and certainly more bitter in many ways. The saga played out during the course of Arsenal's pre-season tour of Asia in the summer of 2011. It was the first time Arsenal, under Wenger, had strayed out of Europe for a pre-season tour and, in truth, Wenger did not really want to be there. He preferred his usual European retreat of Bad Waltersdorf, but no money-making and marketing opportunities exist in a small Austrian spa town.

I was among a small group of journalists who flew over to Kuala Lumpur and on arrival we headed straight for Arsenal's hotel, where a press conference was being held for local media. A private room had then been set aside for us to talk to Wenger and van Persie. Fabregas had stayed in London – a diplomatic injury excuse was offered but not really taken seriously – and Nasri was on the trip but his future was equally uncertain.

The air-conditioning barely eased the sweat and scorching temperatures as Wenger sat back on a sofa with a few regulars from the English press pack sitting around him. It was very noticeable that Ivan Gazidis, Arsenal's chief executive, was hovering at the back of the room, clearly interested in what Wenger had to say. Considering he had just arrived after a long-haul flight, Wenger was relaxed and in good form. He spelt out a defiant message: Arsenal would not sell both Fabregas and Nasri.

'Imagine the worst situation – we lose Fabregas and Nasri – you cannot convince people you are ambitious after that,' said Wenger.

'I believe for us it is important, the message we give out. For example, you talk about Fabregas leaving, Nasri leaving, if you give that message out you cannot pretend you are a big club.

Because a big club first of all holds on to its big players and gives a message out to all the other big clubs that they just cannot come in and take away from you.'

Wenger declared Nasri would 'definitely' stay, despite interest from Manchester City, and he claimed Arsenal would even risk the player running down his contract because they were confident he would sign a new deal. 'For us, on Cesc, it's not a question of money. It is a question of Cesc wanting to be with us. And I think he is torn because he loves the club deeply. We will fight until the last second to keep him.

'I think Cesc has always been torn between his love for Arsenal that I feel is really genuine and, as well and what you can understand, the desire to play for the biggest team at the moment in the world. I think both exist in his head. I am confident because I hope he will see that there will be no greater achievement for him in his life than to lead this team to success and that it will not be the right period for him to leave the club.'

There was another worry: Arsenal's other big star, van Persie, would surely follow them out of the club if Arsenal sold his best team-mates. It was easy to understand just how highly van Persie rated Fabregas from the way he talked about his passing, vision and support from midfield. 'From my own situation, he is the one I first look at to see if he is playing or not. We have a connection together, he knows exactly when to pass, exactly when to make his decisions in the game. He is a really special player, he can see things quicker than others. He would be a miss for any team. That is why I hope that he stays and we can play on a bit longer together because I really rate him. You need investment to keep up because when you look around, Man City is buying loads of good players, Liverpool are doing it now, Man U have been doing it for years.'

That first press conference was the best of the whole two-week tour. Wenger smiled knowingly as we chatted and I asked him whether the previous season – the 2010/11 campaign when Arsenal lost the League Cup final to Birmingham and their title challenge fell apart in the following few weeks – was his hardest to date. He looked ill at times, I told him, feeling that it had definitely taken its toll.

But now, on the heels of that torturous season, Wenger was to endure a cruel summer which, as it began to unravel, became even more difficult. As soon as we got back to our hotel after the press conference, I rang those close to Fabregas, expressed my surprise at Wenger's convincing belief they would be able to keep him – and was immediately told he was still leaving. Wenger had put on a brave face, a defiant face, and yet there was no way back for Fabregas, who had made up his mind.

Fabregas had wanted to leave the previous summer, if truth be told, and was persuaded to stay for one more year – and wasn't going to be denied again. He grew up in Barcelona and always envisaged going back home one day.

It was different for Nasri, as some blame for his departure can be put down to both sides. Arsenal had allowed his contract to run down to just 12 months left and yet discussions had begun the previous autumn. They agreed a deal in principle, Nasri was ready to sign, but they didn't put the contract down on the table and, by the time it was discussed again, Nasri had made up his mind not to sign. The Nasri deal dragged on for weeks, and Wenger was infuriated by Manchester City boss Roberto Mancini admitting publicly he wanted to sign the Arsenal midfielder.

After Arsenal's final game of the Asia tour, in Hangzhou, China, and before they flew home, Wenger, when pressed, finally began to say what he really thought about Mancini and City going public on their desire to sign Nasri and whether it was a case of 'tapping up'. 'We do not make any comments on players who are under contract in other clubs,' snapped Wenger, his patience worn down by the never-ending stream of questions about the impending departures of some of his best players. 'These comments are not allowed and Roberto Mancini should be informed!'

Still it dragged on, and meanwhile Wenger was angered by a series of Barcelona players queuing up to say that they wanted the Arsenal captain to move to the Nou Camp. At least with Fabregas, the situation was resolved quickly. Arsenal maintained a dignified silence when he was agitating for a move, hadn't gone on the tour, and Wenger has never criticised his former captain.

Fabregas eventually got his wish to go to Barcelona and, at the unveiling, a freelance reporter for the *Daily Mirror* says his sister told him how unhappy he was with comments on the transfer made by some English players and media. It was as if Fabregas had signed for Arsenal and then just expected them to one day hand him over to his boyhood heroes.

Ivan Gazidis tried to drive a hard bargain with Barcelona, while Fabregas's agent, Darren Dein (David Dein's son), clearly had only one club in mind. And, there being no bidding war or competition, Barcelona sensed they could get a deal on the cheap.

Eventually, Arsenal agreed a deal worth around £40 million, once you take into account clauses and sell-ons. My own impression is that Barcelona sanctioned the deal – which included a buy-back option and a percentage of future profits – because they never thought Fabregas would leave. It was hard to imagine, in 2011, that Arsenal would ever get to exercise the buy-back option. Had Fabregas really been available in 2013 when Manchester United bid for him, I'm convinced Arsenal would have gone for him and not allowed him to join their rivals. In the end, Fabregas joined Chelsea in 2014 and Arsenal got around £5 million as part of a sell-on fee.

'I don't see why he should not be happy with Arsenal or with me,' said Wenger in October 2014, clearly perplexed by the move.

'We influenced his life in a positive way, that is what we are about. The most important thing is that he is happy.

'I said many times I always understood that he could go back to Barcelona, because he is from Barcelona. It didn't go as well as he imagined it, certainly, because I felt that when he goes back to Barcelona he will finish his career there or come back to Arsenal. It was the fact that he left Barcelona much earlier than everybody expected. Why? I don't know. He can explain that much better.'

Fabregas remained popular with Arsenal fans until he moved to Chelsea. At that point, opinion was split right down the middle. But there was certainly no divided opinion among the fans on Nasri, who were unhappy at the way he left, and who for.

The transfer became a long-drawn-out affair. Arsenal refused to be responsible for a large slice of agent fees, insisting City should pay that, and it came to a head only when Arsenal threatened to include him for the second leg of their Champions League tie with Udinese. That finally twisted City's arm and the negotiations started in earnest as Arsenal prepared to fly to the picturesque Italian city of Udine.

There's no denying it was a grim time for Arsenal: they had sold Fabregas, were about to sell Nasri, and they had a worrying medical bulletin on Jack Wilshere – seen as the midfield successor to the departing captain – who was facing a lengthy lay-off. Wenger admitted to overplaying Wilshere the previous season, which played a part in the stress fracture that ended up keeping him out the whole season.

The press used to travel with the team and, after Wenger had done radio and TV, we would break off into what resembled a small boardroom in the private lounge at Luton airport. Wenger would often relax and be a bit more open and chatty. Not this time. At lunchtime on 23 August, the day before Arsenal played

Udinese – they held a slender 1-0 lead from the previous week's home leg – Wenger was tense, preoccupied; he knew the club was at a crossroads. They had sold their best players, and he was unwilling to spend big until he knew they had reached the Champions League, and he didn't like to be reminded of what he'd said on the Asia tour.

On the official press trips, the English newspapers would see Wenger separately and we'd ask our own questions, get our own quotes, and embargo them for our newspapers the following day to give us something different from the instant radio and TV reports. To us, Wenger didn't deny what he'd said in Asia nearly six weeks earlier about Arsenal not being able to call themselves a big club if they sold Nasri and Fabregas, but, in front of the TV cameras at the official UEFA press conference in the stadium in Udine, his message appeared to be different. He insisted he had never said it. Wenger had done a complete U-turn to save face after eventually having to sell two of his best players in the same summer. It was one of his most difficult periods as manager.

The following night, on a balmy summer's evening in Udine, Arsenal squeezed through into the Champions League and the sense of relief was overwhelming. Wojciech Szczesny saved a penalty, and Arsenal returned to London knowing they would be able to bank the cash windfall from reaching Europe's top competition and that would allow Wenger – in his own mind – to strengthen the squad.

But not before Arsenal faced a trip to Old Trafford with the squad in tatters because of injuries. Wenger still hadn't brought in the necessary replacements and they played Manchester United with a patched-up team that included Armand Traore at left back, who knew he was booked in for a medical the following day and was due to join Queens Park Rangers. Needless to say, Traore came up short, but he wasn't the only one who had a bad game. Just four days after their precious victory at Udinese, they were humiliated 8-2 at Old Trafford, which prompted words of sympathy from Sir Alex Ferguson.

That was a low point for Wenger, as the shambolic and chaotic nature of their transfer business left him horribly exposed to questions about his future. Arsenal were in a mess and, as always, the most obvious person to blame is the manager. Sky Sports reporter Geoff Shreeves, in the interview area in the Old Trafford tunnel, asked whether Wenger would resign or walk away if he couldn't turn it round. 'No, not at all. What is to turn around? We have played three games in the season. We have played two away and we played one at home that we lost and we have qualified for the Champions League.'

Wenger looked shaken and surprised by the question – it even took him a while to forgive Shreeves for asking what was a perfectly reasonable question. But a defeat on that scale begs questions about a manager's future, yet Wenger's expression was one of disdain and disbelief, almost as if it was disrespectful to ask him if he would resign. That is a measure of how Wenger appears to regard his position at the club: untouchable.

The next few days were awash with radio phone-ins, TV debates and fans calling for Wenger to go. Painful though this was, there was never any question of Wenger's future being in doubt. Instead, Arsenal set about rebuilding and, even though Wenger headed off to a coaches' conference ahead of the 2011 transfer deadline, they ended up bringing in Andre Santos, Yossi Benayoun, Per Mertesacker and Mikel Arteta.

Arteta was a deal that was on and off right throughout the day. In fact, it was Arteta who made it happen by agreeing to take a cut in his wages to join from Everton because he wanted to play in the Champions League. 'It was very stressful. At 6 p.m., they said everything had broken down. Then, at 8.30 p.m., everything started again,' Arteta recalled. 'But there wasn't time to have a medical. I went to the offices of the club [Everton] and from there I told Arsenal to trust me and that if some medical problem was found it would be my responsibility.'

The 2011/12 season became the van Persie season as the Dutch striker enjoyed the best year of his Arsenal career and, almost single-handedly, scored the goals to get Arsenal into Europe. He had joined Arsenal as a youngster with a troublesome reputation, arriving in May 2004 for a bargain fee of £2.75 million. But his career at Arsenal was plagued by injuries until the 2011/12 season, when he really took off and scored 37 goals in all competitions.

Van Persie was voted the Football Writers' Footballer of the Year in 2012 and during his acceptance speech he said he would 'always be a Gunner'. The Dutchman also claimed that he would talk to Arsenal about signing a new contract as, rather ominously, he only had a year left on his current deal. 'That is still the plan. We haven't set a date, but I will have a meeting with the boss like we did before. Now we will be having a meeting about my future, and lots of other things.

'Arsenal is an unbelievable club, the player I am today is because of Arsenal. When I actually signed the deal [to join Arsenal] it was a dream come true. If you ask the likes of Robert Pires how he feels, what he feels like, he will say, "I feel like a Gunner" – and whatever happens with me I will always be a Gunner.'

But, behind the scenes, Manchester United, Manchester City and Juventus were all flirting with him. Arsenal were putting on a brave public face and the Dutchman, taking his captain's responsibilities seriously, convinced his team-mates that he might yet stay. He even organised events like a barbecue for his team-mates as a bonding exercise, and his wife Bouchra arranged a girls' night out for the wives, girlfriends and partners.

But after the end of the season, Arsenal's worst fears were confirmed when van Persie and his agent Kees Vos met with Wenger and Ivan Gazidis at Wenger's house. It was at this meeting, on Wednesday 16 May 2012, that it became clear van Persie was leaving Arsenal. Van Persie suggested a list of players that Arsenal should sign. Wenger told him in no uncertain terms: 'You don't tell me who to buy.' It was dismissed out of hand.

There was a feeling that van Persie had already made up his mind to go – a theory backed up by Sir Alex Ferguson in his autobiography, which claims that Manchester United had been approached by the player's agent – and that meeting was merely paying lip service.

For the next two months, Arsenal unashamedly tried to sell van Persie to Juventus rather than lose him to a Premier League rival. Van Persie had told them specifically that he did not want to join Manchester City and at no point did Juventus ever convince Arsenal that, despite the public bluster, they had enough money to get anywhere close to a realistic fee.

It became a financial decision as much as a football one. Arsenal budgeted on a £70 million 'swing', because they would get £24 million in a transfer fee, save on wages and bonuses and also have money to spend on players, while United would have used up those funds. It was a complex equation, but the balance sheet could not deflect from the anger among the supporters as Arsenal were about to sell their star striker to their arch rivals. Van Persie arguably won United the title in his first season, but afterwards failed to live up to those early standards and that financial equation actually makes more sense in retrospect and he joined Fenerbahce in the summer of 2015.

But the van Persie deal was probably more painful than any other, and for the fans it represented waving the white flag. The saga stretched until the second week of August and van Persie even flew to Germany to play in a friendly against Cologne as part of the deal that saw Lukas Podolski join Arsenal.

It was obvious by that stage to Wenger and everyone at the club that they had to sell van Persie. Any fantasies – and there were some – that van Persie would have a last-minute change of heart and stay disappeared in that pre-season trip. It looked as though he didn't want to be there.

Within 48 hours, the deal with Manchester United was done and a phone call from Ferguson to Wenger was the final piece in the jigsaw. Arsenal had resisted all summer long selling to United and now, finally, Ferguson's intervention saw the deal come to fruition very quickly. Arsenal played in Cologne on the Sunday, they decided van Persie had to be sold, wheels were in motion by the Monday evening and the deal was agreed on Tuesday and announced on Wednesday 15 August.

It was a devastating blow for Wenger; it felt like the lowest point for Arsenal and, to rub salt in the wounds, van Persie's goals helped United win the Premier League title in 2012/13, which was to be Ferguson's final season in charge at Old Trafford. When United came to the Emirates in April 2013 having already won the title, Wenger insisted – despite the vitriol aimed at van Persie from the terraces – that his players formed a guard of honour for Ferguson's newly crowned champions. It was van Persie's first return to his former club and, inevitably, he scored in a 1-1 draw.

The pain that Arsenal suffered with the sale of big-name players as they went through hard times during the transition and move to the Emirates never seemed worse than during the whole van Persie affair. Wenger, recalling that phone conversation with Ferguson, admitted it was the hardest sale he has ever made as Arsenal manager, much worse than losing Fabregas or Patrick

Vieira. 'It was a very professional phone call, and there was more than one. I will tell you the rest another day.

'Yes, of course, it was one of the hardest decisions. But with the player at some stage you have to be realistic. I can explain to you why, all what was around that story one day. I am sure that you will be much more comprehensive about it. It is difficult when the player does not want to be here, to force him to be here and know that at the end of the season the club does not get anything with knowing that he might not contribute as well. So you are twice a loser.'

On the one hand, Wenger said van Persie's move to Old Trafford 'wasn't about money'. So, did he know what van Persie was getting at United? 'Yes,' said Wenger, looking skywards. Van Persie was reported to have joined United on a £200,000-a-week contract. Wenger admitted Arsenal couldn't compete. 'No, because it is at a scale that is massive,' Wenger said, before insisting they did everything to keep him.

'It was the transfer that saddened us most because we have lost some other big players like Thierry Henry, Patrick Vieira; they had won with the club and they were around 30 or 31. He could help us to win because we haven't won for a few years. That he left before that was frustrating for us.'

Then Wenger said what he thought the real reason was that van Persie had decided to leave the previous summer. 'He arrived at the age of 29 and thought, can we win the championship here or do I have more chances to win it somewhere else? There's a kind of timescale like for a woman who has no baby at 39. She starts to think, I have not much time left now …'

Then Wenger made a thrusting motion as if he was having sex just to illustrate the point. It brought the house down. That remains one of my most memorable moments from a Wenger press conference as he injected humour into a very painful subject.

'It was completely honest with Robin. We had a frank exchange of views,' said Wenger. 'He's an honest guy, Robin. He tells you the truth. The truth is what you want. He was respectful until the end and we cannot complain.'

To date, Van Persie was the last big sale that Arsenal made to a rival. They did, though, lose Bacary Sagna to Manchester City in the summer of 2014, which was probably more down to their dithering over his contract and his disillusionment during his seven years at Arsenal. Sagna allowed his contract to run out and, despite being offered a new three-year deal at the age of 31, he left Arsenal on a free transfer.

His departure was a blow but in no way on a par with van Persie, Fabregas, Nasri or even Gael Clichy. The fact was that Sagna, an experienced and top-quality international, had become frustrated and fed up with not winning trophies. He had stayed loyal, not pushing to leave when City had twice tried to sign him previously.

Sagna had become more critical in his regular interviews with the French media, declaring that Arsenal were not competing, they were selling their best players and were allowing players to run their contracts down. Despite Arsenal showing a new ambition and winning the 2014 FA Cup, Sagna had made up his mind. He insisted privately that if Arsenal had rung him the day after they won the FA Cup at Wembley he would have stayed. But the call never came and off he went to City. Arsenal felt he had long since resolved to join Manchester City.

Shortly after joining City, Sagna gave a revealing interview, in which he talked about why he left and his perception of the club's philosophy under Wenger.

I think Arsenal is and will remain a quality side. I think during the transfer windows clubs are used to buying, whether that's right or wrong. Arsenal have a very good team with young players pushing to come through. We proved last year that we had a good team by winning a trophy, even if there wasn't much change in personnel. The club runs more on that kind of philosophy. I think the fans are frustrated because when they see their neighbours buying teams they ask themselves why is that not the case in their club?

I think it was a good time for me to look elsewhere. I spent seven wonderful years with Arsenal. I was very young when I arrived and experienced some great things. I learnt an enormous amount under Arsene Wenger and those who I played alongside. It was the time for me to leave at the age of 31 and boost my career. I thought about it a lot and I had a difficult year psychologically because it wasn't an easy choice to make. I left behind somewhat of a family club, where I felt very at ease and it was very difficult to make the choice but I did.

In that interview, Sagna set out the case some make against Wenger's approach: Arsenal are a family club; other clubs spend big while he prefers to build a team around young players and, ultimately, players will move on to look for consistent success.

Wenger takes some departures better than others, and can defuse situations with humour. Jose Reyes was duped into saying he didn't like London by a Spanish radio station and, when he said he wanted to leave and go back to Spain, Wenger replied: 'It's like you wanting to marry Miss World and she doesn't want you. I can try to help you but if she does not want to marry you, what can I do?'

And when Sol Campbell left in 2006 – allowed to go on a free transfer after telling Arsenal he was going abroad – and ended up at Portsmouth, Wenger smiled: 'It is a big surprise to me because he cancelled his contract to go abroad. Have you sold Portsmouth to a foreign country?'

When former Arsenal keeper Jens Lehmann, a member of the 2003/04 Invincibles team, was interviewed just before the FA Cup success of 2014, he had some bitterness about being dropped in 2004/05, despite not losing a single Premier League game in his first season at the club. But Lehmann has clearly retained a great affection for Arsenal, though he doesn't believe they will regain consistent success unless the structure is changed.

I think in the current condition, it's going to be very hard for them to win something. They have to make changes. Spending alone never wins you something. But it's a good basis when you have money. Money needs to be well spent.

I think Arsene represents the club as no other. But I think, as well, sometimes the structure has to be not only on two shoulders or on one man; but sometimes you need to have a couple of people who define and control and monitor the progress of the club and the philosophy. Because particularly the clubs are always growing and the demands for a manager, they are growing. And if you have to do that always by yourself, I doubt that you can be successful.

The assistants he has are very good. But I think what I've learned from Arsene is you can be fantastic, but if you don't perform fantastically, he gives you a rest. That's his philosophy, and his philosophy on myself, particularly. And right now, I think, yes, he still has to live this philosophy.

I think Ivan Gazidis is doing a great job there, but he came in when the times have changed a little bit. David Dein was supporting Arsene in terms of football, evaluation of players. But at the time, Arsene had the advantage of knowing the French market fantastically well. The markets have changed.

A club like Arsenal, which is mentally dependent on Arsene's view of football and his philosophy and his detection of new players, I think that's not enough any more. Still great, but you can't do everything. A little bit of support in terms of knowledge outside the training pitch, yes, football knowledge outside the training pitch, in my opinion would be helpful.

Wenger is very close to Arsenal's 'transfer fixer' Dick Law; they are friends and colleagues, and there is a mutual respect. But the set-up is clearly different from the Dein era. Dein was an incredibly smooth operator and was vice-chairman. He could push Wenger into a deal and almost insist that he did it. Law, a charming Texan, is equally slick and is very well-connected. He has Wenger's ear, but he's not vice-chairman. Gazidis will also push transfers and is a knowledgeable football man, with a wealth of information.

Ultimately, though, it's the way of English football culture that the final decision at any well-run club must rest with the manager; he has to choose whether he wants a player because he must be free to pick his team. But if any one factor is most to blame for Arsenal missing out on deals then it must be the manager's indecision. However, after a period when it seemed the club was always selling top players, things were about to change. After those difficult times in the summers of 2011 and 2012, Arsenal were about to enter a new period of prosperity on and off the pitch. By the summer of 2013, they had enough financial muscle to buy big players again and compete for trophies once more.

CHAPTER 10

OLD FOES

ARSENE WENGER SAT IN THE LIGHT, airy conference room at UEFA's headquarters in Nyon, Switzerland, with two of his fiercest managerial rivals on the other side of the desk. Sir Alex Ferguson looked immaculate in a pale blue shirt with dark blue tie, now enjoying his retirement and status as the godfather of managers. He was the guest host for the UEFA coaching conference. The Chelsea manager, Jose Mourinho, was more casual, in a suit but with an open-necked grey shirt. He looked sullen, only vaguely interested and, if anything, a little bored as managers from across Europe discussed football's global calendar, refereeing and different ideas on coaching.

It was a well-attended UEFA Elite Club Coaches Forum conference in September 2014. Carlo Ancelotti, Pep Guardiola, Rafa Benitez and even Andre Villas-Boas were all there. I asked Wenger whether all differences were put aside at such conferences. 'Yes, of course,' he smiled back.

But you don't like everyone?

'No, and I must say, not everyone likes me,' Wenger laughed.

That's putting it mildly. A truce has been called with Ferguson, a man who used to so annoy and irritate Wenger that at one stage he would only refer to him as 'that man'. He couldn't even say his name out loud. 'I will never talk about that man again,' said Wenger after one of their public spats spiralled horribly out of control.

These days, Wenger has respect for Ferguson and, in public, they speak admiringly of each other. When Ferguson announced his retirement in 2013, Wenger was one of the first Premier League managers to send him a text to wish him well. It is hard to imagine that ever happening nine years previously when the Wenger–Ferguson warfare was at its most intense. Hostilities eased as the years went by.

If hatred has turned into mutual respect between Ferguson and Wenger, the same cannot be said of relations between Wenger and the Chelsea manager. Far from it.

However, when the time comes and people reflect on Wenger's career, his rivalry with Ferguson is the one that will be remembered as the most entertaining to the neutrals. It began from the moment Wenger arrived in 1996, reached its peak during 'pizzagate' and then diminished as Arsenal – and in turn Wenger – became less of a threat to Ferguson's success.

Ferguson, the son of a Glasgow shipyard worker, initially ridiculed Wenger during press conferences in Manchester. 'What can he know about English football?' he once asked.

The question just about captured the mood and highlighted the difficulties, distrust and resentment facing foreign managers 20 years ago. The fact that Wenger had been nicknamed Le Professeur and portrayed as highly intelligent, spoke several languages and was scientific in his approach, was also a cause of mockery. Ferguson told journalists: 'Intelligence! They say he's an intelligent man, right? Speaks five languages. I've got a 15-year-old boy from the Ivory Coast who speaks five languages.'

Such was Ferguson's influence that he didn't have just a clique of journalists, but also a group of fellow managers who appeared to follow his every word and move. If Fergie disliked a new manager on the block, then the others fell in line.

Arsenal's former press officer Clare Tomlinson remembers confronting one manager about the clique ostracising the Frenchman because he refused to follow the very British tradition of coming for a drink in the opposing manager's office after games.

> The whole Fergie clique they were all horrible to him. One said: 'Why won't he come for a drink?' I said: 'I'm sick of this from you lot. You're like children. Have you asked him?' He said: 'No, because he won't come.' No one had actually asked him! He doesn't know, he doesn't know that's the routine. I remember Arsene saying after they asked him: 'That would be lovely.' And they went and had a drink.
>
> He didn't have a long drink afterwards because he believed in the players rehydrating, taking on food and refuelling within an hour after the game. He wouldn't want to hang around; he wanted to get on the bus and go. His media commitments, because of so many foreign commitments, would take longer than anyone else. But the point is, he went for a drink.

Ferguson also wasted little time in picking a fight with Wenger. The hostilities began in April 1997, sparked by an innocuous remark from Wenger when he was asked at a press conference about Ferguson's accusation that the Premier League did not do enough to support English teams in the Champions League. Tomlinson recalls:

I remember the row he had with Fergie in the April. Fergie had made a big fuss about the fixture list surrounding European games. The Premier League put Arsenal–Man United on the Saturday before. Arsenal were only in the UEFA Cup, we had a press conference afterwards which was going nowhere, and winding down, when one of the journalists, Kevin Moseley, just said: 'What do you make of what Fergie said?' Arsene absolutely agreed 100 per cent with what Alex said, 100 per cent, but he said one thing which the boys picked up on and became the headline.

Fergie saw this and blew his top: 'This guy has been here five minutes and now he's telling us how we should run our football!'

I saw Fergie at the Football Writers' awards night that year and said: 'Alex, you know how it works.' He agreed with everything he'd said but said something like: 'You can't change it now.' The headline was along the lines of Wenger telling Ferguson to forget it, it can't be done now. I said to Fergie: 'You'd like him, you'd get on.'

That was just the start of it. During the 1997/98 season, Ferguson could see Wenger was a genuine threat and tried to play some mind games. Fergie claimed the pressure was all on Arsenal as Manchester United's lead slowly but surely ebbed away, Wenger's men going on a spectacular run to clinch the title.

Wenger looked completely unfazed, studious in his glasses and measured in his responses. Ferguson found he could not get under Wenger's skin as easily as he had done with Kevin Keegan, when United overhauled Newcastle in the 1995/96 season. Ferguson had suggested that teams tried harder to beat Manchester United than their title rivals Newcastle, with the intention of trying to egg on Leeds United before they faced Keegan's men.

Keegan famously cracked on Sky TV when the watching nation witnessed the Newcastle manager's emotional 'I'll love it' tirade aimed at Ferguson. It was game over for Newcastle and United won the title.

There is no doubt that Wenger and Ferguson were both guilty of whipping each other up with similar comments, but they've tended to do so away from the TV cameras. The key to their major falling-out was a remark made by Wenger in May 2002 after Arsenal had won the Premier League title and Ferguson had claimed that Manchester United had been the best team since Christmas that season. Ferguson dismissively said: '[Arsenal] are scrappers who rely on belligerence – we are the better team.'

Wenger responded with a cryptic but clever dig, which was the tipping point of their relationship. Wenger's stage was the training ground at London Colney, where the media had gathered ahead of the 2002 FA Cup final with Chelsea. On a bright sunny day, as the journalists waited for Wenger, few could have imagined that a quote would cause such a storm between the rival managers.

'Everyone thinks they have the prettiest wife at home,' Wenger said with a typically mischievous grin on his face. It was not, of course, intended to be in any way disparaging of Ferguson's wife, Cathy. It was meant to be a general remark, suggesting everyone is blinkered and believes theirs is the best. But Ferguson took it badly and personally and, from that moment, their rivalry went up a notch.

A few journalists had heard how upset Ferguson was and relayed the message to Arsenal and Wenger. Wenger called Ferguson to clarify the 'prettiest wife' remark but it would appear that it didn't work. In fact, the football writer Henry Winter recalls bumping into Arsenal's press officer at the time, Amanda Docherty, as they both queued up for their press passes at the Millennium

Stadium for the 2002 FA Cup final. 'Fergie's furious with Arsene!' came the warning. Winter was at the press conferences and recalls the fallout.

The context of that remark to those of us who were listening to him was that you are going to defend what you've got. Your wife is the prettiest, your kids are the best and brightest, your centre half is the best, the team's the best. All Wenger was doing, from my perspective, was saying what any manager would and was defending his own team.

When that got back to Fergie, I think Fergie took it literally and took it to be critical of Lady Cathy. That just gave an extra needle. I think he was asked about it and went back to it and said it was being disrespectful to Lady Cathy. But if you look at Wenger's interviews down the years, he'd actually used it before.

After Vieira had a brilliant season, there was a television documentary. Guy Mowbray asked Wenger about Vieira and how good he was. Wenger used the same analogy, said he thought he was the best but then everyone thinks they've got the prettiest wife. Wenger was not using it as being disrespectful to Ferguson's family, he was just defending his own.

I think Fergie became annoyed when Arsenal became a threat. When he saw some of the players they had, like Vieira, Henry, and they saw how Vieira stood up to Roy Keane, that was the point.

Fergie was sniping at Wenger from the start, even saying: 'He should keep his opinions to Japanese football.' He was niggling from early on because he realised that this man was a threat. The thing about Wenger was that in that first five- or six-year spell, his buying was really good. Anelka came – Anelka absolutely slaughtered Jaap Stam in the Charity Shield. Henry came good, Vieira came good. All of the sniping was because Ferguson realised that Wenger was a big threat.

In Wenger's early years, Arsenal and United were going toe-to-toe for trophies each season. The Battle of Old Trafford occurred in September 2003 after an ugly and bitter clash spilled over when Ruud van Nistelrooy smashed a disputed last-gasp penalty against the crossbar. His miss meant that Arsenal snatched a goal-less draw. The most memorable image of that day is surely Martin Keown screaming in van Nistelrooy's face; he openly called the Dutchman a cheat at the time and has done so again subsequently.

It also prompted a great line from the *Guardian*'s legendary chief football writer David Lacey: 'Martin Keown will have to answer for his gargoyle expression as well as for bringing down an arm on Ruud van Nistelrooy.'

That day – and the amazing let-off from the penalty spot – perhaps laid the foundations for Arsenal's Invincibles season. Wenger apologised after that incident but had the last laugh when Arsenal went unbeaten for the rest of the campaign. Surely that day at Old Trafford was the closest they came to losing all season.

Not surprisingly, the subsequent headlines made difficult and embarrassing reading. The *Daily Telegraph*'s was 'Humiliated Arsenal in the Dock'. Henry Winter captured the mood in the press: 'The shameful serial offending of Arsenal under Arsene Wenger will today bring this proudest of clubs the humiliating charge of "failing to control their players" following this skirmish at Old Trafford. Arsenal may have worn yellow yesterday but they were tainted with red.'

The FA hit Arsenal with a record £175,000 fine for failing to control its players and Lauren, Keown, Ray Parlour and Patrick Vieira were individually fined and received suspensions as well.

Arsenal – and Wenger – were rightly hammered that week in the aftermath of the match.

It was still at a time when Wenger, despite the very public outcry in the press, seemed to enjoy jousting with journalists. He would often come into press conferences wearing a mischievous smile, almost as if he'd known his players had been naughty. The first press conference after the Battle of Old Trafford was at London Colney. As Wenger came up the stairs from the dressing rooms towards the canteen on the first floor, someone asked if he was worried because he might say the wrong thing. 'Don't worry,' he said with a big grin. 'I am looking forward to it.'

But United gained revenge in October 2004 when they won 2-0, after Wayne Rooney won a penalty but was accused of diving under Sol Campbell's challenge – Wenger has never forgiven referee Mike Riley for that decision. Arsenal's record-breaking and remarkable 49-game unbeaten run was ended by their fiercest rivals, the managers nearly came to blows and it all descended into a food fight.

Van Nistelrooy was, again, a central figure as he came into the United dressing room complaining about something Wenger had said to him after the game. Ferguson lost his temper, rushed into the Arsenal dressing room and told Wenger to concentrate on his own affairs. Ferguson then claimed the row escalated and the tunnel descended into a 'rabble'.

Ferguson ended up being covered in pizza and soup as Arsenal's players completely lost their tempers. As with the game in 2003, the unsavoury episode acquired an instantly recognisable nickname: the Battle of the Buffet. And the subsequent enquiry into who threw the food became known as 'pizzagate'. It is certainly the most memorable of the many public spats between Wenger and Ferguson.

Henry Winter recalled: 'I thought Arsenal were a little bit tacky after the Battle of the Buffet. Even if you lose a game like that, you don't throw pizza at people. Ferguson, in his book, made a comment that would have hurt Wenger to the core. He said he smiled within as they were throwing pizza because he knew he'd won, he had control, he was in control. That, for the previous four or five years, Fergie had probably felt control was slipping away from him and he wanted it back. So all that stuff in the tunnel actually made Fergie feel like saying: "I've got him."'

The Battle of Old Trafford and, in particular, the Battle of the Buffet, simmered under the surface for months, if not years, afterwards. And in January 2005, it boiled over again when Ferguson did an interview with Glenn Moore of the *Independent*.

Sometimes words look harsher on the page than when they are spoken, but Ferguson had no hesitation about being so outspoken about Wenger. It was acrimonious and deeply personal; no niceties or excuses were offered. Ferguson talked about Wenger in the most disparaging way – and he wanted Moore to include them in the interview.

In the article, Ferguson called Wenger a 'disgrace' and says Arsenal are 'the worst losers of all time'. He went on: 'In the tunnel Wenger was criticising my players, calling them cheats, so I told him to leave them alone and behave himself. He ran at me with hands raised saying, "What do you want to do about it?" To not apologise for the behaviour of the players to another manager is unthinkable. It's a disgrace, but I don't expect Wenger to ever apologise, he's that type of person.'

At first, Wenger refused to react. But after a defeat at Bolton, Wenger could not resist responding. 'I have no diplomatic relations with him. What I don't understand is that he does what he wants and you [the press] are all at his feet. The managers have a responsibility to protect the game before the game. But in England you are only punished for what you say after the game. I don't respond to anything. In England you have a good phrase. It is "bringing the game into disrepute". But that is not only after a game, it is as well before a game.'

The *Guardian*'s chief football writer Daniel Taylor was one of the journalists at Bolton that day and, despite witnessing Wenger lose his cool on several other occasions, he says that was by far the worst he has seen him.

> He did the main press conference; we went into the next room to do a 'Mondays' where the daily newspapers talk to him. It was in the north-west; it was largely people he didn't know and he seemed to think we were Fergie's henchmen or something.
>
> I remember going to the press conference before the Bayern Munich game where he was angry with the *Sun* – they'd written about his contract after they'd gone out of the FA Cup. People said he was angry then. But he was far worse at Bolton – he was literally grey with anger.
>
> It was the first time I realised how tall he was. I was thinking: 'Wow, this guy has got a proper intimidating presence.' He was pointing his finger and I've referred to it as an ET finger. He said diplomatic relations were off and he said: 'I will never talk about that man again.' He wasn't in the slightest bit composed; he was utterly rattled so if Fergie's intention was to get under his skin then he did that ...
>
> It did also come at a time when Arsenal always seemed to do badly in the north-west and they had lost at Bolton. So we weren't really needing to press any of his buttons. He made this comment about us being at Fergie's feet. That made us laugh afterwards because that's the last thing that was true. But it was one of the all-time managerial temper tantrums. But, with many

of these rows, it was off camera and if it had been filmed it would be shown every time that people talk about Wenger and Fergie.

The relationship between Wenger and Ferguson remained frosty until 2008 or 2009. In his autobiography in 2013, Ferguson claimed that Wenger was more angry than he was during the 'pizzagate' confrontation. 'His fists were clenched. I was in control,' wrote Ferguson.

If that is hard to imagine, just remember that Wenger nearly came to blows with Martin Jol when the Dutchman was in charge of Tottenham and the pair locked horns in a particularly fiery north London derby in April 2006. Wenger was incensed when Robbie Keane scored after Tottenham refused to put the ball out of play following an injury. Wenger, immaculately dressed in white shirt and tie, squared up to tracksuited Jol, swore, accused him of bad sportsmanship and lying. When quizzed whether he thought they might come to blows, Jol smiled: 'He obviously hadn't seen the size of my fists.' For such a studious man, Wenger has a street fighter's temper.

Wenger and Ferguson shook hands after games, observed the niceties for the cameras, but relations only really started to thaw in 2008. In fact, the rapprochement was such a public event that when it eventually happened it almost seemed like world news. The League Managers' Association held a dinner in September 2008 at which Ferguson and Wenger were the two guests of honour. Broadcaster Richard Keys was the compere.

Keys was seated to the left of them on the stage as they conducted a question-and-answer session for the assembled guests. Ferguson laughed at Wenger's rather stunted jokes. 'The manager is the most important man at the club – if not, why do you sack the manager when it doesn't go well?'

Keys said: 'Could we now say that you get on and there is a respect there?'

Ferguson, smiling and looking relaxed after a glass or two of red wine, said: 'Of course – until the next game!'

Henry Winter added: 'If you talk to any Arsenal fan they will tell you that the time they started worrying about Wenger was when Ferguson started being nice to him. I remember them being all lovey-dovey on stage when the LMA brought them together and it quickly became obvious that Ferguson only has a snipe when he is worried about opponents.'

Wenger, who enjoys fine red wine, never entirely bought into the very British tradition of sharing a post-match drink in the host manager's office. And even Wenger's assistant Pat Rice, loyal to a fault, stopped going for a drink in Ferguson's office during the cold war years from 2004 to 2008. But in 2009 Wenger broke the ice by inviting Ferguson into his office to congratulate Manchester United on winning their Champions League semi-final.

Ferguson clearly no longer felt the need to try to wind up Wenger and use mind games because United were now far superior on the pitch. In fact, friendship broke out in 2011 when United thrashed Arsenal 8-2 at Old Trafford and Ferguson felt sorry for Wenger. How it must have hurt Wenger to be defended and yet patronised at the same time by his one-time rival.

Ferguson said: 'I think it is unfair to criticise him. The job he's done for Arsenal and the philosophy he has – he has given Arsenal some very entertaining players. He's also sold well and looked after the Arsenal coffers. People forget these things. It's a cynical world now and when you lose a few games the judges come out.'

Wenger, reflecting upon the change in their relationship, recalled: 'It got milder and more respectful that's for sure. Maybe because we were less in a fight with them recently, so the tension was a bit smaller, and we are a long time in the job as well, so a bit more respect maybe. He is different away from football, because he loves a good Bordeaux. In a competition you never really have exchanges with people, you say, "Hello, how are you?" and after the game, "We played well", "You played well", advice and "See you next time". The exchanges are very, very small.'

Wenger also admitted he may one day follow Ferguson's example and write a warts-and-all autobiography – but only after he's retired. And that day, he insists, is not set in stone.

You can never rule anything out. I believe a life is made of how you feel about the situation. You listen to your gut feeling. It looks like Ferguson had all that prepared. He had prepared his book while he was managing. I suspect he had written some of it at home at night, remembering things and thinking: 'That goes into my book ...'

I say no [I won't write a book] at the moment. Maybe one day I will be inspired to do that, but at the moment I do not. I do not say never, but at the moment I do not have that need at all. The past is history and history has to be written. In France, we say it is not only important to make history, but also to write the history. It is good.

It is a legacy of his career. I think that is important, especially in England where he was a manager at Manchester United for 27 years. It is not just anonymous. It is huge what he has achieved, but it is difficult for me to answer anything on the book because I have not read it.

We are in a job that is a good teacher of humility, I told you that already. Because we have to accept that everybody can judge our job at any minute, at any moment, without completely knowing all the ingredients of our job. But it's part of it, with the positive and the negative, sometimes they give us credit we don't deserve as well. But we have to take both sides.

I just think we have gone through some years that were a bit more difficult. But honestly, in our job, it is quite simple just to think about tomorrow or the next game, and that's it. And after that, people judge.

Wenger's barbs aimed at Ferguson down the years show that he is as much poet as football manager. Ferguson promised to apologise to Wenger after he claimed, in January 1999, that Arsenal's style of play was 'belligerent' and Arsenal's players liked a 'scrap'. Ferguson said: 'The number of fights involving Arsenal is more than Wimbledon had in their heyday.'

However, Ferguson was only apologising because the comments came out when, as he claimed, they were 'off the record', and not for what he actually said. Ferguson promised to drop Wenger a line. At the next press conference, we asked Wenger whether he had received it. 'No. Perhaps he sent it by horse,' smiled Wenger.

The feud went through phases of being good-natured, angry, bitter and jovial. Wenger positively enjoyed it for the most part. 'Ferguson should calm down. Maybe it would have been better if he had put us against a wall and shot us,' was another Wenger riposte – humour mixed with sarcasm in equal measure to make a serious point. Their verbal jousting was always entertaining, but by the end mutual respect had won out, as Wenger made it very clear when Ferguson retired that football and the Premier League would be poorer without him. 'The Premier League will continue, of course, but a huge personality has retired.'

Wenger's other long-standing rivalry has been with Jose Mourinho, and as with Ferguson he has had his ups and downs with the Portuguese manager. However, their fallout was so serious after Mourinho's return to Chelsea that it is hard to imagine them sharing a convivial relationship ever again.

Interestingly, Mourinho and Wenger were on better terms when the Portuguese left Chelsea after his first spell in charge. And, on his return to Stamford Bridge, Mourinho spoke in glowing terms about his counterpart. 'He's a nice guy. I had a chance to meet him much, much better when I left England and I started meeting him in UEFA [coaching meetings], at the Euros, the World Cup. I think I met him a few times; we had dinner and so on. And when you are not in the same league and when you are not playing against each other, it is easier to get to know people; it is easier to go deeper. It is easy to speak about football.

'I'm back in the Premier League, yes, but he's still a nice guy. I respect him a lot and I will show it always. In football, things like this happen. Sometimes, even if you are friends and respect each other, sometimes you say something the other doesn't like and you react, but at the end of the day I respect him a lot and I have the feeling that he is the same in relation to me. I wouldn't bet for one single problem between us.'

How misguided that final comment from Mourinho looks now. But it does clearly show that it is the intensity of football that sees rational, charming and intelligent men completely lose the plot.

Their battle began in October 2005 when Mourinho made his infamous 'voyeur' comment, after claiming that Wenger was obsessed with Chelsea. The suggestion that Wenger was some sort of Peeping Tom or pervert was incredibly hurtful, particularly in view of the false rumours that had forced Wenger to defend himself on the steps at Highbury when he first arrived at Arsenal.

Wenger had started the spat by merely responding that Mourinho's men had lost a 'little belief' when asked a question about Chelsea drawing at Everton and then being knocked out of the League Cup by Charlton. Mourinho, struggling to hide his delight in answering back, delivered a sensational response when asked about Wenger's remarks by a small group of newspaper reporters. It was to become one of the most memorable jibes of all and Wenger took it particularly badly.

The *Daily Star*'s David Woods and the London *Evening Standard*'s Leo Spall were the two journalists who were given the famous quote. Woods recalls:

> To be honest, Wenger's remarks hadn't actually made much of a big story so Mourinho had clearly been looking out for it. It seemed pre-planned because he had obviously had enough of Wenger having what he saw were constant digs at him and Chelsea and this small insult was the final straw. None of the Sundays had asked about it and we went into the tunnel. I mentioned Arsene Wenger in one question and it all came out.
>
> I remember, after Mourinho had spoken and had spoken at length, asking him another question. Mourinho replied: 'I think you have got enough.' It seemed as if it was pre-scripted, he was very intense and, more than anything else, he knew it would hurt Wenger.

Mourinho's words hit the target all right. 'I think he is one of these people who is a voyeur,' said Mourinho in that interview. 'He likes to watch other people. There are some guys who, when they are at home, have a big telescope to see what happens in other families. He speaks, speaks, speaks about Chelsea. It bothers me because the guy is speaking all the time. We never speak about them. He's worried about us; he's always talking about us. It's Chelsea, Chelsea, Chelsea, Chelsea. I don't know if he wants my job, I don't know. He loves Chelsea.'

It came at the very height of Wenger's displeasure at the way Chelsea were splashing the cash since the arrival of Roman Abramovich, whose spending in the transfer market had suddenly seen Arsenal and Manchester United overhauled at the top of the English game.

At the press conference following Mourinho's comments, Wenger was so angry he could barely get the words out to respond. After doing his TV press conference, when he'd been wound up by the incessant questions from the TV reporters, he came to talk to us newspaper guys and he was furious even before he sat down. On days like these, you can see the look of disdain on his face. He hates these sorts of press conferences. The 'voyeur' comment had really annoyed him. It got under his skin so much that Wenger threatened legal action, which he never pursued. He seemed to seize on that particular word and was deeply offended.

It was not helped when one reporter, Matt Scott, insisted on asking him whether he really owned a telescope. When he wouldn't answer at first, Scott repeated the question. Wenger looked utterly bewildered. 'No, no, Arsene, do you really own a telescope?' was the question that really tipped Wenger over the edge. He looked incredulous and turned his head away in disgust. It is incredibly rare to see Wenger quite so riled. He will stomach many of our strange questions but, when he's in a bad mood, he looks contemptuous when he's asked anything he doesn't like.

Wenger did, however, make it clear exactly what he thought of Mourinho's remarks: 'He's out of order, disconnected with reality and disrespectful. When you give success to stupid people, it makes them more stupid sometimes and not more intelligent.'

Mourinho tried to defuse the row by sending Wenger a Christmas card in 2005. He sent a card to the other 18 managers in the Premier League as well, but wrote a personal message to

Wenger to apologise for the voyeur comment. But, in true school-boy fashion, the subsequent events only made matters worse.

A member of Arsenal's staff checked to see if the card was genuine; Chelsea told Mourinho of the suspicion and the Portuguese refused to shake Wenger's hand when the clubs met on Sunday 18 December. As he saw it, his attempted apology had been thrown back in his face. Arsenal had simply wanted to make sure the card really had come from Mourinho. It does show just how childish things had become. For the record, Chelsea won the game 2-0 and that, more than petty squabbles and mind games, probably upset Wenger more than anything else. The fact is that Chelsea, under Mourinho, had overtaken Wenger's Arsenal.

Their relationship never recovered after that, so no tears were shed by Arsenal when Mourinho left Chelsea in 2007. At first, when he returned in 2013, it was all very cordial. Wenger even claimed that he always knew that Mourinho would be back one day. 'It's like Mourinho opened the door, went out for a drink and came back. It takes you a few months when you first join a club, six to eight months, before you become accepted, before you know how everything works inside the club, all the links to know the players well, how they respond under stress situations. On whom you can rely. But he knows Chelsea straightaway.

'With all competitors there are ups and downs, because we put our whole heart into every single game. Sometimes we go overboard and that is part of the job. With the distance after, it always settles. It is impossible to be friends. You cannot be friends. You can be friends at the start of competition. The real sport on that front is rugby. They don't kiss each other before the game when they walk in the tunnel. They go out and are ready for war. They become friends after the game.'

Their antagonism had clearly softened. In fact, in Mourinho's first season back, Arsenal lost to Chelsea in the Capital One Cup in October, drew at the Emirates in December (extending Mourinho's unbeaten record against Wenger to ten meetings) and both managers avoided any real flare-ups. Ironically, however, on Valentine's Day 2014, they fell out of love again.

Arsenal had suffered a bad week, losing 5-1 at Liverpool the previous weekend and then being held at home to Manchester United. Wenger's mood was not helped by these two poor results and Arsenal's form hadn't been good. It had also been a week of silliness on the mind games front. Mourinho had kicked it off by claiming that Chelsea were a 'little horse', not ready to win the title. Liverpool boss Brendan Rodgers carried it on by saying his team were like a 'Chihuahua that runs in between the horses' legs'.

Basically, both managers were trying to play down their own chances to ease the pressure on their players. But then Mourinho – in an interview with the *Daily Mail* – attempted to turn up the heat on Arsenal by saying they were no longer a work in progress, their young players had 'matured' and they had added 'fantastic players like Mesut Ozil, Santi Cazorla and Per Mertesacker'. It did seem that all the managers – barring Wenger, whose team had dominated the top of the table – were desperately trying to suggest someone else was favourite. It's much easier to be the underdog.

In his main TV press conference, Wenger was asked why some managers seemed to be afraid of saying they were title favourites. 'Why are other managers saying they are not contenders? It's fear to fail. If you declare yourself not in the race you cannot lose it, simple as that. I think that our job is to be ambitious and to try to win, and if we do not win, to take full responsibility for that. It's as simple as that and that's how I see it. I say yes we are in it, yes we will have a go for it. We will absolutely give everything to go for it and if we don't do it I will take responsibility for it.'

Wenger wasn't talking specifically about Chelsea or Mourinho.

But that comment 'fear to fail' quickly became toxic. In no time it was all over Twitter, it was written up on websites by reporters who were not even there, and suddenly it had turned into Wenger accusing Mourinho of being afraid to fail.

At Chelsea's training ground at Cobham, Mourinho had barely sat down in the press conference room before Wenger's words were put to him as if he had aimed the comments directly at Chelsea. Mourinho snapped back with venom:

Am I afraid of failure? He is a specialist in failure. I'm not. So if one supposes he's right and I'm afraid of failure, it's because I don't fail many times. So maybe he's right. I'm not used to failing. But the reality is he's a specialist because, eight years without a piece of silverware, that's failure. If I did that in Chelsea I'd leave and not come back to London. I don't fear anything in football.

Do I think I have rattled Wenger? No. If Mr Abramovich gives me eight years to prepare a team, which I don't want – I just want my four years of contract and, after that, to deserve or not deserve the next contract. But in eight years you have to build so much, so much, so much.

I am sorry for that voyeur comment. But he loves to look at this football club. I thought between 2007 and 2013 would be enough time for him to forget this. But it looks like he always likes to look at us. Why is he so obsessed with Chelsea? Ask him.

Why has he not won a trophy in eight seasons? Ask him. Would I get eight years to win a trophy? No. What I have said will go around the world but it also goes around the world what he said before that. Yes, it has annoyed me. Am I afraid of failure? What is that? I believe at the end of the day I'll be the impolite guy in this, the one who's aggressive in his words.

But of course not: he is saying we're not title candidates

because we're afraid of failure. Failure of what? Not winning a title this year? Or in two years? I have a lot of respect for him but failure is not winning a title in seven or eight years. That's failure.

Mourinho's angry response, his attempt to rile Wenger and also take a dig at Arsenal's failure to win a trophy since 2005, had spectacular consequences. War was declared.

After Arsenal beat Liverpool in the FA Cup on the Sunday, Wenger said Mourinho's comments were 'embarrassing'. My own paper, the *Daily Mirror*, used the headline: 'Wenger: Chelsea are Embarrassing.' Three days later, after they lost at home to Bayern Munich, the back-page headline screamed: 'Specialists in Failure'.

I've often heard it said that Wenger doesn't read the press. For someone who doesn't look at the newspapers, he always seems to have a very good idea of what's in them – maybe because some of his coaching staff would often leave them around the training ground to make sure he saw the headlines (football people take a perverse pleasure in doing such things). He'll regularly pull up individuals on pieces. He took exception to a piece in the *Daily Mail* on the lack of home-grown players being produced and took the reporter to task. 'We give them good careers,' Wenger argued, even if they don't make it at Arsenal.

But Wenger went through those few weeks adopting more and more of a siege mentality, believing the media favoured Chelsea, Mourinho, Liverpool and even Manchester City. He assumed a defensive attitude. The good-natured banter slipped away, and my attempts at small talk and humour at the start of press conferences fell on deaf ears. He wasn't in the mood, despite Arsenal's decent run of results that set them up for a trip to Chelsea and, of course, a meeting with Jose Mourinho, which just happened to be Wenger's 1,000th game.

Wenger's pre-match optimism, when he'd afforded us more time than usual and looked back on some memories from those 1,000 games, evaporated quickly. Chelsea ravaged Arsenal, destroying them. Wenger looked a broken man. Arsenal lost 6-0, and Kieran Gibbs was sent off in a case of mistaken identity – it should have been Alex Oxlade-Chamberlain, as he'd handled the ball.

Arsenal's bench looked shellshocked. Chelsea's assistant manager Rui Faria has enraged Arsenal's coaching staff down the years – along with most of the Premier League – with his histrionics and wild celebrations. To further spice up the animosity between the managers, there was a feeling that Mourinho and his men took particular delight in seeing Wenger humiliated on his 1,000th game in charge.

Predictably, more controversy followed. Mourinho did not shake Wenger's hand, claiming afterwards that he often leaves his dugout before the final whistle and waits for his opposite number in the tunnel. He claimed that he 'congratulated' Wenger on his milestone, something that is unlikely to have gone down well with Wenger.

Wenger, pacing up and down the tunnel in frustration and anger at his players' capitulation on this landmark occasion, did not attend the post-match press conference. He claimed that he couldn't get in the room before the team bus departed as Mourinho was taking so long. But he did speak to one or two broadcasters in the tunnel after the game, insisting people should 'blame me' for the defeat.

Wenger then decided not to do a pre-match press conference for the game with Swansea three days later. He did not want to share his embarrassment with anyone. Arsenal drew 2-2 with Swansea, throwing away all three points with a late own goal by Mathieu Flamini. Those close to Wenger believe he was actually in a worse mood after the Swansea game than at Chelsea. Wenger took his anger out on the coaching staff, shouting in frustration at the goalkeeping coach Gerry Peyton.

Towards the end of the season, with the title still undecided, it was noticeable that Wenger missed off one candidate when asked who would be his Manager of the Year. 'You have plenty of candidates. You have two kinds of candidates: those who win the league and those who do not go down. Among those who do not go down, you have Pulis, Bruce, Poyet now, who has done a magnificent job because he got to a cup final as well. Then after that, you have Pellegrini who will win the league or Brendan Rodgers, who has done remarkably well because both played as well a very attractive game.'

It was, by then, a three-horse race for the title between Manuel Pellegrini's Manchester City, Rodgers' Liverpool and Mourinho's Chelsea. But, as far as Wenger was concerned, there were only two teams in it. It stored up animosity for when Wenger next played Mourinho, in October 2014 – and the sideshow was ex-Arsenal captain Cesc Fabregas facing his former club for the first time since joining Chelsea. The game brought the latest in a long line of Mourinho–Wenger spats, perhaps even the most memorable.

On a sunny Sunday afternoon at Stamford Bridge, with the dugouts and technical areas just in front of the press box, the pair had a remarkable confrontation in which Wenger pushed Mourinho. Wenger claimed that he left his technical area and strayed into Mourinho's because he was trying to get to Alexis Sanchez to see if he was badly hurt after a crude foul by Gary Cahill. Mourinho, in contrast, said he was angry because he felt Wenger was trying to get Cahill sent off. Referee Martin Atkinson gave Cahill a yellow card while his fourth official, Jon Moss, split up the warring managers. That was the main story dominating the back pages the following day, *The Times* calling Chelsea's win 'A Pushover' and the *Sun* branding it a 'Disgrace'.

Wenger came into the press conference pleading innocence and suggested it was not much of a push. The most striking thing about it was that it highlighted how tall Wenger is as he towered over Mourinho. Sadly for Wenger, in footballing terms Arsenal barely laid a glove on Chelsea. The 2-0 defeat was better than the earlier 6-0 thrashing, but it was the first time that Arsenal had not managed a shot on target in a game since October 2003 – an incredible stat which highlights perhaps that, while the game was a closer affair, Arsenal were never going to win it.

Maybe that was the explanation behind Wenger's performance in the press conference. When asked whether he regretted the push, he insisted it hardly merited the description, almost as if he was saying, 'Call that a push? I'll show you a push!'

'You would see if I really try to push [you]. Come on,' said Wenger. 'Honestly, I don't listen to what he says. I trust you to teach me all the moral lessons in the next two weeks, and I can accept that. I'm long enough in the game to see things the right way.'

Mourinho, who later claimed he would have got a 'stadium ban' had he pushed Wenger rather than vice versa, said: 'It becomes heated because it's a big game, big clubs, big rivals, an important match for both teams. I think these conditions make a game of emotions. After that, there are two technical areas. One for me, one for him. He was coming into my technical area and not for the right reasons, to give some technical instructions. He was coming to push the referee for a red card, and I didn't like that.'

But Wenger, strangely, was quite relaxed afterwards. In fact, he was smiling and managed to exchange a few words of greeting when I saw him on the pitch after the press conference. What would have pleased him less was to see that Mesut Ozil, Arsenal's

£42 million midfielder whose performance had been savaged by TV critics Graeme Souness and Gary Neville, hugged Mourinho on the pitch after the Arsenal players had showered, changed and were heading towards the team bus.

Mourinho, who had coached Ozil at Real Madrid and proclaimed him the best number 10 in the world, called out 'Messie!' before giving him a big hug. They chatted intently in the middle of the pitch, and at one point Mourinho even squeezed Ozil's biceps as if he was telling him to build up some muscle.

A week later, Wenger – having initially insisted he had nothing to apologise for – said sorry to Mourinho, even though he insisted the story had been overblown by the English press. 'They gave too much importance to this story. In hindsight I think I should not have reacted at all; it's not a way to behave on a football field. I always regret any signs of violence and I apologise, but that's part of games where everything is manic – and then we have quite a substantial past. Did Mourinho provoke me? That is how I felt. I did not enter Chelsea's technical area.'

It will be interesting to see how this rivalry continues to develop, especially if Arsenal can close the gap in the future. And, of course, it is not just with Ferguson and Mourinho that Wenger has had his differences. There was another incident, which also involved a shove, that happened in November 2006.

On this occasion, he pushed the West Ham manager Alan Pardew as he celebrated a late winner. Wenger was fined £10,000 for 'aggressive behaviour', while Pardew apologised. Since then, there has been a simmering undercurrent between the two managers, Pardew once criticising Wenger for having too many foreign players. Wenger was unable to resist biting back when Arsenal had bought British. But the underlying reason for Wenger's disgruntlement was that he had invited Pardew to the Arsenal training ground several times to observe training to help him complete his coaching education. Wenger felt that deserved more respect than he received from Pardew.

There is no doubt about it: Wenger has an angry side when it comes to certain managers. The rivalry with Ferguson was born out of the fierce competition between their respective clubs. The dislike of Mourinho springs from Wenger's years of frustration. Wenger used to be the main man, the best manager out there, then along came Chelsea with their cheque book to allow Mourinho to buy success. It was an unfair advantage. Or at least that is how Wenger sees it. Then he gets caught up in the heat of the moment, which explains his other run-ins. He is intense, strained and focused on the touchline. It's part of his make-up.

But the flipside is spelt out by one of Wenger's closest friends in the business, Sven-Goran Eriksson, who was keen to give him a glowing reference when I rang him in China. They go back a long way and Eriksson, the former England coach, has a huge amount of respect for Wenger as a manager:

I think we first met in Italy, in Rome maybe, long before he took over at Arsenal, many, many years ago. I always knew he would be a success because he's a very clever man, very intelligent, and his knowledge about football is fantastic, of course. He lives for football ...

I wasn't surprised that he was successful [at Arsenal] because he is such a talented manager and the team that he put together was very good, they played wonderful football. For many years, they had the same back line, for a whole decade, I think.

He then implanted the style of play in Arsenal, a different way of playing; they move the ball like nobody else. For years, no one else played like Arsenal. They had fantastic football, fantastic results and took in French players like Pires, Henry,

Vieira. They were top, top-class players. He had Bergkamp, fantastic football players.

I've never known him get really angry. I've rarely seen him lose his temper. He is a very nice man. Many times we went out to dinner together when I was in London; we'd go out together and also with David Dein, quite often at David's house.

The good thing about Arsene is that he doesn't speak about football 24 hours a day. He can speak about other things, politics, music, whatever. He's very good company, always entertaining. He can speak about whatever subject, he knows about it! He is a very good conversationalist.

It's also a club with a healthy economy which, I guess, very, very few clubs have these days because of pressure and financial pressure. But Wenger is a very sensible, clever club manager.

Wenger and the club, the fans and the players have enjoyed great success for a generation. They have built a dynasty and something which will remain successful for many years. Some years recently have been very hard years, but that is something to admire in Arsene Wenger because his philosophy has kept the club very stable. They reached the Champions League every year. Every single year. It's a remarkable achievement. To always play in the Champions League is incredible. He has done it despite moving to a new stadium, and it's been difficult for him.

Of course, supporters want trophies. How do you judge success? Of course, you want success but so often clubs buy expensive players to do that and it still doesn't guarantee success. You must be happy to be a top team in one of the best leagues in the world, to be playing Champions League every year and to be playing great football. That's fantastic. They are also not in debt. It's an incredible achievement.

We used to talk a lot and we used to joke about what we would do after football. Arsene lives for football. More than once he told me he could never retire. We'd talk about players, who was fit, who was ready for England. Of course, people still talk about Theo Walcott going to the World Cup in 2006 [Walcott had yet to play for Arsenal since joining them as a 16-year-old a few months earlier]. It was a big decision. He always told me everything about his English players, fitness, how they were playing. That was important for me to know. How they train and so on. Of course, Theo Walcott was another example and when he said he was ready, I was willing to listen.

It's so difficult to rank the great managers, but he is among the very best. He's a top manager because of the success that he has brought, so much success, plays great football. Arsene is a legend, a living legend. If you speak about him then you immediately think of Arsenal, the attractive style of play that he produces. It can be very easy in our job to be frustrated or angry, but Arsene is not like that. He always has a very good personality and is a wonderful man.

Similarly, from a different school of managers, Phil Brown, who has endured battles, bust-ups and a few football matches with Wenger down the years, also speaks highly of him. Brown was Sam Allardyce's number two at Bolton, managed Hull (and got the sack after Arsenal won there in 2010) and tells a different story of Wenger, which is at odds with the common theory that he does not like to mix or share a post-match drink with other managers.

He didn't get me the sack at Hull City; it was the straw that broke the camel's back. In the manner in which they won – they scored a 93rd-minute winner and we'd been down to ten men after about 35 minutes. After the game, he shook my hand, came in for a drink afterwards and then I got the sack on the Monday. And then five days later he is writing about me in his home programme notes and the good job that I'd done at Hull City.

He didn't have any need to do that. It was just testament to his empathy towards a fellow coach or a fellow manager. His sympathy towards the job that I'd been doing and yet had lost my position. It's the sign of a great man, for me.

I've heard people say he's aloof, but maybe it's his style or even a tactic of his. He would utilise everything he possibly can to get an edge. That's testimony to him as a tactician or even a strategist. He reminds me of a general in a war, in the way that he plans. He tries to give his team the best possible opportunity to win games. Over the long term, he probably sees it as a battle, like a war, and he strategises things.

I don't think he did come in for a post-match drink that often. But each to their own. We're all different in our own ways. It's a very English tradition. If you go abroad, they don't do it. It's a cultural thing and some of the foreign coaches have found it hard to understand why we do it.

Brown also recalls some tough battles during his days as Allardyce's number two, when Arsenal had a furious rivalry with Bolton. Brown, whose Hull side also became embroiled in a tunnel row with Cesc Fabregas at Arsenal, believes Wenger did not enjoy the physical side of the English game at times but says he has adapted since.

Sam got under his skin a little bit. Again, you've got another guy who plans and strategises how he can work against the opposition. Sam used to set traps for Arsene and also for Arsene's team. Rather like Arsene, Sam would look for weaknesses in the teams, the staff or the club itself. Anything he could do to really make a difference.

There were some battles, big battles. You don't really look at Arsene's teams as battling teams, but they were battles in a different way. Arsene would have a beautiful way of winning a game of football and sometimes myself and Sam would have an uglier way of winning games of football.

That was the hardest part perhaps for Arsene to stomach about the English game. I think he's got over that by a long way. He's got more strings to his bow. He understands the English game a lot better and Arsenal are getting the benefit of that long-term.

What happened with Hull at Arsenal wasn't really a problem with Arsene Wenger; that was more to do with Cesc Fabregas. Obviously Cesc Fabregas was an extension of Arsene Wenger. He was his club captain. The incident was unsavoury by any stretch of the imagination. But I don't like bringing it up; it's in the past now and it's not synonymous with Arsenal Football Club, Arsene Wenger or even Cesc Fabregas.

Brown believes that Wenger's record and managerial ability rank him alongside some of the all-time greats:

He's got to be classed as one of the great foreign managers to have worked in this country, for sure. In terms of stature among the all-time great managers – I class the greats like Sir Alex Ferguson, Sir Bobby Robson – I think it's difficult to compare. He's definitely one of the great managers.

If you look at his first eight years, what they won, how they played football, it was incredible. Great managers, be they foreign managers, English, Scottish, whatever, can go through times when they win trophies and then through periods where they don't.

Look at Billy Shankly and Liverpool – he won so much and

was so successful early on and then went seven years without winning anything. But he, like Wenger, came back again. Wenger went eight seasons without a winning a trophy before the FA Cup. You are talking about one of the greats in Shankly and if you are putting Arsene Wenger in the same breath then he must be one of the greats as well.

These comments all highlight the respect that Wenger has managed to earn from his rivals and his peers, earned over one of the longest managerial careers ever seen in England. He might initially have been treated with some suspicion as a foreigner with very different ways, but he has become very much a part of the English scene – something that the press has also discovered about him over the years.

CHAPTER 11

PRESS RELATIONS

Arsene Wenger settled into his seat for the charter flight to Trieste in August 2011, looked into the seat pocket in front of him and picked up the inflight magazine. Within the pages of *BMI Voyager* was a fascinating but less than flattering interview with Arsenal's former captain Tony Adams. 'I love Arsene dearly,' Adams said in the piece. 'But coaching is not his strong point.'

The timing was not good. Arsenal were flying to Italy for their Champions League play-off second leg with Udinese, Wenger was under all sorts of pressure, Cesc Fabregas had been sold, Samir Nasri was about to be sold, and here was Adams seemingly attempting to explode a few myths about Wenger.

In the extensive interview with journalist Peter Watts, Adams insisted that Wenger's diet revolution was overrated, that he got lucky because he inherited good players and that he wasn't even a good motivator.

'We were reading books on diet in 1987, ten years before Arsene

walked into the club. Arsene came with his own ideas and strate-
gies, and brought in an osteopath and acupuncturist. But there's no
secrets. Diet won't change anything if you don't have great players
and I still ate fish and chips every week for the last six years under
Arsene Wenger. Every Friday on Putney Bridge I went and got
battered cod and a chip sandwich and sat there looking at the
river.'

Adams made disparaging remarks about Wenger's coaching
and, while he stressed he 'respected and loved' Wenger, Adams
said George Graham's 1991 squad was the best Arsenal team he
played in.

Adams had even asked Watts to tone down the interview and
originally a much harsher turn of phrase about Wenger's coaching
ability was used in the piece. For the journalists travelling on the
same charter flight, Adams's comments only added to the growing
storm surrounding Wenger and Arsenal. The club went to the
second leg at Udinese in danger of going out of the Champions
League; they were losing big players and had not done much business of their own in the transfer market; and serious questions
were being asked about Wenger as a manager, and if indeed he was
losing or had lost his magic touch. And here was one of his former
captains seemingly twisting the knife.

Needless to say, by the time we flew home on the same plane –
Arsenal beat Udinese and went through – the inflight magazine
had been removed from the seat pockets. That's typical of how the
club treat him; they try to shield him from criticism.

Despite Wenger's claims that he doesn't read the papers or care
what is being written, when he moved to England he started
having the *Daily Mail* delivered to his house every day after David
Dein recommended it as a newspaper he might enjoy reading. You
can always tell if something in the *Mail* has upset him because
he'll bring it up.

There's often some mischief at the training ground. They usually have every newspaper knocking about. If one of the coaches or staff wants to make a point, they'll leave a paper where Wenger is sure to see it. 'Look what they're writing now,' they'll say, in a bid to curry favour with Wenger while trying to denigrate the press. Wenger is not obsessed about what is written in the press – but it's wrong to believe him when he says he doesn't care. He does.

Wenger watches *Match of the Day* but is rather dismissive when it comes to the points made by the pundits. He is equally disparaging when it comes to radio phone-ins and football chat shows, and says he's never looked at Twitter.

The only thing I can say on social networks is anybody can insult anybody even if it's not true, and that is maybe a weak point of the modern social networks. You can tomorrow be insulted by anybody without any defence. I don't believe it's affected how managers behave, not at all. People are better informed, more informed today. We had that debate at the [League Managers' Association] meeting recently, where some people felt victimised by the social networks, but we cannot stop that.

We have to live with that and maybe reinforce our solidarity and be stronger inside the clubs. And maybe this is a time as a manager to have stronger beliefs than ever, because you are questioned more than ever, and that's maybe the new challenge we face. Everything we do is questioned, and sometimes people are right, we make mistakes.

I never look at social media. Never. You know there is a thing, on the radio, a debate where people call in. I didn't even know it exists. I am here for seventeen years.

I took a great lesson in Japan, because in Japan at the start, I could not understand, or read, anything. So even a journalist who said I was absolutely useless, I welcomed him the next day in the press conference.

So, what does he listen to? 'Classical music or pop music – 1970s or 80s,' replied Wenger.

Wenger knows who the 'regulars' are in the press pack. There are no cliques at Arsenal yet he's friendlier to some reporters than others. That would suggest to me that he knows who is more sympathetic both in questioning and in writing or broadcasting.

His press conferences can be incredibly entertaining; he is engaging, humorous and enjoys some banter. But, over the years, his relationship with the press has changed, and he has changed too.

Back in the successful era when Arsenal were winning trophies every year, Wenger lapped up the praise and did far more media work. His pre-match press conferences would start with him being interviewed by TV; he'd then do a separate set of radio interviews, followed by another separate interview for the daily newspapers. When he first arrived, he'd do all of this at the training ground, then at Sopwell House in St Albans when the old training ground was burnt down. Eventually, when the new training ground was built, a separate 'media building' was constructed where all the interviews were conducted, and the main training ground building was kept sacrosanct.

After a match, Wenger will do various TV and radio interviews, then go into the lavish main press conference room at the Emirates and then, if it's a Saturday, he will go into a small room that resembles a padded cell to do a 'Mondays' for the daily newspapers. But it's pre-match where Wenger has, over time, cut back on what he does with the media, giving less time and it's much more rushed. It has coincided with Arsenal being less successful and getting less praise.

However, Wenger is normally cooperative and patient. Occasionally, though, his patience will wear thin. 'For fuck's sake, Mark,' he snapped at Arsenal's director of communications Mark Gonnella in November 2014. 'This is too long.' He was complaining that the 17 minutes given to every TV and radio station and website was excessive. Then Wenger had to do a separate 'newspaper section' to give us a different angle. We got seven minutes.

These days we huddle round a table at the front of the room. Back in the day, we would go into a separate room, we'd get more time, even have a laugh and occasionally, just occasionally, he'd go off the record and give us some help and information.

I remember when Arsenal were desperate for a new centre forward in December 2009 and plenty of names were being bandied around ahead of the January window. I cheekily wrote down a list of strikers and put the piece of paper on the table for Wenger to see when he sat down. One of the names was Eden Hazard. Wenger opened the door, stepped inside, sat down and immediately looked at the piece of paper.

'I was just trying to give you a shopping list, Arsene,' I smiled.

'Ah, interesting,' Wenger said, pointing at Hazard's name. Another name caught his eye and I said: 'Do you like him?'

'He's a good player,' said Wenger. 'I like him. But we already have too many players who have injuries and can't play two games a week.'

Wenger was often good fun in those press briefings, particularly back in the days of the separate room where we'd sit and talk. When someone told him that Jamie Jackson of the *Guardian* had got married, he asked him where he'd been on honeymoon. Jackson told him he'd gone to Thailand. 'What a waste,' smiled Wenger with a twinkle in his eye.

Wenger will often make a joke of the fact that many of us have his phone number. 'I'm sure you will ring me,' he will smile. These days he's better at responding to texts than taking calls. But I will always remember ringing him after the Premier League tribunal into the Ashley Cole 'tapping up' case at the end of the 2004/05 season. Wenger answered the phone and was clearly at a funfair (you could hear the noise in the background), and it sounded as if he had his daughter Lea with him.

After insisting he didn't want to talk about the case, I apologised for interrupting his family holiday and said I'd let him get back to them. Wenger, however, was in no rush, was polite, made small talk and asked how I was, was I going on holiday? If he's in a good mood, he's great company and will indulge the press.

We'll often see him at tournaments – World Cups or European Championships – and have a chat. After Brazil in the summer of 2014, on the Monday following the previous day's final, Wenger spotted some familiar faces from the English press at the airport and made a beeline to come over.

Wenger did look rather embarrassed once when a few journalists saw him bounding out of a wine bar with Gerard Houllier during a tournament. He likes a drink and a night out – just not in front of us. He is incredibly private like that.

Of course, there will be fallouts. My paper, the *Daily Mirror*, got banned from the training ground for a week after a succession of headlines upset him – although I always wonder whether it's him or the press officers who take offence. My colleagues, as a joke, put an A4 piece of paper on one of the chairs at the table. It read: 'Crossie's seat' and they made a point of keeping it empty. Wenger laughed along. Before he cut back on this aspect of his job, it was all very jovial, and he was always generous with his time. He provided soundbites and most of us really wouldn't care that he was infamous for being late; sometimes he'd be as much as two hours later than scheduled if training on a Friday afternoon overran.

When he turned 60 in October 2009, I organised a collection to buy him a nice bottle of red wine. I found out what he liked and cobbled together more than a hundred pounds. Then, one Friday after his press conference, we waited outside and made a small presentation. He seemed genuinely touched and smiled. Mind you, the following day, the press officer, Amanda Docherty, did ask how much we'd paid for the bottle. 'Was it OK?' I asked. 'I'm not sure,' she replied, with a look that suggested even a £100 bottle might not satisfy his palate.

Wenger moved his press conferences to before training as well as scaling them down over the years. These days he will do as little as he can get away with. The arrangement of having the separate room for the daily newspapers went in February 2011, when Wenger was unhappy about headlines that appeared following a tunnel bust-up after Everton boss David Moyes alleged Cesc Fabregas made comments to referee Lee Mason that he felt warranted a red card.

I made representations and Wenger promised he'd sit down and talk about it at the end of the season. But he refused to relent. Now, a few of us gather round at the top table in the press conference room, but it's rather hurried and is less entertaining. By contrast, Jose Mourinho regularly does 20 minutes with the national newspapers after his pre-match broadcast press conference, and other managers do more.

For years, Wenger did punditry work with French TV station TF1 and used to be controversial, making strong remarks as a co-commentator. After Thierry Henry's infamous handball during the World Cup play-off with the Republic of Ireland in November 2009, which helped France reach the finals, Wenger was honest and critical of his former protege as he urged him to show remorse and apologise. 'One should [own up], but one doesn't, we know, with the pressure and what's at stake,' said Wenger on air. 'The goal we scored was hard to swallow if you were in the opposite camp. We would have preferred to qualify in a different manner. All the stadium has seen the handball, but the referee hasn't. This isn't the French way and football should learn from this.

'I have spoken to Titi [Henry] after the game and he knows it was not correct but it is up to the referee also to stop the play. In the end we qualified because of a referee's mistake, the strength of a wrist and also the clumsiness of the Irish in front of their goal.'

But when Wenger's often strong remarks bounced back to the English media, he became less and less forthright. Perhaps as a result, Wenger no longer co-commentates for TF1 – and Bixente Lizarazu does it more often – although he does still do some work for TF1, conducting regular interviews.

Despite often complaining about the level of media work he has to do, Wenger does a monthly sit-down with beIN Sports (formerly Al Jazeera), as he is friendly with Nasser Al-Khelaifi, who is chief executive not only of the TV network but also of Paris Saint-Germain. When linked with PSG, Wenger will say his association with the club's hierarchy is because of his work for Al Jazeera and beIN Sports, advising them on their football coverage. Wenger's willingness to do paid-for interviews with a cash-rich TV station while complaining about the level of media duties in every other aspect of his work, suggests that he is money-motivated.

Wenger does admit to using the media; he has confessed to lying about injuries, and his vagueness about timescales and when players will return from injury is a constant source of frustration for Arsenal's medical team. These days, they will sometimes advise that an injury may take longer to overcome than is the case, because Wenger may say something different. An example of that is when Alex Oxlade-Chamberlain suffered a knee injury on the opening-day defeat to Aston Villa in August 2013. He was out for more than three months, but Wenger said at first it would be a month, which resulted in the fans then getting angry because the player took so much longer to recover.

On this subject, Wenger said in October 2010: 'If you are asking me if I have lied to the press to protect a player, the honest answer is yes. I didn't do it and feel comfortable afterwards. But if it's for one of my players, it's a good cause. When I lie to the press, I always speak to the player concerned beforehand to get our story straight.

'If you ask the players, they want to play every three days, but if you ask the managers, sometimes they feel they have to rest players. A player's mind can become tired as well as his body. If you look at the statistics, it is surprising that players don't drop their performance when they play every three days, in terms of how far they run and the distance covered in sprints. The mental sharpness is what changes.'

Similarly, it's not just 'white lies' about injuries that can cause embarrassment in the media building at the London Colney training ground.

Ever since the row involving an agent who was accused of hanging around in the training ground building to entice a player away from their existing representative, agents have been banned from the training ground building and now hold their meetings about players in the media building.

The training ground at London Colney is vast. The pitches are glorious. In fact, there's a theory that Wenger's priority is to have better pitches at the training ground than the stadium because the players use them more often.

They are behind the main training ground building and that vast white and glass structure is rather sheltered by a huge white indoor arena where the players can train under cover. Almost adjoining the indoor pitch is the media building, which also houses the offices for the Arsenal Ladies manager, the education officer for the youngsters, the player liaison officer and, perhaps most interesting for us journalists, the office of Dick Law, Arsenal's transfer fixer.

Like everyone in the transfer business, Law is always discreet –
especially around journalists. But when we look out of the media
building window and see a smart Bentley, Ferrari or Porsche in the
car park outside, we know straightaway that another agent has
arrived. There's even the odd occasion when a player will turn up.
Arsenal are so secretive about transfers, but it is possible to catch
them in the act if you know who to look out for in this part of the
complex.

There is often a 'Wenger code' when it comes to transfers.
Those of us who have covered his press conferences for many
years have learned to read his levels of denial, from completely
dismissing the rumours, to a gentle rebuttal that frequently hints
at interest, and then the rare one: confirmation. A smile for a possible; nervous grin for a transfer at a delicate stage; and a flat denial
for a definite banker.

My favourite transfer saga and game of Wenger transfer bingo
began back in December 2008. Cesc Fabregas had just been ruled
out for a long time with a knee injury. Arsenal had been monitoring
Andrey Arshavin for a while and, when asked in a TV interview,
Wenger categorically denied the interest. But as the weeks of the
January transfer window passed, Wenger began to show signs that
they were interested after all. 'We're a long way apart,' he said.

I rang Arshavin's agent, Dennis Lachter, to see if anything was
moving. I rarely quote agents but, on this occasion, I made an
exception – largely because it sounded a lot like something
Wenger would say. Lachter, a real character, remarked: 'We know
that Arsene Wenger likes the look of Arshavin. But I like the look
of Angelina Jolie and it doesn't always mean you get what you
want.' In fairness, Wenger will never duck a question and that's
why he remains so popular with the media.

There are definitely feisty press conferences. In fact, there have
been a number in recent times. After a defeat he can often be

snappy and take questions badly. I was staggered to see so many journalists think that he was rude or patronising in his post-match interview for *Match of the Day* following Arsenal's draw with Hull at the Emirates in October 2014. The BBC called it an 'uncomfortable' interview. Frankly, that was him in a good mood after a bad result.

When Arsenal lost their opening game of the 2013/14 season to Aston Villa, they had not made a significant signing, the fans were fed up and the heat was really on Wenger. During the game fans held up banners with 'Spend, Spend, Spend' written on them. There was poisonous, personal and deeply hurtful abuse, too, and those on the bench near Wenger said at the time that it was as bad as he has ever had to endure. Wenger always insists he doesn't listen – but this was horrific and from his own fans. Bearing in mind the regular chants at away games, it is a measure of the nastiness of the taunts that some of his coaching staff were genuinely shocked.

Wenger was feisty, wound up and annoyed when he came into his press conference after the 3-1 defeat. 'You got what you wanted, you should be happy,' he said to the assembled media in the vast press conference room at the Emirates. 'Before the start of the season that was all you write in the papers, so what do you expect?' Wenger was steaming and could barely conceal his anger at the media and also at the officials as he claimed Villa were lucky with some refereeing decisions.

It was even more aggressive three days later in Istanbul when, at the pre-match press conference ahead of the Champions League play-off with Fenerbahce, Wenger lost his patience with the press and it turned into a full-on finger-pointing exercise.

Newcastle manager Alan Pardew had rounded on Arsenal for their attempts to sign Yohan Cabaye, with negotiations going particularly badly. When Dick Law rang Newcastle owner Mike

Ashley to make an offer of £10.2 million for Cabaye, Ashley immediately responded with a quip: 'Which part of him do you want to
buy?' Law assured him the offer was genuine, but Ashley said they
should come back with at least £20 million if they were serious.

Nothing was going right for Arsenal and the obvious questions
for Wenger concerned the lack of signings, Newcastle's anger and
the growing pressure on the club. He was particularly prickly and,
with the pre-Fenerbahce press conference running late, there was
no time for pleasantries. It was combative, angry and Wenger got
increasingly annoyed. 'We don't want to hurt anybody, not
Newcastle, not anybody. You can't reproach us on one side for not
buying and yet on the other side, when we try to buy, reproach us
as well. That is a bit contradictory.

'I would just like to reiterate to you that in the last 16 years we
have been very successful with transfers. And if you look at the
players who will play here, they are top-quality players. And you
should never forget that. Do not always think that what is outside
is better than what you have. What is important is to rate what you
have and our fans have to understand that.'

This was the first time that we had not travelled with the team
on a European away trip – Arsenal had changed travel agents and
the press and fans no longer went with the team – and there was a
suspicion that we had turned 'nasty' because we were sulking at
having to make our own way. We got a ticking-off from one of the
press officers for being too aggressive. Nothing could have been
further from the truth. Arsenal were struggling and questions
needed to be asked.

Things actually began to improve in the next 24 hours as
Arsenal won in Istanbul and, perhaps even more importantly, word
began to filter out that they were talking to Real Madrid about
signing one of their three available players – Mesut Ozil, Angel Di
Maria or Karim Benzema. Real would have done business on any

of the three; Arsenal were only ever going to get one, and it was
Ozil who ultimately decided to leave for the Emirates.

Nothing improves the mood of a manager like a victory and
Arsenal's season turned around quite quickly, with Ozil's arrival
being heralded as a turning point in the club's whole history. The
club record-breaking £42.5 million transfer fee catapulted Arsenal
back into the major league, as it was the first time in a few years
they had done a deal at the very top level.

Similarly, nothing upsets a manager like a really bad defeat.
Arsenal desperately needed a trophy. The drought had lasted since
the 2005 FA Cup and, by the time of the 2012/13 season, the fans
were getting restless and impatient for silverware. It began to open
up in the League Cup as Arsenal were drawn away to Bradford in
the quarter-finals. Wenger seemed to appreciate the mood and
dispensed with his habit of fielding the kids by using a near full-
strength line-up against the League Two club. Sadly for Wenger, it
backfired and they lost on penalties.

Few weeks have been as uncomfortable for Wenger as that
period during December 2012. He lost his cool with Sky's post-
match interviewer Guy Havord at Bradford. 'Is this the most
humiliating defeat since you've been at Arsenal? You've lost to a
team in the fourth tier of English football? Is it a lack of quality?'

Wenger looked shaken as he was asked again about how difficult it would be to get over such a 'humiliating defeat' and said:
'That's our job to get over it,' before quickly walking out on the
interview.

Three days later at the training ground, Wenger certainly hadn't
got over it. As he walked into the press conference and sat down,
he muttered a disparaging remark about the journalists under his
breath. Wenger fielded the questions from TV and radio before we
broke off into the newspaper section. He was quizzed in particular
about Gervinho, the Ivory Coast international, and his poor form,

after he'd missed a sitter at Bradford. The conversation went like this:

Can you understand the concerns of the supporters generally at the moment?
Wenger: Of course.

Have you seen a reaction from the players since Tuesday?
Wenger: I have had groups who had fantastic results who were less serious than these players, believe me. Players who were less focused than this team.

And they won trophies?
Wenger: Yes.

So are those players hurting if they're underperforming?
Wenger: Of course these players are hurting.

If these players are much better, are you disappointed with some of the players you've bought over the last three or four years?
Wenger: Names?

Well, you don't want to name names, do you?
Wenger: You name them.

Well, Gervinho, then. Gervinho, Chamakh, Santos, Park, Squillaci? Some of those players were big buys. What's happened to Park? It's an extraordinary situation.
Wenger: Who are the big buys?

Well, Gervinho?
Wenger: How much?

£11 million.
Wenger: He was eight million.

Well, do you feel he is fulfilling his potential at the moment?
Wenger: Gervinho?

Yes.
Wenger: Gervinho is a good player, yes.

Is he at the top of his form?
Wenger: I don't want to go into individual assessments.

But generally, are you disappointed with the level of signings? Generally?
Wenger: Generally, what?

These players are nowhere near as good, are they?
Wenger: Chamakh was a big buy? He was free. Squillaci nearly free. You cannot say that we have a squad of no quality. They are international players.

I could miss from two yards, but Gervinho is not supposed to ...
Wenger: You can and everybody can.

Things went from bad to worse that season as Arsenal suffered their first defeat to lower league opposition at the Emirates in the FA Cup, losing to Blackburn. It came just three days before they played Bayern Munich in the Champions League and, on the Monday, the *Sun* ran a back page saying that Wenger was close to signing a new two-year deal. This was a rumour doing the rounds for a couple of weeks, but it had been shot down by any journalist who had rung to check it.

Rarely since Wenger was asked whether he actually owned a telescope after the 'voyeur' row with Jose Mourinho have I seen Wenger so irate at a press conference. And this time it was in front of the TV cameras. Wenger's point was that it was a delicate time: the fans were already angry and the timing of the story was, to Wenger's mind, mischievous because it would make an already upset group of fans even more upset and raise tensions before a big game. Basically, the message was that, when Arsenal were ready to announce Wenger's next deal, then it would have to be at a good time. Now wasn't. And they were also adamant that nothing was imminent.

The mood was frosty at the training ground as Wenger would undoubtedly have seen the story and the *Sun*'s back page. When the players came out on to the training pitch – the first 15 minutes of training for Champions League games are open, largely for the benefit of photographers and TV crews, but all the media can watch – you could see Wenger turning towards the press pack and fixing them with a stare.

As soon as he came into the press conference, which was packed ahead of such an important game against a huge club, Wenger sat down alongside Mikel Arteta at the top table and you could tell he was in a bad mood. Wenger needed no encouragement and immediately snapped in response to a question about whether the players believed they could beat Bayern Munich after losing to Blackburn. 'Why, why do you ask that?'

He was then asked whether the reports were true that he was about to sign a new contract. 'This is the wrong information. I have been here for 16 years. I deserve a bit more credit than wrong information. There's only one intention and that's to harm. It's completely wrong.'

Wenger then turned on Neil Ashton from the *Daily Mail*, either forgetting who he was or thinking he was from the *Sun*.

'Why do you look at me?' Wenger fired at him.

'Because it's your press conference,' came the reply.

'I thought you gave this information out.'

'It wasn't my story,' said Ashton.

'OK, thank you very much,' Wenger shot back.

It was a snappy 15 minutes in front of the cameras and Carrie Brown from Al Jazeera, now beIN Sports, who had earlier been shut down by Wenger, came back and said: 'The point I was trying to make was that it's your last chance to win a trophy ...'

Wenger quickly interrupted: 'Thank you for that question – it's a long time since I've been asked that.'

He continued: 'Look, I have been accused of not taking seriously the FA Cup. I've won the FA Cup four times. Who else has done that? I have also been accused of not putting out a strong team. We didn't lose the game with the players who started; we lost the game in the last ten minutes. There's a lot of superficial analysis that we cannot accept.'

Brown then went back for another attempt to get an answer: 'So, Arsene, your desire is to reach the final?'

'I want to lose it. I want to lose tomorrow so you can all be happy tomorrow,' Wenger retorted testily.

Edgy though it was, that press conference was perhaps not quite as bad as before the Fenerbahce game. However, it was a tricky period for Wenger and the club and, rather inevitably, they went out – but only on away goals, and their 2-0 win in Munich in the return leg proved to be a morale-boosting victory. It was the catalyst for a run-in that took them from being seven points behind Tottenham in the battle for a place in the top four to eclipsing them on the final day of the season.

UEFA rules state that clubs must do a press conference with a manager and a player the day before a game. One of Wenger's quirks is that he will never put up a player of the same nationality as the opposing team for a Champions League match. So, for example, Per Mertesacker would never talk before a game against German opposition. The intention is definitely to avoid whipping up the opposition and giving them any ammunition or an excuse, as some managers do, to put up material in the dressing room to motivate the players. George Graham famously did that before the title-winning game at Anfield in 1989, when most of the papers had given Arsenal no chance.

Wenger is anxious to avoid giving any help to the opposition, and it's become a standing joke among the Arsenal regulars that he is always very guarded before a big game because he does not want to say anything that will fan the flames or make the back pages.

Although he watches *Match of the Day*, Wenger admitted he doesn't really take the comments too seriously, especially when it comes to Arsenal's defending. When every pundit was writing off Arsenal's title chances in December 2013 despite them being top of the league, he said:

Sometimes I watch it [*Match of the Day*], sometimes not. Sometimes it's just someone saying their opinion without an argument on something. That can make sense. But if it's something based on hate or love, or just gut feeling, then I just say, 'OK, it's an opinion – he might be right, he might be wrong.' But I have enough experience to analyse what we do and how well we play. I don't need someone else to tell me. I'm not upset by that at all.

Often, [the pundit] doesn't sustain his opinion by some work he has done to support that argument. Of course, [I have gleaned things from a pundit] – if you make an article tomorrow saying, 'I think Arsenal will win the championship because of that, this or that' or 'Arsenal will not win the championship because of something else. Look at these numbers or statistics, they always repeat the same mistake' or offer something that is in there.

If you just say, 'Arsenal will win the championship' or 'Arsenal won't win the championship because they haven't won it for eight years', then I think it's just an opinion.

When I arrived here, people explained I couldn't win the title as I am foreign. Everybody has their own logic. I just think you win the title through your quality. If we didn't win for eight years it is because we weren't good enough in the important moments of the season. We have a good opportunity to show we are good enough, so let's take it.

Wenger was also dismissive of Alan Hansen's savaging of Arsenal's defending and their tendency to get caught on the counterattack.

'You can find that. One specific incident,' said Wenger. 'It was right on the night – we were caught on the counter from a corner. Gibbs went forward, but he was supposed to be at the back. The ball was kicked to him and he went forward, and we were caught on the counterattack, and it ended up with Arteta being sent off. It was an accident but it was, a little bit, the desire for us to play.

While Wenger can be incredibly late for press conferences at times, he very rarely cancels them. However, he did so ahead of a game against Swansea in March 2014, just two days after Arsenal had been thrashed 6-0 at Chelsea. That certainly set tongues wagging, with press officers having to ring round to deny rumours that Wenger had told the players in the dressing room that he was leaving at the end of the season.

By all accounts, Wenger was angrier and more upset after conceding a late equaliser against Swansea than he had been at Chelsea, when he failed to turn up to the post-match press conference. Wenger looked shellshocked in the tunnel at Stamford Bridge, angrily pacing the floor, waiting to get into the press room, but Jose Mourinho was busy lapping up the questions and praise, so Wenger turned on his heels, did a quick TV interview and left the newspapers waiting while he got on the team bus.

Journalists want decent quotes from a press conference; they don't want monosyllabic answers. It's rare that a feisty press conference will actually be the story. The story from a press conference comes from the quotes. And better to have a manager in a good mood with good quotes than a manager in a bad mood who gives bad replies.

Wenger takes a keen interest in politics and, ahead of a French election, I asked him whether he would be voting and which way he would vote. I even joked whether he put the champagne into champagne socialist.

'I vote here,' he said, explaining that he could cast his vote in the French elections in London. 'Which way, I won't let you know.'

In August 2013, Wenger said he had spoken to Sir Alex Ferguson who had retired at the end of the previous season. What did Ferguson say to you? 'That he loves you. He misses the newspapers. You will miss me when I'm gone!'

He displayed his softer side when he heard that former BBC Radio 5 Live commentator David Oates had died. Wenger made a point of seeking out his widow, Charlotte Nicol, who also works in the media, to pass on his condolences and convey some nice private words.

Over the years, Wenger has picked up on who all the journalists support. He knows, for example, that Jim van Wijk from the Press Association supports Norwich and Wenger always ends up calling them: 'Nor-which', which has become a standing joke. When van

Wijk asked about his determination, Wenger said: 'I will go out with you and play one-on-one and if I don't beat you, I will want to beat you.'

Van Wijk: 'My knee is not what it was.'

'Don't make excuses even before we've started!'

Wenger commands respect from journalists – be they lifelong reporters or former players – and he is always polite and smiling. He'll take a call even on a Sunday and, if the subject appeals – like paying tribute to a player – then he'll happily talk. Former Arsenal striker John Hartson, now a media pundit, said:

> When I went over to a European game, I had a really good chat with him for about an hour and a half in Istanbul. It was the night before the game, all the players had gone to bed, around half past nine, quarter to ten. We talked about everything.
>
> He said I did great at West Ham; he told me I'd done great at Celtic. I asked him about players, Ramsey, Wilshere, and why he was so adamant on not spending, his philosophy, and he gave me some great insight. We had a really, really long discussion.
>
> I told him about my kids, what I was doing now and was interested in media work. He is one who doesn't get uptight or upset about what is written or said in the media. He said there's nothing that's not been said about Arsenal. If Manchester United, Manchester City, Chelsea have a nightmare then nothing is said on the same scale if Arsenal have a nightmare. That brings everyone out of the woodwork.
>
> I was at West Brom and I looked at the local paper there and they were always highlighting on Birmingham. Arsenal seems to be the same and it's everywhere with Arsenal. But he's not too concerned about it because he knows that the media has a job to do. He gave me a real insight into what he's achieving, trying to get at Arsenal and bring regular success to the club.

Similarly, Sky commentator Martin Tyler remembers his first meeting with Wenger and the polite manner in which he was greeted. 'I had met him at the 1992 Cup Winners' Cup final when he was in charge of Monaco and they had lost to Werder Bremen. They had lost and I remember going on to the pitch and saying to him: "I'm really sorry, I'm commentating on this and can you tell me how to pronounce your name?" He tolerated me with a smile and that was the first contact I ever had with him.'

Tyler recalls going to see Wenger within days of him taking over at Arsenal and it was a two-way street as the Frenchman wanted to know about the workings of the English media as much as Tyler wanted to find out about Arsenal's new manager.

I had asked to go and see him when he took over. We saw him at Sopwell House and I felt that he brought something, not just to Arsenal, but to English football. It was a very nice hour or so. He was very engaging. I really admire and respect him.

We've often talked about other issues. I remember talking about the American presidency before a game. It was at Wigan. There had been some riots in Paris and we were both standing outside in this open forecourt area near the dressing rooms and tunnel. We were chatting away and then I suddenly went: 'There's only half an hour to kick-off! I've got to get upstairs, you've got to get into the dressing room.'

You could stop him and say: 'What about the Ebola crisis?' I'll tell you what, he would know all about it. He's very independent on what he wants from football, but he's also the most wide-ranging manager I've ever come across.

Tyler has covered Wenger and Arsenal through good, bad and indifferent. And now he talks as if he genuinely hopes Wenger's legacy will remain intact even after comparatively lean times:

I suppose the debate since then is whether the magic has faltered, when it faltered or if it's still there. I had very happy memories after they won the FA Cup [to complete the 1998 Double] and I said to him: 'In football terms, you're immortal.' Back then in 1998, it was still quite rare. Tottenham were the first ones to do it in 1961 and then Arsenal in 1971 and I grew up with the Double being something very elusive.

I hope his legacy is not spoiled by the latter years. It's pretty hard to invent the telephone and then go and invent penicillin. To finish in the top four of your division for 18 years in a row is incredible. It really is incredible.

It is the same for football writer Henry Winter, who has a very chatty, friendly relationship with Wenger that dates back to when the Frenchman took over. Winter has seen all sides of Wenger, from temper and charm, to success and failure.

'I was at the first press conference when David Dein organised something. We didn't know too much about him. He talked for about 45 minutes and was absolutely spellbinding, talking about his philosophy and his wry sense of humour came out,' said Winter, who also recalls Wenger losing his cool with the Arsenal press officer, Amanda Docherty, after a European game in 2004.

He does have a temper. I was in Celta Vigo, Edu had scored twice, was in the doping and Wenger had to leave bang on 12 o'clock. He was standing in the background going absolutely mental. Edu had been promised to Sky and partly to me because I was staying over. Wenger had steam coming out of his ears and then he swore. I wrote a piece a few days later saying that some of the professor reputation is a bit strange when you see him lose his temper. I linked it in to why he is one of the great managers because all great managers have that.

My wife has met Wenger and she has met a few people in football and says that he has the best manners of anyone she's met in the game. He is the most charming man, remembered her name.

Wenger also has a genuine interest in the off-the-field and charity work that the club does, and is a great supporter of the Arsenal Foundation, as Winter explains:

Arsenal became involved in Chernobyl and the areas around there. They sent some kits as well. Wenger spoke well about it and the need to reach out around the world. I got a letter about a year later and he was talking about helping the kids of people who had been affected by the nuclear fallout and who had died. One of the girls who was dying of cancer asked to be buried in her Arsenal top because they were the only ones to have shown her any love in her life. All clubs do that but Wenger was very, very aware of that.

I remember doing something at an autism charity, TreeHouse, with Nick Hornby. He spoke so well about autism, what it means and he got it all. It was interesting to see him walking around the autism place. You could see he really cared, there was eye contact, he spoke to the people there and was interested in what they had to say. It wasn't just for show. It wasn't done just to keep his paymasters at his club happy; he realised the impact that Arsenal had on people's lives. He also had this intellectual interest in it and I've not met a brighter person in football.

These days Clare Tomlinson is known as one of the best presenters on Sky Sports News, but before that she was a press officer at the Football Association and also at Arsenal for two years from 1996 to 1998. Her admiration for Wenger is clear:

He never ducked a question. The only time you knew he'd been riled a bit was when he went: 'Listen, listen ...' When he said that you knew he was annoyed. He'd never bully anyone in a press conference, even in the early days. He never did one-word answers – even though he's getting better at those these days. He was so polite, so gracious and always answered every question.

What would happen was that he would come in on a Thursday, I'd have this big pile of requests for things for him to do and he'd say: 'What's that?' He couldn't believe the sheer number of requests. After about three months, I remember going in one day with only two pieces of paper. He said: 'Where is your big pile of papers, Clare?' I told him I'd said no to everything else and he replied: 'Now you begin to understand!'

He asked me what's the minimum he could get away with. I told him he'd have to do a Friday press conference, a separate Sundays if it was a Sunday game, pre-match and post-match. You have to do separate for broadcast, separate radio, separate TV and separate written. Whatever he wanted to do in a foreign language was his choice.

But I told him that if he did one one-on-one interview then he'd have to do them all. I told him my life wouldn't be worth living. I told him: 'If you do the *Mirror*, you have to do the *Telegraph*.' He said: 'I won't be doing one-on-ones!' He stuck by that. He understood the idea of doing separates, something different for dailies and Sundays, radio, TV and so on. They all want something different. He was so single-minded, so focused on football; he understood his responsibilities for the media and was excellent.

Tomlinson, a self-confessed Tottenham fan, remembers telling him that she was leaving in 1998, straight after the FA Cup final when Arsenal completed the Double. 'I remember when I left, we were talking as we walked around the pitch and he said: "So, Clare, your last game. Will you miss it?" I told him I could go and watch Tottenham play. He was joshing me about that and said: "So you're off to do Sports News. You'll have to talk about cricket. Cricket? No, I just can't get my head round it."

'He then asked me: "Do you like football?" I said to him: "Arsene, you've worked with me for two years and you ask me if I like football!" Then he said: "But you're a Tottenham fan." He found that very funny. I've got nothing but respect for the man.'

CHAPTER 12

THE INTELLIGENT ONE

'I MET BILLY BEANE, yes. I am completely uncultured in baseball; it is very difficult for me to understand. I was a bit in touch with it in Japan; it is a big sport there. In Nagoya there was a team so I met the coach a few times. Of what I have heard from Stan Kroenke, Billy Beane has done exceptionally well in baseball. He is obsessed by statistics.

'I like the numbers as well, because what is repeated is not a coincidence. If you think you have a good defence, if you are always conceding goals the numbers will tell you the truth. But what is more difficult is to number the performances.'

Like most football managers, Wenger looks to use statistics to play down a defeat – they still had shots on target and so on – and focuses on the performance when they win. Such was Beane's success with statistics and baseball economics at Oakland Athletics that he became the subject of a book that was later turned into the Hollywood film, *Moneyball*. Beane is also a major fan of Wenger and his methods, as Arsenal's majority shareholder Stan Kroenke has pointed out on several occasions. It further underlines the esteem in which Kroenke holds Wenger. His faith in the Arsenal manager is unshakeable.

Clearly, part of Wenger's appeal has been his ability to guide Arsenal into the lucrative Champions League year after year. That brings rich rewards and guarantees the club will remain on a sound financial footing. Furthermore, Wenger has, down the years, been able to spot young players or raw talents, develop them and sell on at a big profit. Emmanuel Adebayor, Nicolas Anelka, Samir Nasri, Marc Overmars, Emmanuel Petit, Robin van Persie and Kolo Toure are just some of those who are proof of that. They encapsulate Wenger's economics. Beane's philosophy relies more heavily on statistics in the first instance when identifying talent and potential, but is also about taking a chance on undervalued players and then selling them on for a profit. This has become known as the Moneyball effect.

Those close to Wenger don't believe he truly buys into Moneyball, despite his acknowledgement of the use of statistics. But the club certainly buys into it. Chief executive Ivan Gazidis brought in Hendrik Almstadt to be head of business development. They also appointed Gero Kahlen in the summer of 2013 to work alongside Almstadt, with Kahlen describing himself as an 'in-house consultant'. Almstadt, now Aston Villa's sporting director is mostly based at the training ground and is viewed with some suspicion by old-school members of the coaching and scouting staff. They weren't disappointed when he left in the summer of 2015.

Arsenal also bought a US-based data company, StatDNA, for £2.165 million in December 2012. According to Gazidis: 'The insights produced by the company are widely used across our football operations – in scouting and talent identification, in game preparation, in post-match analysis and in gaining tactical insights.'

The interesting part about this is that the number-crunchers can look at stats and analyse players but, and this is the crux of the issue for the old-school scouts and coaches, does it really work on a practical level? For example, Tom Cleverley was identified as a potential target in the spring of 2014. His stats, according to the number-crunchers at the training ground and StatDNA, were outstanding. But can the system really analyse beyond the accuracy of passing? Therefore, will it really understand how many of those accurate passes actually drive the team forward? Judging by the fact Cleverley didn't join Arsenal, the old-school scouts might have proved the stats don't always work.

But in January 2015, Wenger admitted that Arsenal signed Brazilian defender Gabriel from Villarreal for £15 million, at least partly due to his statistics. Clearly, Arsenal also watched and scouted Gabriel – a relative unknown who was signed as a 24-year-old even though he had not represented Brazil at any level – but it was the statistics that had flagged him up. That Wenger may not be altogether comfortable with such a heavy reliance on statistics was clear from the way he reacted when questioned about it in his press conference. He appeared almost embarrassed when quizzed.

One of the journalists, Gary Jacob from *The Times*, had heard from a contact about the statistics being the basis of the signing and raised it with Wenger, who smiled: 'I cannot tell you. I am not saying no. But he has good stats! We look at interceptions, defensive errors, winning tackles – what we call tackles is committing to win the ball. Set-piece receptions. These kind of things. But the most important thing is through the eye.

'It is difficult to watch all the games. But what I mean is that if the numbers confirm the eye, it gives you more. If a guy comes home and says, "I've seen a good player," you can statistically observe this player for five, six, seven games. You send him again, he comes back and says he's a good player, and the numbers confirm, you can say the risk is limited. Though there is always a risk.'

The interesting question is whether the stats or the scouting report came first. I suspect, from the way Wenger looked so uncomfortable, it was the former. But a remark made by their French scout, ex-Arsenal player Gilles Grimaldi, who is very close to Wenger, perhaps highlighted the fact that Wenger and old-school scouts really don't respect stats too much. In an interview with *L'Equipe* in December 2014, Grimandi said: 'Stats take a greater and greater role. You really have to put your case forward to argue against the numbers. In a club, stats give the possibility to exist to people who have a very limited knowledge.'

In the summer of 2014, Arsenal were left desperately short of defenders. But the stats told them that, in the previous few seasons, the fourth-choice centre back had played an average of four games a season. So they decided they didn't need to buy another defender to replace Thomas Vermaelen after he joined Barcelona. The stats did not legislate for the fact Arsenal suffered injuries to Mathieu Debuchy, their new right back, Laurent Koscielny, one half of the first-choice centre-half pairing, and both left backs. So, on this occasion, the stats were proved horribly wrong.

When it comes to scouting for a keeper, one of the key considerations is the length of time between mistakes. You can judge whether the keeper is strong mentally, recovers quickly, or is vulnerable to making more mistakes after committing an error. Again, that is a stats-based assessment rather than the old-school method of scouting performances alone.

So when Arsenal signed Emiliano Viviano, an Italian international, in 2013, it was because he was seen as being at the top of a batch of 'B list' keepers and so ideal as a back-up. It was a typical Moneyball strategy: don't go for the best, but choose the best in that category. Viviano joined on a season-long loan, but he didn't play a game and didn't impress the club enough for them to want to make it a permanent deal, so he returned to Palermo, at which point he was immediately loaned out to Sampdoria.

Basically, the stats work to a degree and the scientific aspect of analysing opponents, as well as Arsenal's own players, is something the club has embraced. Wenger regularly refers to players being in the 'red zone', meaning they are vulnerable to injury because they are tired, but when it comes to actually resting players in the red zone, Wenger often ignores the recommendation and plays them anyway, especially if there isn't an obvious alternative. He also judges on what he sees for himself on the pitch and on the training ground. He brought a new scientific approach to diet, fitness and stretching when he took over at Arsenal, but doesn't now like his own theories to be challenged.

However, Wenger's intelligence goes way beyond your average football manager. He surely is The Intelligent One. You always have the feeling that he has a depth of knowledge about many subjects.

He speaks several languages: English – even if occasionally idiosyncratic and often punctuated by strange Wengerisms like 'footballistically', which probably means addressing an issue in football terms – as well as German, Spanish, some Japanese and, of course, French. He is quick-witted, well-informed and interest-ing – far removed from the typical tracksuited football manager, barking orders at players and trying to motivate them.

On the other hand, there are moments when he can appear cold. When former Arsenal physio Gary Lewin knocked on his office door with Theo Walcott alongside him to ask whether it was OK for the Arsenal winger to go and have a shoulder operation, Wenger looked up from his desk and said: 'Yes, yes, of course.' But he failed to wish the player well or didn't offer him any support at that moment.

While some of his early scientific methods and new techniques have been matched – and some would say overtaken – since he took charge back in 1996, he still embraces different ideas such as psychology and intelligence tests for players. He uses a psychologist and insists on knowing a player's mentality and motivation before signing them.

Beyond the club, Wenger has strong views on Financial Fair Play, doping in football and the future of the English game. He also clearly believes that many of his management techniques are universal and similar if not the same as those in big business. It is noticeable that he often takes part in business seminars when Arsenal go on tour. Other managers would leave the speeches and business meetings to their chief executive, but Wenger takes the microphone, addresses the audience and then takes questions.

Wenger did just that while on tour in Saitama, Japan, in the summer of 2013. The questions were short, the answers long, considered and revealing. It was a fantastic insight into what makes Wenger tick as he discussed developing young players, managing egos in football, what makes a good team, why Europeans aren't always good trainers, playing under pressure, timekeeping, the importance of teamwork and even getting lost while out jogging.

Q: In a highly competitive, globalised, market, how does Arsenal find the best talent?

A: One of our strengths is young people know we will give them a chance. But what we look for is their motivation to be successful. But what is motivation? How can you tell if somebody is motivated? How can you remain motivated? Well, for me, motivation is the person who has the capability to recruit the resources he needs to achieve a goal.

For example, earlier today I went for a jog in Saitama, but I couldn't find my way back. I was motivated to come back to the hotel, but I couldn't find my way. So, I was highly motivated and slowly I found my way back. But what does that show? It shows that motivation is essential but not enough. You also need consistency in your motivation and that is what we try to test in players as well. For me that is a very underrated quality.

I could have said: 'Right, I can't find my way back to the hotel, so let's see if I can find a taxi.' But because I'm a sportsman I decided not to get a taxi and that I would find my way back no matter how long it would take me, so I continued to run. That's what I mean in the consistency of your motivation. The stamina of your motivation.

When you look at people who are successful, you will find that they aren't the people who are motivated, but have consistency in their motivation. You have many people who start diets on 1 January. Some of them last until mid-January, some give up mid-June and some of them last. We are interested in the ones that last because that makes a successful sportsman.

That doesn't necessarily mean successful sportsmen are happy people, but it means they are determined and they are ready to hurt themselves to be successful and that's the type we are looking for. The people who are very demanding with themselves and each other for a long time. That consistent motivation is applicable to football, business, anything you do in life.

Q: But where do you look for that talent?

A: We look all over the world. It's simple as that. I've spent a long time in the game, and I still think it's a little miracle how popular this game has become on a worldwide level at such a high speed. Today, when something happens in London, they know it in Saitama at the same minute. So that means Arsenal are a worldwide club and we are interested in worldwide talent. The world is small. Previously a young boy in Saitama never had the chance to become a world-class player, but today he has that chance. Because if he has the talent and determination then he will get the chance somewhere and that's what we try to do. We try to look all over the world to find players who have the talent and desire because unfortunately, in football, there is more money than talent.

Q: What is your experience of nurturing talent into world-class players?

A: I believe one of the best things about managing people is that we can influence lives in a positive way. That's basically what a manager is about. When I can do that, I am very happy. That's not the only part of my job, because the essential part is to win on a Saturday afternoon, but it is an important part. In a world where we only care about stars, it is important to say to players: 'You are not a star yet, but you can become one and I will give you a chance.' At Arsenal we are proud to do that, and we have fought against the policy of only buying stars. You have to understand that a player who is a star was at one stage an unknown person who had talent. We want to be the club who gives this guy a chance.

Q: You are working with some of the most highly paid athletes in the world, so how big is the factor of egos in your job as a manager?

A: If you're asking me if the egos are big? Yes. You must know that a person, no matter how big a star he is, is ready to listen to you if it meets his needs. The condition for him to know if you meet his needs is to test you first. Is the manager capable of making him the player he wants to be? Unfortunately in management, you cannot cheat for a long time. When you are in a squad of 30 people, the players detect at a huge speed the weakness in your personality. So that's the moment of truth, when a person sits in front of you. They observe you and then they try to decide if you can help them. If they think you are the man who can help them, they will respect you. The next step for them is deciding whether they are in a squad who can help them to be successful. We had that problem when we were under financially restricted conditions. For some players we didn't have enough stars to be successful as quickly as they wanted to be. Of course, that's one of the problems we face in our job.

Q: *Is your ideology of football art only achievable by results on the pitch?*

A: A manager is a guide. He takes a group of people and says, 'With you I can make us a success, I can show you the way.' But first you have to have a clear idea of what you want. You have to have a clear concept and make it understandable so they can work with you, and that's not very easy. That's why it was very interesting for me to work in Japan when I did, because you have to make your ideas as clear as possible and you have to adapt to the difference of culture. And sometimes you have to maintain your own ideas against the results.

Q: *Is there a difference between man management in football and in business?*

A: Not really. The only difference is that most of the time in business you manage people who have maturity. In football, you manage people who are 18, 19, 20 years old. The responsibilities are quite big for them. We forget that these players have to perform under huge public pressure, in front of 60,000 people, with a huge responsibility to win games. I'm not sure how I would have responded to it if I was 20, rich, famous and a big star – it's not easy to handle. That's the main difference between man management in football and business.

The other big difference is that you can work in an office and be at 70 per cent of your potential and do your job well. You can't be a footballer and be at 70 per cent of your potential and play well. And that's where the stress comes from. One player being weak can cost you the game, the player knows that. That's where the pressure comes from. Every minute of every day a footballer tests himself – that puts the body under pressure, because you know you can only perform in a game if you're 100 per cent. Look at the Tour de France. Chris Froome won, but he can lose it in one day, by just having one bad day in the office. That's top-level sport.

Q: *What are the key ingredients of a winning team?*

A: You can't have any weak positions. You need players who can make the difference. You need a team who can stop the other team from scoring goals, so a good goalkeeper and good defence and you need to score. You need one guy who can pass the ball, the quarterback, to one guy who can score the goal, the receiver. Once you have a guy who can give passes to score, you will always have a chance to win football games. The rest is based on teamwork and attitude.

Q: *How do you cope with having a multicultural squad?*

A: By creating a culture of our own. I've had years with people from 18 different countries. For example, being on time isn't the same for a Japanese man as it is for a Frenchman. When a Frenchman arrives five minutes late, he still thinks he is on time. In Japan when it's five minutes before the set time he thinks he is too late. That means you have to create a new culture and identify how we all want to behave, create a company culture. That way, when someone steps out of line, we can say: 'Look, my friend, that's not what we said.' So it's important to have clear rules and everyone knows and agrees with it.

Q: Do you have a go-to method to inspire your team when they are feeling down?

A: We live in a life where everyone tells us what we don't have. Most of the time, I remind my team and my players the qualities they do have. None of us have all the qualities in life, but the good thing is that we can all be successful without having all the qualities. Players shouldn't forget the qualities they don't have.

Q: In business, a lot is dependent on individuals meeting personal objectives and often penalising those who don't meet those objectives . . .

A: Success in life is a balance between individual achievement and co-operation with others. The West is totally focused on individual achievement; you have to be successful no matter what. Even if you have to kill your partners, even if you have to cheat a little bit – only one thing counts and that is individual success at any price.

But the Japanese culture is geared more towards co-operation with others. Your success is graded on how much you integrate into the collective spirit of your company. And sometimes even that can be to an excess because individual performance is not acknowledged as much as collective success. But in Europe we have gone completely the other way; the sense of co-operation with others has dropped dramatically.

The sense of happiness is linked with a good balance between the two. That's what team sport is about. A good footballer should feel he can express himself, but also be helpful to the group. If one of the two is missing you will never be completely happy. That's the magic of team sport.

Q: How do you deal with those who aren't meeting their objectives?
A: If they are underperforming, our biggest power is to drop the player. One of the difficulties in our job is that we have 25 people who fight to play on Saturday and on Friday night we have 14 who are unemployed, and we tell them on Monday, 'Let's start again, you have another chance.' That's the difficulty with our job.

After years of covering Wenger and Arsenal, the most amusing quote for me is the one on timekeeping, for as we have seen Wenger is very often late for press conferences. So the irony of Wenger talking about the importance of timekeeping is rather amusing.

But it's clear that Wenger places a great deal of emphasis on man management, mental attitude and developing players – even if, as some say privately, he is taciturn in the dressing room and shies away from confrontation if a player is out of the team or on the training pitch. However, rather like in the dressing room at half-time, Wenger clearly has a very precise philosophy of not saying very much so that when he does speak, the players are more likely to listen and take it on board.

It is a clever approach, which has helped players develop in the first team and take confidence. In the case of Arsenal's England international Kieran Gibbs, Wenger gave him his first-team debut at Sheffield United in 2007 as a left back, even though he had never played in that position before. Wenger did not even tell him until the day before so as not to allow him time to get nervous. Wenger has a habit of seeing something in a player that he believes will make them suitable for different positions, just as he did with Gibbs, Thierry Henry and Lauren, who was converted from midfielder to right back in the Invincibles team.

When I interviewed Gibbs, he had an intriguing take on Wenger's methods and what makes him such a clever man manager:

He has got something special. When you're first coming into the team, he's got an ability to make you feel like you deserve to be there. He doesn't have to do a lot because of who he is. If he tells you something, whatever he tells you, if he pays you compliments then you think: 'It's Arsene Wenger telling me this ...' You go home and you think: 'Wow, Arsene Wenger has told me this.'

You think he must be right and you take it on board. He's not a manager who is constantly on your back; he just lets you take it in and learn for yourself. He always tells you to play free, do what you feel that the game deserves. That has helped me a lot. I'm quite like that. If someone tells me to do something, and they tell you in a certain way, I react differently to if someone tells you just to get on with it and lets you learn. He tends to just throw you in and you learn by yourself. I'm my own biggest critic so I will know what I need to do and what I don't need to do. He can read someone's personality as well. He will leave you when you need to be left and tell you when you need to be told.

That is a view echoed by Ray Parlour, who believes it is also the reason why very few players leave Arsenal and then publicly criticise Wenger – unlike, for example, the feud between Sir Alex Ferguson and Roy Keane. Wenger remains on great terms with his own Captain Marvel, Patrick Vieira.

'I believe his football management is absolutely superb. He loved it day to day,' said Parlour. 'But off the field he was quality. Any problems you had, he'd always be willing to sit down, help you as a manager. Man management is so important. You'll find it very hard to find a player who has a bad word [to say] about him. That's fantastic, the best testament you can get.

'Lots of managers are successful but don't have that. What a quality to have ... Managers and players fall out. Some players say: "He was terrible, he was this, he was that." I think you'll find it very difficult to find a player who worked under him who won't say he's a top manager or a nice man. Because he was and is a genuinely nice man.'

It would be fair to say that Wenger is more prone to bad moods than angry outbursts, though he is capable of those too, even occasionally shouting at his players – but not too often as it dilutes the effect. If a player has made a mistake then he is just as likely to aim a verbal volley of frustration at one of his coaches as he is at the player himself. The anger is more likely to be shouted in their presence rather than directly at them. Generally, the players are spared so that when team meetings or dressing-downs are needed, they remain effective.

Wenger admits he uses a psychologist but always refuses to discuss it in anything but general terms. In fact, for a long time he shied away from confirming he used one – David Dein would insist that Arsenal didn't need a psychologist as they already had one in Wenger – but Wenger now says: 'We have one, yes. No, I don't want to talk about that. Because what we do inside ... Well, nobody tells you how to make Coca-Cola.'

Just like the recipe for Coca-Cola, what goes on inside the club is a closely guarded secret, and Wenger absolutely hates the idea of the press getting information or an insight that he does not approve of. So, while on the one hand he confirms he uses a psychologist, on the other he downplays the effect.

'The players are like everybody else. When they win the game they say everybody is great; when they lose the game they say everybody is not so great. Yes, I believe in mental help. Nobody is perfect. We can all take some advantage from mental help. But a guy who has come to that level at the start means that he has mental strength. And that he can deal in adversity, or he would not be there.'

Wenger was typically unimpressed when a group of journalists – myself included – happened to stumble across some details of a team meeting in which psychology was used in September 2008. It was just his luck that we were attending a wedding reception in the same Manchester hotel Arsenal used before an away game at Bolton. They won the match but that didn't matter. Wenger didn't like the story coming out.

The players had been given a briefing on an A4 sheet of paper with just 224 words and it was remarkable because it was so simple. But the idea was surely just to emphasise the key messages. Arsenal had endured a poor run away from home, particularly in the north-west. Words such as 'driving force' and 'dynamic' were used. It also stressed the need for a 'positive attitude' and included a demand to 'stay humble and grounded as a player and a person'. It highlighted, too, the need to 'play the football we love to play at home', even when they are visiting grounds like Bolton, which was a notoriously unhappy hunting ground for Arsenal.

Here is the briefing put to the players at the pre-match meeting.

The team:

- A team is as strong as the relationships within it. The driving force of a team is its members' ability to create and maintain excellent relationships within the team that can add an extra dimension and robustness to the team dynamic.
- This attitude can be used by our team to focus on the gratitude and the vitally important benefits that the team brings to our own lives. It can be used to strengthen and deepen the relationships within it and maximise the opportunities that await a strong and united team.

Our team becomes stronger by:

- Displaying a positive attitude on and off the pitch
- Everyone making the right decisions for the team
- Having an unshakeable belief that we can achieve our target
- Believing in the strength of the team
- Always wanting more – always giving more
- Focusing on our communication
- Being demanding with yourself
- Being fresh and well prepared to win
- Focusing on being mentally stronger and always keeping going until the end
- When we play away from home, believing in our identity and playing the football we love to play at home
- Sticking together
- Staying grounded and humble as a player and a person
- Showing the desire to win in all that you do

Enjoy and contribute to all that is special about being in a team – don't take it for granted.

The building of the Emirates Stadium was to transform Arsenal's prospects, as the huge cost meant that for several years Arsene Wenger had to become more accountant than manager. (*Getty Images*)

Before they moved from Highbury, however, there was one last trophy when Wenger for once sent out a side to defend. After reaching full time at 0-0 in the 2005 FA Cup final, the manager urges his team on for one last effort against Manchester United. (*Getty Images*)

Wenger and Jose Mourinho have had a fiery relationship ever since the Chelsea boss accused him of being a 'voyeur' of the Stamford Bridge outfit in 2005. (*PA*)

Samuel Eto'o is sent tumbling by Jens Lehmann during the 2006 Champions League final, and Arsenal were down to ten men in the biggest game in their history. (*PA*)

Wenger watches on from the touchline during Arsenal's first game at their new stadium. (*Getty Images*)

Theo Walcott was part of the new era, but David Dein, who had formed such a close partnership with Wenger would soon be sacked. (*Getty Images*)

When stories emerged that Wenger might leave the club after the 2008/09 season, fans gathered to persuade him to stay, but a lack of trophies would soon bring unrest. (*Mirrorpix*)

Arsene Wenger at a press conference in Kuala Lumpur in July 2011, when he insisted that the club would not sell both Cesc Fabregas and Samir Nasri. They both left, and 12 months later so too did Robin van Persie. (*Getty Images*)

Boro Primorac has been working with Wenger for many years now but his old-school methods have remained the same on the training ground. (*Getty Images*)

Ivan Gazidis (left) and Sir Chips Keswick (right) present Wenger with a gold cannon to mark his 1000th game in charge of the club. The match itself was a crushing defeat to Chelsea. (*Getty Images*)

The unveiling of Mesut Ozil early in the 2013/14 season showed that Arsenal were back in the market for world-class players, and that the club would aim to buy the best it could afford. (*Getty Images*)

At the end of the season, Wenger celebrated like never before when he got his hands on his first trophy in nine years, after Arsenal beat Hull City in the 2014 FA Cup final. (*Getty Images*)

Alexis Sanchez is in clear pain after a foul on him by a Chelsea player in October 2014, and in the aftermath the simmering feud between Wenger and Mourinho erupts again. *(Getty Images)*

Jack Wilshere goes past Carlos Sanchez as the Gunners recorded a thumping one-sided 4-0 FA Cup final win over Aston Villa to reinforce the sense that the Arsenal side of 2015 were only going to get better. *(Getty Images)*

Wenger moves on after another victory. (*Getty Images*)

Psychology in football – as compared to other sports – is often mocked or not taken seriously enough. In football, it is still regarded as a quirky new concept, even though many players appreciate it. Wenger has known French psychologist Jacques Crevoisier for more than 40 years and Crevoisier has regularly worked with Arsenal's players. One of the exercises he uses is a set of multiple choice questions to test a player's intelligence, confidence and belief.

Crevoisier has given regular interviews, despite the very private nature of his job and Wenger's desire for secrecy. In one interview for Swedish magazine *Offside*, Crevoisier revealed an amusing account about the Arsenal striker Nicklas Bendtner, whose self-confidence was off the scale. 'One of the categories is called "self-perceived competence" – i.e. how good the player himself thinks he is. On a scale up to nine, Bendtner got ten!

'We have never seen that before. Pat Rice was sitting next to me and couldn't stop laughing. When Bendtner misses a chance, he is always genuinely convinced that it wasn't his fault. You might say that's a problem, and to a certain degree it can be. But you can also view it as this guy has a remarkable ability to come back after setbacks.'

Crevoisier is clearly close to Wenger and believes that the Arsenal manager has overcome his own barriers at the same time as putting a huge amount of faith in the importance of mental strength in his players. Talking in 2011 during Arsenal's barren spell, Crevoisier said:

I've tested all the young Arsenal players and they were outstanding psychologically. A mental barrier? For me, the problem is not there. What people must understand is that Arsene Wenger had a special philosophy and policy. He couldn't put the money into players because he had to pay for the new stadium.

It is unfair for Arsenal to compete with clubs who don't have the same rules. At Chelsea, Roman Abramovich gave Jose Mourinho the money to buy the best players in the world. Rafael Benitez took 68 players in five years at Liverpool. For Arsenal, the problem is to keep their players as long as possible. If you keep players like Fabregas, Wilshere and Szczesny for three or four years, what they do must be special.

When Arsene leaves Arsenal – and he will finish his job there – he will leave a new stadium, a new academy, a great team and enough money for the club. It will be an incredible legacy. Each time I see Arsene, I'm so impressed by his intelligence and the new aspects he brings to our conversations. Arsene Wenger always tells me that you have to be clever to play for Arsenal and that is where he starts. Without that, you cannot fit into his system.

For a long time, Arsenal used psychologists on a casual basis. As a result, players would joke about mixed messages. One psychologist would say one thing, another would have their own message and then the coach or manager would be preaching something different. When they went away with their national teams, many would also see an additional psychologist there. After one session, Ray Parlour joked: 'I've got one parrot on this shoulder telling me one thing and another saying something different on the other shoulder.'

Some players bought into it, others less so. One player who embraced it wholeheartedly was Jack Wilshere, who saw a psychologist, Pete Lindsay, at Arsenal on a consultancy basis. Wilshere admitted every player is different, every manager is different, and his own issues on the pitch often came down to anger and frustration rather than injuries or a lack of confidence. He spoke about how Lindsay supported him while he was away on England duty, helping him to channel his aggression and overcome his frustrations at his bad luck with injuries:

> Players are different. Some take time to adapt and some others will jump at the chance straightaway. I don't think it was ever the confidence. It was the worry. Not confidence. Not the worry, the frustration if you like. Now I've learned to enjoy my football while I can.
>
> Every time I'm on the pitch I just enjoy it. I'm not as aggressive, not as angry. If something goes wrong, a couple of years ago I would have gone to the physio: 'Look, my ankle's not right.' Now I'm on top of it, enjoying my football and I've grown up. I realise things aren't going to go my way every week. Of course they're not. You can't expect them to. But the main thing is to give your all and enjoy.
>
> I think there was a time I realised I had to change. I can't put a finger on when it was, but there was a time … I've worked with, not Steve Peters [England's psychologist] but another psychologist at Arsenal [Pete Lindsay] and he's really helped me. He's taught me that, if your head's not right, it can affect other parts of your body. So get that right and enjoy your football, and that's what I'm trying to do.

It all comes down to man management and, in the summer of 2014, there seemed to be an acceptance that change was needed within the coaching structure at London Colney to keep up with the times, formalise their use of sports psychology and also address concerns about their fitness department.

In came Shad Forsythe, who had worked with the German FA since 2004 as a fitness coach, to try to improve the club's injury record and recent problems. His arrival created quite a buzz as the American fitness guru had been part of Germany's World

Cup-winning set-up and even Mesut Ozil tweeted his delight: 'Another world champion for the Gunners!'

To less fanfare but equally important was the appointment of a full-time psychologist, David Priestley, who joined from rugby club Saracens where he was head of psychology and personal development. Up until Priestley's appointment, Crevoisier and the rest had been employed on an ad hoc basis and were called upon regularly but only when required. While at Saracens, Priestley made a point of never stepping onto the pitch, but instead drew up personal development plans which preached confidence, honesty and humility. His strategy includes visits to children in hospital, talks by inspirational speakers, and building team spirit and confidence.

Clearly, Wenger believes in a combination of coaching, fitness work and psychology – and in keeping up with new developments in these areas – to get the best out of his players, and he is particularly keen on giving the younger ones their chance to shine. As Jack Wilshere explains:

> One thing with the manager here is his ability to get the best out of young players. He makes the young players believe in themselves and to play with confidence. Once you've got that as a young player, if you've got the right technical and physical ability then that's pretty much it.
>
> I think the main thing is that he believes in young players and gives them their chance. Not just that, but it's easy for managers to stick a player in and then if they have a bad game or they make a mistake then just throw them out.
>
> You see that at teams in the bottom half of the table, but in the top half and for a club like Arsenal, to give young players a chance gives you great belief as a young player. You are playing with world-class players and fighting for the title at 18 years old.

Although these changes in the support staff came after Arsenal had broken their trophy drought with winning the FA Cup in 2014, Wenger recognised that the fans were getting frustrated that the club no longer seemed capable of challenging for the Premier League title. With Manchester United struggling to come to terms with the end of the Ferguson era, he recognised that there was a chance for the club to put that right. As far as the fans were concerned, this couldn't happen soon enough.

CHAPTER 13

FAN UNREST

FOR MANY ARSENAL FANS, Arsene Wenger is a bit like a favourite uncle. Still lovable, he has given some great memories and it's difficult to dislike him. But there was a point in Wenger's career, probably in 2008, when the magic began to fade. It was a small yet vociferous minority at first. Slowly, though, the groundswell of opinion has gained momentum to such a degree that sometimes it seems as if the small minority has turned into the vast majority. Of course they tend to quieten down or disappear when Arsenal win trophies.

But the truth is that Wenger is probably his own worst enemy. He set incredible standards in those early years, sweeping all before him, his team playing the most incredible football, and it was always going to be difficult not to fall below that benchmark. Up until 2008, Arsenal had consistently challenged for trophies, even if they lost the 2006 Champions League final, lost the 2007 League Cup final to Chelsea and blew a five-point lead in the Premier League title race in late February 2008. Wenger had kept going close – but was making a habit of falling at the last hurdle. Having an all-conquering team of superstars one minute, then a team that always seemed to come up short the next was difficult for the fans.

Sadly for Wenger, fan unrest is not a new thing and Arsenal supporters, with the seemingly endless number of blogs and the huge interest on social media, whip themselves up into such a frenzy after every draw, let alone defeat. It has become a key facet of Wenger's reign because Arsenal charge extremely expensive ticket prices, they have a huge fan base accustomed to success and now they are struggling to revive those glory days.

The problem for Wenger is how he will be remembered in years to come and whether his remarkable legacy will be overshadowed by the apparent malaise of the second half of his reign. It is hard to imagine any manager at any top club being allowed to go nine years between trophies, and Wenger certainly wouldn't still be in a job had he not been so successful in the early part of his tenure. To a degree, he was living off his past achievements, but the hope must be that the future will see him recapture that golden period while serving up the wonderful football that was such a key part of Arsenal's early success.

That is the reason why Wenger is allowed to carry on. That, and of course, the fact that Arsenal are so consistent in finishing in the top four, which guarantees not just Champions League football but also the lucrative revenues it brings. But therein lies the other problem. Somewhere along the way, the lines seemed to get blurred as to what was most important: the football or the finance.

That Wenger is almost seen as more accountant than football manager infuriates supporters. But when he eventually looks back on his Arsenal career, no one can pretend that the fans – who once worshipped him – falling out of love with their favourite uncle won't be one of the most abiding memories of his reign.

Arsenal fans have occasionally gone too far. After Arsenal's 3-2 defeat at Stoke City in December 2014, a group of their fans chanted foul-mouthed abuse both at Wenger and his players. One of Wenger's closest friends insists that, no matter what the Frenchman said publicly, it really hurt and upset him. Similarly, when Arsenal lost at home to Aston Villa on the opening day of the 2013/14 season, the abuse was so loud and so personal that many in the dugout that day believe it was the worst that he has ever heard and, again, it really upset him.

It has gradually got worse. When whispers of discontent began in the 2008/09 season, one of the biggest fans' groups, Red Action, actually staged a march in support of Wenger on the final day of the season in May 2009, a game Arsenal duly won, beating Stoke 4-1.

Generally, Arsenal fans are quite a reverent, middle-class bunch, or the 'latte-sipping classes', to use a familiar nickname. And even when some of the more vociferous fans produced a banner calling for Wenger to go, it was done very politely: 'Arsene – thanks for the memories, now it's time to say goodbye.' You really can't fault such a courteous approach – unless, of course, it begins to seep into the players' confidence and affects them during the game.

One of Wenger's biggest critics, former *Daily Mirror* editor turned showbiz star Piers Morgan, has been respectful of Wenger – but claims he has stayed too long. As a staunch Arsenal fan, Morgan actually had a very good relationship with Wenger as they are both friendly with David Dein. When Arsenal won the Premier League title at White Hart Lane in 2004, Morgan was a guest of former Spurs chairman Sir Alan Sugar and he recalls a wonderful occasion in the boardroom:

When we won the league at White Hart Lane after a 2-2 draw, my dad, who is a lifelong Spurs fan, and I were in the boardroom as Alan Sugar's guests. Everybody left because we were all celebrating winning the league in their backyard and in walked

Wenger and Pat Rice and we were the only four people in the boardroom, ordered the most expensive bottle of wine that they had, and we sat there for an hour in one of Arsenal's greatest moments. I loved him then with a passion that I could rarely imagine having for any man alive.

I saw Pat Rice again recently – we were back in the Spurs boardroom after Arsenal won there in 2014 and we were laughing about it. It was great to see him because he'd been ill recently, but we had a wonderful time, drinking some wine, sharing an hour and talking about the glory that Wenger had brought to the club.

That's what it's like with all Arsenal fans. It feels a bit like you're cheating on your wife when you criticise Wenger because we all love him so much. But I'm just taking a much more pragmatic and ruthless view as to where the club needs to go and I've reached the conclusion after quite a number of years that we're not going to do it with him. It's heartbreaking. But it's fact.

Morgan sums up the feeling among many Arsenal fans. He is as passionate about Arsenal as he ever was when he was my first Fleet Street editor and, when he talks, he does so with regret because he still clearly likes Wenger, but believes the magic has gone.

It's nothing personal about Wenger. I come from a position where I think Arsenal should always be competing for the league. That's the ultimate yardstick for any supposed big club in Britain. The frustration is that it seems to me that the focus of Wenger's mind, the board and many fans, has drifted away from being competitive to win the league to trying to finish top four and qualifying for the Champions League. That's all we hear, again and again, is Wenger saying 18 years of Champions League football.

I don't give a stuff about Champions League football, I really don't. It would be different if we'd ever won it. But one final and our performance in it has been pretty woeful. The fact we qualify for a tournament we never come close to winning is not something that should be celebrated. Can you ever imagine Jose Mourinho or Sir Alex Ferguson boasting about qualifying for something they'd never won? I don't think so.

It seems to me that Wenger's mentality since coming to Arsenal was that of an absolute winner. He shook up the way English football did things, changed everything from diet to training, preparation, the way we played football.

But he was flattered by the fact that he inherited one of the great back fives of English football history. People forget this. He built his early rock around players he inherited. He inherited Bergkamp, Bould, Adams, Seaman, Dixon and Winterburn. You forget that. His early success – he did brilliantly to get Anelka – was founded on a rock that he inherited.

He bought great players – Henry, Vieira and Campbell. He got a reputation for turning round players who were underperforming and making them world-beaters. He also bought Overmars, Pires, who were already world-class players. There's a slight mythology about Wenger and the teams he built because he was fortunate to get this incredible defence, which was the bedrock of all his trophy-winning years.

Now, let's be perfectly fair and say that Wenger was, for eight years, one of the two or three greatest managers in Arsenal history ... He was also one of the greatest managers in Premier League history and won everything there was to win, apart from the Champions League.

But look at the way he won those trophies. He won them with tall, skilful, aggressive and powerful footballers. Look at what's happened in the last ten years. All of the Invincibles were shipped out within two years and he replaced them with smaller, lighter, physically less aggressive footballers. They had great ability, but they had less power to compete with Chelsea, Manchester City, teams with great powerful teams. Frankly, even struggling away to places like Stoke, who had big powerful players.

I got increasingly frustrated. I wrote a column for the *Mail on Sunday*, that I instantly wished I hadn't written, but we lost 3-0 away at Manchester City and I wrote a whole piece about how we had become this smaller, physically less imposing team and it was ruinous strategy and Wenger should perhaps consider going. I was ridiculed but if you go and read that column, really nothing has changed in the last seven or eight years ...

If you ask me what the real problem is then, anyone will tell you, it's that Wenger is incredibly indecisive when it comes to transfers and to buying players. David Dein would cut through that indecision and make big deals happen. He was the guy that brought Bergkamp. He acted quickly, understood how the market worked. The two of them were a bit like Lennon and McCartney. Together they would make sweet music and apart it's just not been the same.

Wenger has ... bought far too many mediocre players for big money. He's used endless excuses, notably the cost of the stadium when Manchester United were also developing their stadium, had American owners, had huge debts and similar problems to Arsenal. That didn't stop them from winning trophies ...

Everybody loves Wenger as a man. Everyone thinks he's erudite, intelligent, a smart guy, but that's part of the problem because it means he's able to talk his way out of a lot of tricky situations in a way that the fans accept and fall back in love with him over. I think you have to distance Wenger the man from

Wenger the manager ... Wenger the manager is simply not the manager that he was eight or nine years ago. For people to try to pretend that he is and to try to equate him to someone like Mourinho, I think they're living in cloud cuckoo-land ...

Arsenal fans have been guilty of mass sentimentality ruling their ruthless heads. If we want to get back to competing for the league, Champions League and serious trophies – and we've got the money to do it – then we have to be less sentimental. Wenger was a brilliant manager a decade ago. This guy is no longer a brilliant manager ...

Could you imagine Ferguson going ten years with one FA Cup? Mourinho going ten years with one FA Cup? Could you imagine even going five years? The longevity of the honeymoon period for Wenger is unprecedented. We've got the money, got the stadium and they have begun to spend money and it's still not good enough.

If I'd have been him, I'd have gone after the FA Cup in 2014 ... All the fans would have loved that moment to have been his send-off. The great manager, Arsene Wenger, left finally clutching silverware again, even if it was second-tier silverware, and we could then rebuild with a new manager. That would have been perfect for everyone.

For several years, Wenger dismissed any notion of fan unrest as something stoked up by the media, claiming in particular that it was because there was a group of loud fans near the press box. Time and again, he has been quite clear in his view that the media are to blame for any fan discontent.

'If our fans go the way the media want them to go we have no chance,' he snapped, when a few of us at London Colney quizzed him about whether the fans were turning. 'The people behind me and around the press box do not necessarily represent the majority of the fans. They are the ones you [journalists] hear the most but aren't necessarily the majority. They make your opinion maybe but they aren't necessarily the opinion [of the majority].'

It's difficult to agree with Wenger on this one. Less than a fortnight later, after Arsenal were thrashed 8-2 at Manchester United, *The Times* actually ran a leader column in support of Wenger. Leader columns are normally reserved for heads of state, not football managers. It was 293 words of some of the most glowing praise you are likely to read in a national newspaper:

'His brand of living within-your-means book-keeping is an example to all governments striving to cut spending without undermining the competitiveness of their economies. Arsene Wenger has won more trophies for Arsenal than any previous boss of the north London club. And Wenger's reward? To be booed and pilloried by Arsenal supporters.'

It was a remarkable piece and, as this extract shows, it reflects the admiration and respect in which Wenger is held within the media – not that he ever seems to notice. Radio presenter Adrian Durham, whose *Drive Time* show on talkSPORT features a light-hearted slot called the Daily Arsenal, regularly pokes fun at the media for lapping up everything he says. There are two sides to every story and the perception as to whether Wenger gets a fair, unfair or even generous press causes endless debate.

Wenger was honoured by the Football Writers' Association in 2007 at a glitzy ceremony at the Savoy. It is perhaps the case that he is admired more by the media than his own fans at times, which probably frustrates the supporters and is clearly not appreciated by the manager anyway.

Wenger, of course, doesn't see it like that. But Arsenal do drive a lot of media interest because they are a leading club, have been successful under Wenger, have moved to a new stadium and are still regarded as one of Europe's super powers.

More recently, Arsenal fans seem to have followed their manager's example and become rather obsessed with the club's balance sheet as well as their results on the pitch. They tend to take a great deal of interest in what Wenger spends, Arsenal's finances and the way their club is run. It never seemed to be like this in the 1970s and 1980s, although Arsenal did run a controversial bond scheme in the 1980s and early 1990s to try to raise funds to rebuild Highbury.

Wenger's own preoccupation with money and success related to finance seems to have rubbed off on the fans, making them more interested than most in what is happening on and off the pitch, particularly when it comes to judging their manager. One of the best-known supporters is Tim Payton, of the Arsenal Supporters' Trust, who is a lifelong fan, lives in the heart of north London and is often quoted on Wenger's troubles and where next for the club.

When we meet in a coffee shop, Payton is in typical mood – bristling with enthusiasm about the club while also struggling to hide his frustration with Wenger and his lack of spending:

> I think not spending has become something of an obsession. He sees himself as a modern-day Brian Clough or even Robin Hood. Taking money from the rich like a modern-day hero. There were 18 months when money was incredibly tight. But after they sold Emmanuel Adebayor and Kolo Toure there was always more money available than actually spent.
>
> It's a myth that the Emirates has held him back financially. It hasn't. What's changed has been the arrival of Chelsea and Manchester City and rich owners. If Arsenal had stayed at Highbury, they'd have less money to spend and would be competing on the same level financially as a Tottenham or Liverpool, for example.
>
> Arsenal also pay big wages. Ozil on £200,000 a week, Sanchez

on £140,000 and, to keep on the socialist structure, you've got the likes of [Calum] Chambers earning around £25,000 a week, with the incentive of earning more as he progresses.

Payton also believes the second half of Wenger's reign has sullied the achievements of his early days.

If he'd left in 2006 then he'd be regarded as Arsenal's greatest ever manager. But because of what happened after that, I think Herbert Chapman is Arsenal's greatest manager. What happened later on has tarnished what he achieved in the early days.

What happened in the boardroom, David Dein going, Danny Fiszman sadly dying, has changed things so much and meant that the football infrastructure has changed so much. When Wenger arrived, he changed the game so much and the set-up. He arrived with ground-breaking techniques and technology. But now Sam Allardyce is using more science and technology. Wenger still uses Boro Primorac, who arrived with him in 1996; he didn't want to lose Pat Rice, and I really think it's an Arsene Wenger of two eras.

The fans and the way he is viewed is ever so volatile. If I look at things in December 2014, I think the majority view is that it's time for a change. But the majority view is probably split in half between putting banners up, protests and strong words in social media. But the other side of the split is that Wenger has done so much for the club that, while they'd like him to go, they would like a bloodless coup so they can say: 'Thanks very much, but time to go,' and it would all end happily ever after.

Payton, who keeps a close eye on the club's finances, is also adamant that the bigger issue for Arsenal in the second half of Wenger's reign was the emergence of big-spending Chelsea and

Manchester City rather than Arsenal not having money available. In fact, he makes the point that Wenger had more to spend than he chose to.

The most difficult time for the club was when they were raising the funds, persuading the banks to lend to them. A player could only come in if another went out. You might remember the debate over Ashley Cole and the way he was lost over £5,000 a week. It became a moral dispute over who should pay his wages. Money was tight as well and they were looking at every penny.

Then Roman Abramovich turned up and David Dein said that he had arrived, parked his tanks on his lawn and was firing £50 notes. That then prompted David Dein to go and find his own billionaire. He ended up finding two but, despite that, Arsenal had new competition and not the billionaire owner that David Dein envisaged.

Arsene Wenger did become obsessed with not spending money. During the Invincibles season, they had the biggest wage budget, so he was not against spending money. But there's a rule in football which says the highest wage bill wins the title. That is normally always the case.

It's certainly true that, for five or six years, Arsene Wenger has not spent all the money available to him. The best example is when it was widely known that Luis Suarez was available – in fact, it was even briefed by Liverpool – that Arsenal could only persuade Wenger to bid £40,000,001. He tried to even save himself £1 million when trying to sign Mark Schwarzer. In the summer of 2014, they had plenty of money left in the bank but still started the season with six defenders ...

If Wenger goes away, makes a complete split, then comes back he will get a rapturous reception; the fans will welcome him back for the good times, the success and the football he played. The man has contributed so much to football. It's a shame in many ways – a bit like in politics, which is his other great passion – that they tend to get pushed out of office ...

I'm not sure whether any other club in world football would ... be as patient as Arsenal fans. You can't tell me that if he were appointed in 2006, he would still be manager now. He's stayed in charge because of what he achieved in his first era of success. It shows the respect the fans have for him. It's a quiet crowd, a much more corporate crowd now ...

The point is that Arsene Wenger is not failing. He's just not succeeding. But he's performing to his budget and he does just enough to stay in a job. He's probably got his own personal standards. Finishing top four is his bread and butter. If he had one outstanding trophy it would be the Champions League. Even in his successful era, you can criticise him for not actually achieving more with the team.

The club throws open the doors to its Annual General Meeting, which allows the chance to gain an insight not just into those on the board, but also into Wenger's behaviour. He often stays behind at the end of the meeting to sign autographs, shake hands and pose for selfies. It's hard to imagine many other clubs or managers being so open and friendly. He recognises not only the well-heeled executive punters, but also addresses a few long-standing supporters on a first-name basis.

But woe betide any fan who dares to criticise individual players. Wenger just won't tolerate it. Back in May 2009, he snapped and had a row at a supporters' meeting after a fan described one of his poorer signings, Mikael Silvestre, as 'geriatric'. Wenger's explanation for why he got so upset was enlightening about his attitude towards supporters.

There are two things in our job. Criticism I accept with respect. Disrespect, I don't accept and I don't respect. Maybe one day you will have worked 25 years in the media and people will claim you don't understand anything in your job. Maybe they will be right, but you have to distance yourself from that.

I accept everyone's opinion, but what was not enjoyable in that meeting was that it was disrespectful to some players and I don't accept that. No matter even if you lose 38 games on the trot I won't accept that.

You have never heard me complain about the money that was available. But I do not accept that people think I am stupid enough to have £100 million at my disposal and just put it in the bank because I am afraid to spend that. I do with what I have as well as I can and I do not complain. But if I tell you I have £250 million to spend, every player I call will cost three times more.

Wenger's stance is essentially that fans don't have the right to question his judgement, because they are not in possession of all the facts. He was annoyed when the Arsenal fans chanted: 'You don't know what you're doing' after he replaced Alex Oxlade-Chamberlain with Andrey Arshavin in January 2012 and also when he took off Olivier Giroud at Aston Villa in November 2012.

When the jibe was put to him after that Villa game, Wenger fired back: 'I've been lucky. I've only managed 1,600 games and in 200 matches in the Champions League.'

He can be similarly touchy when fans start questioning his ability in the transfer market. In the summer of 2013, when Arsenal were struggling to get any deals done while Tottenham were doing a series of transfers, Wenger was asked whether he could understand the frustration of his own fans. 'Honestly!' exhaled Wenger. The truth was that Tottenham's mammoth £100 million-plus spending spree did not get them above Arsenal that season.

When questioned ahead of Arsenal's Champions League qualifier with Fenerbahce in August 2013, and hot on the heels of their 3-1 home defeat to Villa, Wenger didn't take kindly to the suggestion that his failure to make a significant signing in the transfer window represented poor planning.

'I could get lessons on how to put on training sessions from everybody at the moment,' said Wenger. 'I live in a public job, where there are opinions of everybody. I do my job with full commitment to what I believe is important for the club and the team and prepare for the next game.

'What is important in football is to go out and see a good football game. All that other stuff is good for the newspapers, but it is not real football. What is real football is the quality of the game and for me that is always the most important.'

Within a few days, the club had signed German international Mesut Ozil from Real Madrid for a club record fee of over £42 million. It was the sort of landmark signing the fans had been waiting for, and it gave out the message that the ambition had returned, after a period when Arsenal had appeared to be a selling club. In 2013/14 the quest for another trophy would finally succeed.

CHAPTER 14

A NEW DAWN

'THE BEST MOMENTS ARE every important game you win and the worst moment is every defeat, basically, because I experience every defeat like a death. Defeat has to hurt you very much to survive in this job because you learn a lot about yourself. Every defeat is terrible in our job.' Arsene Wenger was about to enter a new era in the summer of 2013 but, as he made clear when he did a sit-down interview on Arsenal's pre-season tour of Asia, the pain of defeat and self-inflicted pressures of the job never get any easier.

The 2013/14 season was a real mixture for Wenger. It culminated in the FA Cup success and saw him pass the remarkable milestone of managing 1,000 games for Arsenal, but also produced some of the worst and most humiliating defeats of his entire Arsenal managerial career.

It is difficult to balance such starkly contrasting highs and lows. Arsenal were top of the Premier League for 128 days – more than any of their title rivals – and yet conceded five at Liverpool, six at

Chelsea and six at Manchester City. Those heavy defeats were probably the reason why the media never really got swept along by Arsenal as serious contenders, much to Wenger's frustration, although he could see why so many people doubted Arsenal's challenge. 'We haven't won the title since 2004 and last year we were not in contention, so I can understand that completely. It's down to us to create that belief for our performances, we can only do that.'

There can be no doubt that, more than anything else, from the heady days of the Invincibles, Arsenal's level of quality had dropped over the following nine years, many of the signings had been bargains, gambles and second rate, or youngsters who had taken their time to blossom, unlike the signings that had been so inspirational in the past.

But now things were changing. In fact, everything was supposed to change from the day Arsenal's chief executive Ivan Gazidis invited a few journalists into the Arsenal boardroom to outline the club's plans and make it very clear that there was big money to spend. As Gazidis said, Arsenal now had the funds to compete with Europe's elite.

It was a bright, sunny day on Wednesday 5 June 2013, even if the wood panelling in the boardroom – the old decor and furniture from Highbury having been transported to the new offices – at Highbury House in the new stadium always tends to make it seem very dark.

Gazidis is a really engaging, bright man who, it seems, has been dismissed by some as not knowing about football because he talks with an American accent. That's such a lazy English mistake. An Oxford University double football Blue, Gazidis grew up in Manchester from the age of four but spent much of his football life working for the MLS in the United States. He is incredibly knowl-edgeable and interesting on football, players, philosophy and the politics and future of our national sport. Unlike many in the game, he's a genuinely nice man – no side, no agenda, always friendly, polite and considerate. He is also generally quite discreet and doesn't give too many press interviews, so when he invites a few journalists into the boardroom, you can bet he's got something important to say.

Gazidis spoke for nearly an hour. He always gives lengthy and informed answers, thinking carefully about what he says in every sentence, and sometimes, after an interview, you will have to transcribe it, read it back carefully and then pick out the message. However, on this occasion, although there were more than 5,000 words of transcription, the message was really quite simple: this is a new dawn for Arsenal, we've got serious money to spend – and we're ready to spend it.

It was the culmination of new and upcoming commercial deals, the stadium finances being ahead of schedule and Arsenal, proud to be self-sufficient and self-financing, were ready to show that success can be achieved – and, ultimately, bought – without a sugar daddy. Gazidis said:

We want to be a club that is competing at the very top end of the game and that means competing to win the Premier League and competing to win the Champions League. On that basis, we are not where we want to be yet.

We're going to be emerging into the new period in our development, a very exciting period, I think, which will mean if we think we can get the right value and a player is really special and Arsene believes in it, we can make some exciting moves, and I think our fans will be pleased over the next couple of years to see the club making some progressive steps.

I think fans want to see a real form of progression. I think they want to see good players being added to the team. The fact is, this year we are beginning to see something for which we have been planning for some time, which is the escalation in our financial firepower. And that's going to happen partly into next season – it's partway available now in the summer but the following season as well. It's a progression over the next two seasons. It's quite significant for the club.

Gazidis couldn't have been more upbeat, more direct and more determined in getting his vision across. Arsenal had a new 'escalation in financial firepower' and Wenger was the man to spend it. The immediate issue for the newspapers, of course, was to find out who Arsenal were planning to spend it on.

Some columnists took their turn to criticise Gazidis for going public on Arsenal's new-found wealth. After all, wouldn't that start pushing the prices up on transfers? As one member of staff, a regular filmgoer, said: 'The first rule of Fight Club is don't talk about Fight Club.'

Sure enough, Wenger was quite animated when talking to a confidant and complained that it would force prices up and make deals more difficult. He didn't think the club should be so open with the press.

So, why did Gazidis do it? Well, perhaps because he felt there should be no grey areas, excuses or false accusations. Arsenal had money, wanted to compete and the club actively wanted Wenger to be able to spend it on big players.

The other interesting aspect of Gazidis's message was that there had been money in the past, but it depended on how much Wenger wanted a particular player. And that's the issue. It's clear from what Gazidis said that the board felt there hadn't been a huge amount of money available in the past and, by the same token, Wenger had often decided against going to them to ask for a 'critical player' at an 'extra special price'.

After buying Sylvain Wiltord for £12 million in 2000, Arsenal had bought the likes of Andrey Arshavin, Alex Oxlade-Chamberlain, Samir Nasri and Santi Cazorla for similar fees in the period up to the summer of 2013, with Arshavin remaining a club record buy at £15 million – a sum matched or beaten by nine other clubs in the Premier League. Wenger's spending graph had flat-lined even though, by Gazidis's admission, there was money available for a special case.

So perhaps – either consciously or subconsciously – Gazidis was giving a nudge to Wenger, urging him to start spending money and also making it crystal clear to supporters that there was money in the coffers. As it transpired, Gazidis's interview definitely set the agenda for the summer and shaped the Arsenal narrative as they then flirted with signing Luis Suarez, Gonzalo Higuain and even Wayne Rooney.

Arsenal thought they had a deal for Higuain – and then the price went up. Wenger is very demanding when it comes to hon-esty on transfers. It's difficult to work out whether the new fee was down to Real Madrid or, more likely, third parties suddenly becoming involved and demanding their share of the pie. Arsenal steadfastly refused to pay the extra and Wenger saw it as a point of principle, so the player moved to Napoli.

Wenger has become embroiled in a few agent disputes over the years, none more so than with Samir Nasri's transfer when the deal was held up because Arsenal – and, in particular, Wenger – refused to meet Nasri's agent fees. Eventually, the £24 million deal went through, with Nasri's agent fees still reported as totalling around £2 million. The hangers-on were demanding a huge slice of the Higuain deal and, while that dragged on, Arsenal switched targets and became embroiled in one of the most ugly transfer sagas in Premier League history.

Arsenal had been made aware by the end of the 2012/13

season that there might be a chance of Luis Suarez, Liverpool's brilliant Uruguayan striker, becoming available because the Merseyside club had not reached the Champions League and Suarez wanted a fresh challenge at a club that could win trophies. Also, he had become involved in a string of controversies, from biting Chelsea defender Branislav Ivanovic to an FA ban after being found guilty of racist abuse towards Manchester United fullback Patrice Evra.

Suarez was, as Arsenal saw it, 'damaged goods' and therefore his price should reflect his off-the-field problems, no matter how brilliant he was on it. Liverpool, meanwhile, had almost certainly seen Gazidis's comments and had no doubt that Arsenal could afford top dollar. But Suarez and his agent Pere Guardiola were driving the move, and Liverpool were aware they might lose him.

First came a phone call to Liverpool and a fee of £30 million was mentioned. It was only two-and-a-half years since Suarez had joined Liverpool for £22 million, so it was quickly dismissed. Arsenal insist it was only a 'conversation' between the clubs. Liverpool say it was an offer and one that was rejected out of hand. Whatever the precise nature of the contact, news of it leaked out and Liverpool took a strong stance that they were not selling.

The clamour for Arsenal to sign a big name was overwhelming and was the topic of conversation when the club touched down in Jakarta on 12 July 2013 for the start of their Asia tour. As Wenger sat in the airport lounge in the sweltering Indonesian heat, the Frenchman looked slightly uncomfortable talking about transfers, his future and Arsenal's finances. Gazidis was sitting next to him at a table and four journalists were firing questions from the other side.

We immediately asked about Suarez. It was the burning issue. 'At the moment I cannot give you any names because you work on many different cases and it's very difficult. It could damage our chances if we say something,' said Wenger.

But are Suarez, Rooney and Higuain realistic targets?

'They are all realistic targets quality-wise, not all of them are available to join us,' said Wenger. 'First of all, all those players are under contract and it is the club that decides their contract who decides if they can go and after, if they go, if they can join us.

'We have better financial resources than the years before and, financially, resources we have created ourselves. That is massively important to us. We will see what we can do until the end of the transfer period and certainly before the new season starts. That's what we are working on at the moment. The fans, the players and everybody is reassured by big names always. But what is important is that we don't need numbers, we need quality.'

Throughout that tour, Suarez dominated conversations – from post-match interviews with Wenger to publicity events with players. Suarez was the only topic. Arsenal, renowned under Wenger for being cautious with money and losing their big players, were now throwing caution to the wind and were about to try to sign one of their mains rivals' biggest players.

As the tour continued, the players were also becoming anxious to find out whether the club – with the clock ticking in the transfer window and it being the best part of two months since Gazidis's press briefing – could in fact deliver a big signing. One player even sent a text asking: 'Are we really going to sign someone?' Doubts were creeping in from all angles.

Having flown straight from the game in Jakarta to Vietnam, Arsenal hosted another press conference at their luxury hotel in Hanoi. Money was the topic that also dominated a discussion with Mikel Arteta, an eloquent and deep-thinking player who is surely destined to be a manager one day. He said:

The club have said they are going to be very ambitious in the market and have got the financial resources to get big players. I think it's about time. When you compare us to the other top English clubs and the money they have paid, we are very far apart. The value of this club is the class and what it means is very difficult to match. There has never been a tradition at Arsenal to pay crazy, crazy money.

But now, financially, they are very strong, so maybe we will be more aggressive in the transfer market. I am excited. They made it public that they are going to go big. The sort of players they have been linked with makes me happy.

I believe we can be contenders again but it also creates a genuine atmosphere for the fans and they need that because we haven't won trophies in the last years. It will be unbelievable to win trophies. We really enjoy playing with this club, so imagine if we are able to win trophies. I don't think we're that far away. The fact that we haven't won it for eight years makes it harder mentally to believe. But that's what we need to do.

The problem with this saga was that, while Arsenal were trying to pull off the biggest deal in their history, they weren't doing any others. Wenger was adamant, and said so in conversation, that his squad was unified, together, and he didn't want a raft of new signings to upset the dressing room. There was a method and reasoning behind his decision to keep a small, tight squad. The only player he really wanted was a star striker.

As the tour rolled on to Japan, it became increasingly obvious that Arsenal were about to make a new bid for Suarez. With the time difference a major factor, I filed a story saying Arsenal had bid £40 million. By the time I woke up in the middle of the night English time, I could see that many back pages had gone with a similar story: Arsenal had bid £40,000,001. It became the most notorious transfer bid of all time. And it quickly alienated Liverpool, prompting their owner, John W. Henry, to tweet: 'What are they smoking at the Emirates?'

Arsenal made the offer during a telephone conversation between Gazidis and Liverpool's managing director, Ian Ayre. In retrospect, it was a mistake on Arsenal's part, but if you look at the reasoning then you begin to understand. Some believed that Wenger, renowned for his conservative transfer valuations, did not want to bid more than £40 million. Furthermore, Arsenal had been told quite categorically that there was a buy-out clause in Suarez's contract, which Henry himself, in March 2014, had confirmed publicly.

But who fed Arsenal the information about what it was? The suspicion of many was that it had to have come from the Suarez camp, and that it was an indication of the player's determination to leave. But Liverpool sat tight, refusing to budge, while Arsenal expected, perhaps naively, for the clause to be activated immediately and, if Liverpool didn't oblige, that Suarez would force the issue.

Having given three interviews at the end of the season, in which he suggested he was 'uncomfortable' in England, and keen to go to Real Madrid, Suarez then stated in interviews at the beginning of August that Liverpool had agreed he could leave them if they didn't qualify for the Champions League, and withdrew from the squad for a pre-season tour.

At this point, Arsenal were absolutely convinced that it was only a matter of time before Suarez became an Arsenal player. After all, in the past they had seen what happened when big players had left them when the club had wanted to keep them, so that perhaps assuaged any sense of guilt they may have felt over the way they were conducting the transfer.

Arsenal stayed quiet publicly and much of the information was gleaned from sources in and around the deal rather than from the club. It was largely the same for Liverpool, other than the fact that Brendan Rodgers had spoken about Arsenal's bid during the course of his club's pre-season tour. 'There's been a lot of speculation over the course of the close season, but the reality is that he's a player who is very much valued at Liverpool,' said Rodgers. 'And unless there's any sort of offer that comes in that's anywhere near his value, there's nothing to consider. We haven't had that.'

Asked what that value was, Rodgers said: 'I didn't say we would sell him. I said that every player has a value and a worth. Doesn't mean you've got to sell them.'

It was clear from what Rodgers said, that Liverpool weren't ruling out selling Suarez, but it was about the price. If Arsenal had gone to £45 million or even £50 million, there was a feeling that the deal would have been done. After Arsenal's last game in Asia, a couple of us almost pinned Wenger up against a wall to try to get him to talk about Suarez and the £40,000,001 bid.

'I don't know who gave you that information,' said Wenger. When we replied it was Brendan Rodgers, Wenger smiled: 'He talks a lot.'

As the situation dragged on, it got to the point where it became clear Arsenal were not going to get their man. Yet, this was against a backdrop of Arsenal publicly declaring that they had a lot of money to spend. The questions were becoming more frequent and Wenger was getting more impatient, a situation not helped by Arsenal's opening-day defeat to Villa and the fans' 'Spend, Spend, Spend' banners. No wonder he was becoming frustrated: they had the money but were actually struggling to spend it, and their only deal as the window neared closure was signing Mathieu Flamini on a free transfer.

Tensions were becoming increasingly high in the closing days as Arsenal enquired about Schalke's emerging German young-ster, Julian Draxler, but the price was deemed too high. They wanted £40 million for him and that didn't sit easily with Wenger. But, elsewhere, a plan was being put into place for Arsenal to pull off their biggest and most audacious transfer of all time.

Arsenal are renowned for trying to keep their transfer business quiet. We knew about the interest in Mesut Ozil with about ten days to go in the transfer window. Arsenal, like a number of clubs, had been sounded out by Real Madrid, who were willing to do business on either Ozil, Karim Benzema or Angel Di Maria to try to balance the books so that they could sign Gareth Bale from Tottenham. But the behind-the-scenes operation to land Ozil was real cloak-and-dagger stuff, like something out of a James Bond film. And it worked perfectly.

Ozil's representatives had begun touting him around and Arsenal had bitten. Their trump card was Gazidis, who knew Real Madrid director general Jose Angel Sanchez from his time working in the MLS, when the Spanish club tried to market themselves in the US. In reality, the first seeds of the Ozil deal were sown in June, when Gazidis made an approach to his contact at Real Madrid. Ozil's name was circulated in mid-August. While other big clubs like Manchester United hesitated, Arsenal pounced. Their interest was made known.

The trouble was that Real Madrid were trying to tie up a deal for Gareth Bale, and they didn't want to let a big name go until they had recruited the Spurs man. Tottenham didn't want to sell Bale and were happy to let it drag on until the last minute, because it was obvious what was going to happen. If Real Madrid signed Bale they would need to sell and offload to help balance the books. Having already signed up numerous players, Tottenham chairman Daniel Levy wanted to leave it so late that Real Madrid wouldn't have time to sell one of their players to a Premier League rival – especially not Arsenal. However, Arsenal went undercover, fooled Tottenham into thinking the Ozil deal was off and then Spurs sanctioned the world record signing of Bale.

Arsenal made renewed contact as late as Thursday 29 August and the wheels began to turn. To complete such a big transfer in the space of three days is very unusual. They got in touch with Mesut Ozil – with the permission of Real Madrid – through his father Mustafa, who also worked as his agent. Wenger called Ozil, spoke to him in German and charmed him. He was confident by the end of the call that Ozil wanted to come to Arsenal.

Then, on the Saturday, Gazidis made a whistle-stop trip to Madrid while Dick Law, Arsenal's transfer fixer and a man who had been thrust into the limelight as a figure of fun by Twitter during the club's quiet summer of transfer inactivity, flew to Munich to see the Ozil family, which was also where the player was due to join up with the German national squad.

On the Sunday morning, Law flew back to London to be at the game against Spurs. The last thing he wanted to do was to arouse suspicion from Levy or his technical director, Franco Baldini, that Arsenal were about to do a deal. Levy and Baldini enjoyed Arsenal's hospitality in the boardroom, sat in the directors' box, saw Arsenal grind out a 1-0 win against their expensively assembled signings and still thought nothing was going on. Shortly after the game was over, and with Spurs believing Arsenal didn't have a deal on the go, the Bale transfer was announced.

Meanwhile, Law had left the Emirates, was whisked back to Munich on a private plane and the £42 million signing of Mesut Ozil was concluded within 24 hours. To get the deal done quickly, Ozil underwent a medical in Munich, which was overseen by German national team doctor, Dr Hans-Wilhelm Muller-Wohlfahrt, and Arsenal's doctor, Gary O'Driscoll, who also flew over.

Tottenham had sold Bale and, in doing so, allowed Arsenal to sign Ozil. Tottenham chairman Levy was furious, while privately Baldini admired Arsenal's amazing transfer coup. From a position of despair and ridicule, Arsenal had beaten Tottenham, outfoxed them in the transfer market and signed a world-class player who would completely transform the mood and expectations of the fans.

There is no doubt that Ozil would not have joined Arsenal had it not been for Wenger. It reinstated the feel-good factor around Wenger among most fans, but the Arsenal manager acknowledged that tensions had run high in the closing days – if not hours – of the transfer window.

'To say it was all under control is a bit exaggerated because not a lot was under control,' said Wenger. 'But I told you two or three days before, I looked a bit lonely when I said I was optimistic but in the end it happened. I thought we had a chance to do it, a small one, but we worked very hard on it until the end.

'It was very complicated in the end because the timing was short, but on Sunday when I came to the Tottenham game, just at two o'clock I thought we will manage to do it. Before the game I knew we were 90 per cent there.'

Wenger insisted it did not jar with him to spend so much money:

Not at all. There are two things that are completely different. One, I fight for the teams to spend the money they had made and not the money they have artificially earned. Once they have made that money I am happy to spend it. As you know as well, what is very important for us is to find world-class players. There are not plenty around.

I think it was linked with the Bale transfer. I don't know exactly what happened inside the club in Madrid. Was it down to financial reasons? Was it down to the fact that when they bought Bale they had Isco and they had to let somebody go? I was surprised [they let him go], yes.

When Mesut went to Real, we were in touch. Even then I wanted to get him to Arsenal, but it didn't work back then. That was the start of our relationship. Now the second time it worked. I think the first contact really helped.

We had to go through some years when I signed a long-term contract where we had some restricted financial potential. And the target was to stay in the Champions League in this period and we managed to do it. We are now in a strong position financially.

Ozil, a third generation Turkish-German, was described during negotiations as humble and very keen to learn, which is what made him particularly keen to work with Wenger:

The coach is a world-class manager – he's demonstrated that for years. A lot of players have developed under his guidance in the past and that's why I decided to join Arsenal. I want to improve myself further and I'm looking forward to the style of play. Arsenal are well known for the strength of their technical game and their desire to play attacking football. I think I will fit perfectly into that. That's why I chose to sign for the club.

The most important thing is that the manager has given me his trust. I want to show my potential and have fun on the pitch. I think that I can help the team through my performances. I spoke to the manager a lot on the phone and he presented his vision and what he thinks about me. That convinced me and that's why I am now at Arsenal.

The manager always wants to play attractive and attacking

football. I think I fit into that because I enjoy playing quickly – that 'one-touch football'. I'm happy to be part of the club and I hope I can help the team.

Ozil joined Arsenal as a world-class superstar and it certainly ranks as the biggest statement Wenger and Arsenal have made in the transfer market. Ozil's arrival also helped give them lift-off in the title race as, after that opening-day blip, Arsenal quickly clicked into gear, led the way for much of the season and suddenly Wenger looked in great shape again.

On Friday 20 September 2013, the *Daily Telegraph*'s Jeremy Wilson and I met Arsenal's majority shareholder Stan Kroenke in a plush London hotel. He came straight from the hotel gym, still perspiring from his workout, to meet us. Although in his sixties, he works out most days and is incredibly fit. Kroenke spoke passionately about his love of Arsenal, England and, most instructive of all, Arsene Wenger. If you spend any amount of time with Kroenke, it will leave you utterly convinced that Wenger will be in charge until he decides otherwise. But it is also clear that Kroenke has a burning ambition to win.

Part of the problem of being involved [with a football club] is that you get drawn so much into it – it can ruin your day, ruin your weekend and it sticks with you. You try to be more even about it; I take my mother's advice and try to strike a good balance.

There would be nothing cooler, I've never experienced it over here, to win the championship of the Premier League. Some of my American cohorts have experienced that and we haven't been able to. I'm not getting any younger. It's something I would like to achieve.

I really enjoy Arsene. Very smart, very intelligent man, as we all know ... He was trained in economics, my undergraduate study was in economics. I enjoy talking with him; he is a very interesting guy. He has an absolute view on how he runs that team and the club. Look, he has earned that right. Don't look for me to interfere with that. I have learned over the years that sometimes owners try to do that and it is not so good. He knows how we feel, what our philosophy is, what we want to do and I feel like we are totally aligned. I think he wants to do it the exact same way as we do.

I don't want to say something about Arsene that is not the way he feels but, to me, I think he seems to love what he does. But that's Arsene's decision. He knows he has our support, there's no one I feel more strongly about and I think he is doing a great job.

I had my son and a bunch of his friends at the training ground last year. A couple of them are NBA players and were over here with us for the Olympics. We were standing out in the rain watching. Arsene is out there all the time. This was going on for several hours. It rained like hell, lightning.

I was getting worried about players getting hit by lightning and Arsene was out in the middle of it. He's up there, coaching them every day. You've got to love that or you can't do it. That's a passion.

There was definitely a change in mood in the 2013/14 season, which was probably fuelled by a number of factors. They had won at Bayern Munich the previous season, which was the catalyst for them going on a great run and pipping their rivals Tottenham into fourth place on the final day of the season. Then came the signing of Ozil, plus the togetherness in the dressing room. It gave Arsenal a platform and a renewed sense of belief and direction under Wenger.

The other point was that, for the first time in some years, there was tranquillity and harmony behind the scenes. Arsenal's biggest shareholder Kroenke was in control, the boardroom struggles and battle for ownership were no longer an issue for Arsenal or for Wenger. The club was pulling in the same direction; there was financial security and a sense that Arsenal were moving in the right direction on and off the pitch. In short, the future was looking good after a long period of uncertainty.

In the autumn of 2013, with Arsenal flying high, Wenger went even further as he set out his philosophy and vision for Arsenal at the club's AGM – it was as close as he's ever come to setting out his template for how to build a team:

We have a huge ambition to win this league again and that is the target of the season, but I still believe our policy has to be based on three different levels and we want to continue that with success.

I don't think without that we will have success. The first level is, of course, continue to defend our style of play, our philosophy of play and our values. That can only be done by developing our own players and the core of our team has to come from the development inside our club. That is why we make huge investments again in our youth policy. I believe that has to be the core and the strength of our club. If you go today through our squad, for example, we have completely or partially educated Szczesny, Jenkinson, Gibbs, Wilshere, Ramsey, Chamberlain, Gnabry – all these players who have made their debut in the Premier League with us. They know how we want to play, they know how we want to behave, and they bring their qualities and these values to the team.

The second level of the development of our club has to be based on the intelligence of our eye. That means players who are unknown and who can become big players here, through our connections, the quality of our scouting, through the quality of what we have seen in them and how they could develop. For example, Koscielny has come here, nobody knew him; today he is an international with France. Giroud has come here, not many people knew him and he has now become an international player with France. Many people have come here and through the quality of our coaching and our development have become international players. They can complete the part of the players that develop inside from the youth level to the top level.

Then, the third part of our development and ambition is to scout and buy recognised world-class players. This season, for example, we have bought Ozil. You don't need any scout to buy Ozil. You just need money! I am quite happy that we have shown to you that we are not scared to spend money when we think the players have the quality and we have the funds available to do it.

Wenger had a new bullishness, a belief that Arsenal could win the league and take their big opportunity after making a flying start, which made the season feel like the start of a new era for the club and their manager. But Arsenal didn't take their opportunity and, to make matters worse, Wenger's 1,000th game in charge was marked by a 6-0 thrashing at the hands of Chelsea and his great rival Jose Mourinho.

Although the 5-1 defeat at Liverpool in February 2014 wasn't their heaviest, it probably marked the turning point of Arsenal's season. It stripped away their belief and they never regained their title momentum. And, adding insult to injury, one fan took pictures of Wenger falling flat on his back at Lime Street station as Arsenal arrived to take the train home. Even *Match of the Day* showed the pictures as Gary Lineker described it as 'one to forget', while Alan Shearer chuckled in the background.

It seemed so cruel that a few of us felt compelled to apologise to him when we next saw him for the way the media – including our own – had seized upon the humiliating pictures. 'It was painful but I was more worried about the defeat,' he said with a rather forced grin.

Arsenal had been blitzed at Manchester City on a Saturday lunchtime kick-off, they were thrashed at Liverpool in another 12.45pm kick-off and so, bearing in mind the game at Chelsea kicked off at the same time on Saturday 22 March 2014, maybe Arsenal should have put the 1,000th-game celebrations on ice. All week in the build-up there had been pieces in the papers, on radio and TV about Wenger's landmark game. Even his old enemy, Sir Alex Ferguson, sent a written tribute:

Having also reached the same milestone at one club, I cannot emphasise enough the level of dedication, resilience as well as sacrifice required and for that I have the utmost admiration. Over the years we enjoyed some fantastic battles and you could say we had survived together and respected each other's efforts to play good football. I always enjoy watching Arsene's sides – Arsenal play the right way.

Playing against them always presented special challenges that I burned many hours over the years thinking about. He has always been a conscientious member of our trade who makes it his business to help other managers. Perhaps the biggest compliment I could give Arsene is that I could never be anything other than competitive with my rival for 17 years.

It was a warm and genuine tribute which made Wenger smile when he was asked about it, probably recalling some of those battles down the years before friendship was declared.

On a glorious sunny morning at London Colney, Wenger was

presented with a golden cannon by chairman Sir Chips Keswick in the training ground car park. Sir Chips congratulated Wenger on '1,000 years in charge'. Wenger immediately picked up on the error and said that the 1,000 matches had made him 'look 1,000 years old!'

Wenger seemed to enjoy the press conference more than usual that morning. It was the biggest story of the day and the papers had sent their main football correspondents and chief sports writers. Inevitably, the first question was about the best and worst moments of his career.

'There have been many,' laughed Wenger. 'I cannot classify the moments of happiness and of sadness, but what is for sure is that every defeat is a scar in your heart that you never forget. The happiness you forget quickly because you find it normal because that's what you work for. Unfortunately, there is a lot of suffering as well in 1,000 games and what is for sure is what you want is the next moment of happiness. You're always expecting the next game and the next game hopefully will be a moment of happiness.'

All the while, the whole 'will he, won't he' debate was raging about whether Wenger would sign a new contract and commit himself as he had been promising to do for months. So, how far into the next thousand games would he go?

'I am an idealist but not a fool, not crazy. I am at the stage of my career where I am extremely passionate, maybe more than ever, to do well for this club. But I have to accept that the next thousand will be difficult.

'The game itself has become, maybe, more physical, faster, quicker, but especially the environment has changed and the pressures. The importance of football has become bigger, the comments on every single event that happens in football has been multiplied. The pressure of the environment is, of course, bigger because we live in a society where we have more opinions, and maybe inside the club today you need to be stronger to resist all that than when I arrived.'

It was also pointed out that it had been 502 games since Wenger last won a trophy, which could have proved irritating. Nothing, however, was going to spoil this particular press conference.

'I can take a distance with that, if winning a trophy is winning the League Cup and finish 12th in the league ...,' said Wenger before trailing off, making the point that Arsenal have remained consistent and finishing in the top four is more important to him than the League Cup. He continued:

I think the most important thing for the quality of the club, of the management of the club, is the consistency of the achievement. After the trophies come and go, but I believe you see the quality of the management in the consistency of their achievement. If you finish one year first and the second year 12th, I don't believe that ... the real quality of management is linked with consistency.

Of course, we want to win trophies, but I think if you look well at the consistency that we have shown in the last 15 or 17 years, and you compare with all other clubs, that is the most difficult thing to achieve. In individual finals it's great players who win you the games, and we have great players, so I'm confident we can win trophies.

But the competition is at the higher level. Look, there's Man United, they suffer as well. Man City, Chelsea, Liverpool, Arsenal, Tottenham, who invested over £100 million, it is difficult. It's certainly more difficult to win. What is important is that with nine games to go we are in the position where we can win.

What is fantastic and difficult in our job is that it is very fragile. Bad decisions can take you down quickly. What people sometimes don't understand is you can go down, you can drop after one decision. Of course, I don't think we are in that position but for years you had to be careful.

And, more tellingly perhaps, Wenger was even clearer when he was asked about what he was most proud of: 'The consistency of our results across 18 years, which is extraordinarily difficult. I'm also very proud of the fact that we have been united within the club, even during difficult times. Also, I think this club has had a positive influence on the lives of a lot of people, especially a lot of players. I am very proud of that because a manager is above all an educator, who has to have a positive influence on people.'

Perhaps surprisingly, Mourinho made no mention of Wenger's milestone in his programme notes when Chelsea hosted Arsenal the following day, which just about sums up the relationship between the two managers. As Wenger went to sit down in his dugout, he managed a handshake but also a look of contempt for Mourinho.

In the stands, one Arsenal fan held up a placard which read: 'In Arsene We Trust for the 1,000th Game.' But that trust ebbed away and Wenger's contempt probably turned to loathing as Chelsea scored goal after goal and they went on to win 6-0. There was no room for sentimentality at Stamford Bridge.

There was also no Arsene Wenger. The devastated Arsenal manager did not show up for his post-match press conference. Mourinho was in the press conference room for 11 minutes (which is quite long by post-match standards) and Wenger gave up waiting.

When Wenger later reflected on that Chelsea mauling, he admitted it was the 'lowest point'. The humiliation of the scoreline was only made worse by the fact that it happened on what should have been a day of celebration and recognition of his achievement.

'It was a massive, massive disappointment,' said Wenger. 'But on the other hand I must say that afterwards we showed great strength. The way we responded until the end of the season would not have happened at many clubs. We were very strong until the end of the season. I will never forget that day, but was very proud with how we responded.

'When we lost 8-2 at Old Trafford [in 2011] we had no team on the day. We had nobody at the back, so that was explainable. But it [the Chelsea game] was the lowest point of the 2013/14 season.'

It was a brutal and painful day at Stamford Bridge and, as Everton closed in, Arsenal were in danger of allowing fourth place to slip away, let alone the title. They then went on to lose 3-0 at Everton in early April and, before they knew it, fourth place was out of their hands. They were having to rely on Roberto Martinez's side to trip up. Wenger still had the FA Cup but even that was becoming a difficult distraction – they nearly lost to Wigan in the semi-final after going behind – and suddenly they were rocking.

During that time, Wenger faced constant questions about whether he was going to re-sign and commit himself to a new contract. He had been talking for months about the new deal; Arsenal were looking at his transfer targets, planning for life with him – and also without him. They definitely made enquiries elsewhere, just in case the unthinkable happened and Wenger left. It would have been foolish not to. But Wenger did drop hints that he was staying, as he insisted he had 'given his word' to the club. However, he wasn't quite saying what his word was.

'My word is my word.' So you will definitely stay? 'Yes . . . unless I decide otherwise.'

Yet, as the season drew to a close, there was still no signature on the contract. And so I put it to him that it would be difficult for him to leave it until the final day, up and leave and simply say goodbye after the FA Cup final. 'Why should you believe that?' Wenger was keeping everyone guessing.

Apart, of course, from beIN Sports, with whom he has a lucrative contract. At the end of April 2014, Wenger told the TV station: 'Look, I've said that many times already, I've given my word to this club and I want to continue where I am.' Then, after a long pause, he added: 'That means to stay.'

Of course, there were some bumps and bruises along the way. Wenger's mood and mind-set became even more difficult to read as Arsenal's season ebbed away, relying on the FA Cup final to end their nine-year wait for a trophy. Eight barren seasons meant so much focus was on one Wembley final that it really turned up the heat, and the doubts lingered.

'I am like everybody else,' said Wenger as he insisted his future would be decided on whether he could be successful. 'Of course, it is important to see how well we do, yes.'

The other interesting element in Wenger's eventual decision to stay lay in his belief that Arsenal could compete again, thanks to the introduction of Financial Fair Play. For years, Wenger felt hard done by because of what he called 'financial doping', which gave the big-spending clubs such as Chelsea and Manchester City an unfair advantage while Arsenal tried to live within their means. FFP quickly took on a new importance when UEFA promised to clamp down and sanction Manchester City and Paris Saint-Germain. City's punishment included a reduction in the size of their Champions League squad.

One of Wenger's favourite subjects is FFP and, while it seems interesting to some journalists and their papers, for others it is a dry subject so it rarely makes headlines. In May 2014, however, Wenger's remarks did make back-page headlines, even for the tabloids, as he effectively declared that if Manchester City broke the FFP rules then they should be banned from the Champions League. He admitted, though, that he doubted whether the rules would be applied, partly because of the TV deals: viewers would not want the top teams excluded, while the TV executives had paid big money for the contracts. He commented:

> There are rules to apply for the Financial Fair Play. One of the rules is that normally you should be banned for the excess of the financial amount that is not justified, that is if you are £100 million overboard, you should be punished for £100 million of your wages bill in the Champions League.
>
> I want to see that respected. If that is not respected, then the Financial Fair Play will have problems to be respected in the future because everyone will just not consider it at all. I have thought about that [clubs being banned] and the media might play a part in that, because when UEFA sells the rights of the Champions League to a French TV station, it is very difficult to explain to them once they have paid the money that the best club in their country will not play in the competition, so that might be one of the reasons behind that.

But, in the longer term, Wenger does believe that FFP will be applied and that is an important reason why he decided to stay on as a manager. Even though UEFA eased their FFP rules in the summer of 2015, Wenger genuinely believes tighter rules on spending make it possible to compete:

> On short term, certainly people will try to find a way to get around it. Maybe longer term, if you imagine tomorrow 20 clubs in the Premier League with 20 multibillionaires. At some stage they have to sit down and say, 'Look, are we killing each other just for the sake to pay higher wages or do we make a rule that makes sense?'

It will happen on the longer term, there's no other way. Until now, we only had one or two billionaires at the start. But once we have ten, they have to respect some rules or they kill each other and it's endless. That's why I think it will happen.

Of course, [breaking the rules] is unfair. Why should I resist? I just defend the idea that you spend the money you have and not the money you don't have. For years I did that. Today we have more so we can spend more. It's as simple as that.

Of course, I am excited by that prospect but what I want to convince you of is that we are ready to spend the money if we feel that the player makes us a better team tomorrow morning. Maybe it's difficult to balance that in a newspaper, but football is not only about that. It's bigger than that. It's about the team, the quality of the play, the spirit and togetherness, and the quality of the players. Therefore, we have to focus on all the rest as well.

What happened for years was the quality of our work has been taken away from us because the best players left for financial reasons. For the first time this year that has not happened and I don't think it will happen again for financial reasons. We have made the first step. The next step is to strengthen the squad and the team by buying the right players.

Fortunately, he was about to have some good news from events on the pitch – Arsenal were up for some silverware at last.

CHAPTER 15

FA CUP WIN 2014

ARSENE WENGER TRUDGED DOWN the corridors at Arsenal's London Colney training ground as if he had the weight of the world on his shoulders. Even those close to him had never seen him like this before. Wenger is often grumpy and uncommunicative after a bad defeat, although he is generally good at hiding any tension and nerves before an important game so that his mood does not spread to the players.

But this was different: for more than a week before the cup final, Wenger struggled to conceal the fact that he was clearly wound up. He knew what the FA Cup final meant to Arsenal, what it represented to the fans, and also, at the forefront of his mind, the huge implications it had for his own future. He was so on edge that he even put off one of his favourite former players from coming to the training ground in the week before the cup final. 'He's not in a very good mood, he says to leave it,' the player was told by one of Wenger's assistants.

Wenger was equally fractious and not very colourful at Arsenal's press day on the bright sunny Wednesday morning three days before the final at Wembley against Hull City. Normally, we can have a laugh and a joke or he'll make a wisecrack once the cameras and microphones are off after his broadcast press conference. But Wenger looked tired and drawn, and he was clearly not in the frame of mind for any pleasantries. Arsenal had invited two or three regular bloggers to come to the press day to see what happens. They didn't catch him anywhere near his best, which was a shame.

'Nothing has changed,' Wenger snapped when someone asked about his contract, why it remained unsigned and whether the result of the cup final would have any bearing on him staying or going.

Stress was etched all over Wenger's face during the run-in to that season. I had also noticed that, as Arsenal toiled and struggled in the battle for fourth and during their FA Cup run, Wenger had stayed rooted to his seat in the dugout. That was most unlike him: he's normally up off his seat, getting animated on the touchline, barking orders, struggling with the zip on his coat.

'Sometimes I try consciously to spend less time on the touchline,' he said. 'Because when you get up there, you know, you're tense. You can have a negative influence. I try to sit down when I feel I am in a negative mood. Because then on the touchline you can become a handicap ...

'This period of the season, you feel much more under pressure as a manager. In September you think, "OK, we lost this game but we still have time to catch up." Now, one, two, three games to go, you look at the table – at the bottom, at the top – everybody feels a bit like you're playing Russian roulette.'

The last few games of the 2013/14 season saw Arsenal, despite having led the title race for so long, in danger of finishing outside the top four, and the FA Cup semi-final against Wigan at Wembley

324 | ARSENE WENGER

nearly went horribly wrong. Arsenal went behind to the Championship underdogs and what was supposed to be a comfortable passage to the final turned into a tense day that went to a penalty shoot-out.

That was as nervous and as bad as it got for Arsenal fans that entire season. Former Olympic champion Denise Lewis, who was sitting just in front of the press box, clearly went through agonies, shouting, screaming and losing her cool as Arsenal so nearly went out at the semi-final stage. I'm not quite sure whether she is a member of the 'Wenger Out' brigade, but she certainly showed she is an Arsenal fan and went through a range of emotions that day.

Arsenal supporters were undeniably split over Wenger, whether he should stay or go, and that semi-final simply highlighted the tensions. Arsenal played as if weighed down by the pressure of expectation, and it needed a late equaliser by Per Mertesacker to take the game to a penalty shoot-out, which Arsenal won 4-2 thanks to Lukasz Fabianski's heroics in goal.

And with that weight lifted from them, Arsenal managed to seal fourth place by a comfortable margin of seven points, which meant they were returning to Wembley with at least their Champions League place safely retained.

However, the semi-final against Wigan was a reminder – if Arsenal needed one – that the final would be just as tense, despite the fact that Steve Bruce's Hull City were huge outsiders. Arsenal had lost the Carling Cup final to Birmingham in 2011 when Wenger's men were red-hot favourites.

Wenger seemed aggravated by the questions that came in about Arsenal's wait for a trophy and, when someone asked him whether he thought the criticism of Arsenal going so long without one was unfair, he shot back:

It's not down to me to judge what is fair; I'm not a judge. I'm a manager who relies on what he's doing, what he's achieving on the pitch and let other people judge and criticise. We can accept that and live with that completely. What is down to the quality of our club is the consistency, and I believe on that front we are better than most of the teams.

No matter what the result will be, this club – and this is always most important – can deal with the consequences of any game. What is important is that we come out of the game and have the feeling that we gave absolutely our best, our total energy to play at our best, and then you always accept the consequences. No matter how much we talk about it, you can win and lose but you want to come out of the game feeling you have done the maximum to win and that is what we want to achieve. Let's focus on a top-level performance.

Wenger had said a few weeks earlier that he had only ever set up a team not to lose a game – rather than go all out for a win, which is his footballing philosophy – once in his entire career. That game was the 2005 FA Cup final, when they bored their way to a goalless draw with Manchester United and won on penalties. The performance went against Wenger's principles.

So I brought up that game again. Would he be prepared to do that once more just to win a trophy? And, indeed, did he see the 2005 FA Cup final as an ugly win?

'Yes. And a lucky one,' he smiled at last. It's quite unusual for Wenger ever to admit he is lucky. His ego rarely allows that.

'We won the Double the year before so I was conscious that it was a lucky win. I realise today that Manchester United had Rooney and Ronaldo in full power. I thought: "How can they create so many goal chances against us?" Now we know why. You don't prepare games with that in your mind. You prepare a game by thinking that the best chance to win is to play at your best, at your top.'

The final itself, on 17 May 2014, was a bizarre game. Hull went steaming ahead with two goals in the opening eight minutes by James Chester and Curtis Davies. They nearly made it three, but Alex Bruce's header was cleared off the line by Kieran Gibbs. It seemed as if the tension had indeed got to Arsenal. But that Gibbs clearance actually proved to be the turning point. Back came Arsenal, as Santi Cazorla scored with a free kick before half-time, Laurent Koscielny equalised with just under 20 minutes left and Aaron Ramsey, Arsenal's best player in the first half of the season, rounded off his campaign with the extra-time winner.

The sense of relief was palpable as players and manager celebrated after the final whistle. Of all the trophies – the first Premier League trophy, the Invincibles season or even one of the FA Cups to complete the Double – this was the one Wenger celebrated like never before. The emotion was plain to see all over his face, the players tried to soak him in champagne and then almost the entire squad lifted him up and threw him in the air. Some of those pictures of Wenger are a sight to behold. They are a mixture of joy, relief, glory and ecstasy.

The dressing room afterwards was a scene of great jubilation as Stan Kroenke, Ivan Gazidis and the rest of the club hierarchy went to congratulate the players. Wenger enjoyed the post-match press conference and, as usual, spoke to the daily newspapers. He was smiling, relieved; he was enjoying his day and there was no getting away from the fact that he saw it as proving a point to those in the media who had questioned him as a manager. Finally, Arsenal had won a trophy.

One of the first questions was about how important it was that Arsenal had ended their drought, and had they overcome a psychological barrier?

'It will force you, first, to be a bit more creative in the press conferences,' smiled Wenger. 'But I trust you will be. I don't worry too much about that.

'We had a horrible feeling for a long time in the game. In the end, it was a relief. But this job is about how it finishes. All the rest, nobody cares about. The quality of the consistency is important for a club – and on that front we've been better than everybody else. There are only two clubs in Europe who have qualified for the Champions League for 17 years consecutively and that consistency demands special values inside the club.'

There was an irony in that Arsenal had won a trophy while Chelsea, whose manager Jose Mourinho had called Wenger a 'specialist in failure', had not. Always looking for a headline, someone reminded Wenger of this. 'Look, I don't want to go into that kind of controversy. We will try to do our best and let people talk,' said Wenger.

Sir Alex Ferguson used to write letters of congratulation. Do you expect one from Mourinho? 'I don't mind at all ...,' smiled Wenger.

But it's still only one trophy in nine years ...?

'I've nothing against this question if you say it to the other clubs as well. You know there are some clubs who haven't won for 20 years and don't get that question at all.'

Wenger believes that newspapers make more of a fuss about Arsenal not winning trophies while they ignore Liverpool's drought, even though they dominated the 1970s and 1980s. I think it's more to do with the fact that he reads more about his own club, analysing every word and particularly seizing on each negative comment, article or headline. Would Wenger take more notice of a column about Arsenal or Liverpool? It's obvious.

Arsenal hired two potential venues for their post-cup final celebrations. One was a modest hotel, the other a more lavish London venue.

Needless to say, Arsenal's players, the staff and the hierarchy partied at the latter. But what it revealed was that Arsenal had braced themselves for a wake. If Arsenal had lost, the pressure on Wenger would have been immense and the fallout would surely have seen the fans turn. But, as it was, there was a new sense of happiness, satisfaction and celebration among the supporters, who were treated the following day to an open-top bus parade through the streets of Islington (which didn't happen when they won in 2003 or 2005).

Some have suggested that this would have been a perfect time for Wenger to have left the club, but very few felt that way then. Those comments tended to come a little later, after Arsenal's poor start to the following season.

It was always my view that Wenger would have stayed even if Arsenal had lost the FA Cup final. They had been discussing a new contract for months. Even though Arsenal were sensible enough to take soundings and make enquiries about possible replacements, I struggle to believe that Wenger would have made a snap decision based on just 90 minutes of an 18-year spell in charge. Furthermore, Wenger would have left them in the lurch and, having fought and worked so hard towards consistency and stability, it is hard to imagine a scenario in which he would have turned round and just said goodbye.

A few journalists, myself included, got wind of the fact that Arsenal planned to announce Wenger signing a new contract within a few days of the cup final. However, we should have known better than to put a timescale on anything to do with Wenger, Arsenal, and a contract. As the delays continued, the press were told that it was a matter of sorting out the formalities. Wenger is not, several people assure me, money-motivated, but money clearly matters to him, which might explain why negotiations dragged on for another fortnight until, finally, Wenger's three-year contract was announced by the club on 30 May 2014.

Wenger had taken charge of his 1,010th Arsenal game in the FA Cup final and it did feel like a new page was about to be turned. Wenger said at the time: 'I want to stay and to continue to develop the team and the club. We are entering a very exciting period. We have a strong squad, financial stability and huge support around the world. We are all determined to bring more success to this club. The club has always shown faith in me and I'm very grateful for that. We have gone through fantastic periods and also periods where we have had to stick together. Every time when that togetherness was tested I got the right response. I think I have shown some loyalty as well towards this club and hopefully we can make some more history. I am sure we can.'

It was pretty standard stuff but the bigger question was whether Wenger would have gone had Arsenal lost that FA Cup final. Some of those who know him well believe that, from spending time with him around the final and immediately afterwards, he might have walked away from the club had Arsenal lost, which appears to be borne out by an interview Wenger gave to beIN Sports some months later, in September 2014.

When asked whether he would have left the club had Arsenal not won the FA Cup, Wenger said: 'I don't know, I honestly don't. It would have been very difficult; it was a very difficult set of circumstances. I'm pleased we didn't have to make that decision. We would have had to assess what the circumstances were and seen whether it was better for someone else to come in.

'I question myself every day. Even when I win a match, I go home and question myself after every game. It's the only way you can stay at the top. I'm very relieved we won a trophy. Of course, it was a proud moment and important for the club.'

One of Wenger's Invincibles, Ray Parlour, sees Wenger regularly; they get on well and talk a lot. He believes there is a good chance Wenger would have gone had Arsenal lost at Wembley:

I think he might have walked if he lost that game. If he had not won the trophy, the pressure on himself, that could have been the final straw. I don't know for sure. It's just my opinion. He might deny it and say: 'I never would have walked.' But I felt he looked under so much pressure, so much strain that it might have been too much for him and too much for the players as well. He might have said: 'Look, maybe I can't take this club forward.' Then he would have walked away ...

I think you could see how much it meant to him. The club had gone nine years without a trophy, but I'd never seen him run on the pitch, cuddle the players, celebrate like that. We've won lots of trophies under him but never seen him react like that. He knew it was a massive focus for the club, a massive trophy for him, the club and a massive trophy for the players. That first trophy is always the hardest to win together. He knew the trophy would be the catalyst to take them forward, to help them start winning trophies again year after year.

Parlour believes that Wenger is still driven by a burning desire to succeed. 'He's still very passionate. I think he'd walk away if he wasn't. If he lost that passion or will to win then he'd give up. You can see that passion even when he does things like push Mourinho [in October 2014]. That's how much it means to him. He believes he has a squad to challenge. He believes he has players of good ages, but once that goes ... Wenger is not doing it for money; he's doing it purely for success and to win things.'

It is a view echoed by Nigel Winterburn, who also questioned whether Wenger would have walked if they had lost the FA Cup final. But Winterburn's view is that Wenger was determined to stay, ride out the storm and prove that he could win trophies again.

Winterburn is realistic and measured in his approach. He has always been a big admirer of his former manager but, at the same time, admits that he still has to get back to winning trophies on a regular basis. His argument is that Wenger has done a difficult job during tough times and financial restrictions and should now reap the rewards of the club rebuilding. 'With the releasing of some of the money, it's going to be so important to see how Arsenal do over the next three years. I think he's as driven as ever, he's still motivated. I think he still wants to prove to people that he can still be successful.'

That certainly felt like Wenger's main motivation for signing a new contract, staying on and leading the club to new success. You can be certain that his great friend David Dein would have been one of the first people with whom Wenger would have celebrated that FA Cup win. He had this to say:

> When you consider that he's now 65, 18 years is, in today's world in modern football, such a rarity and you don't see it any more. I'm not sure that you'll ever see it again. People are more transient now. The League Managers' Association will tell you that the average life span of a manager and how long he stays in charge is 11 months. Arsene has been there for so long, remained so successful and yet no one has any patience any more.
>
> The FA Cup was so important to him. It was at the end of his contract, it was an obvious question as to whether he would leave and there's an argument that you should go out on a winning note. But he decided to stay and he's still as hungry as ever. He's still got the fire in his belly, he's still got the desire, he wants to win, he loves the club. He wants to be successful. It's in his DNA. That's Arsene Wenger.

The whole mood had indeed changed at the club. It meant Wenger could sign the contract without the fans baying for blood, it gave everyone renewed hope and, while Wenger's priority has always been the top four, it gave the fans what they wanted so they could enjoy a celebration.

'I think we are better placed to challenge next season,' said Wenger. 'It is always my target to be successful and win trophies. But it's not as if we had been finishing seventh, 12th or lower down the table. We'd qualified every year for the Champions League, for 17 years. We had also reached finals, gone very close, always been challenging and that is also very important.'

CHAPTER 16

TRAINING AND TACTICS

JOSE MOURINHO STOOD on the edge of the pitch in the March sunshine as Arsenal launched an early attack. He turned away from the action after Olivier Giroud wasted a great chance as Arsenal made a bright start to the London derby at Stamford Bridge. The Chelsea manager took a couple of paces back to the bench, clenched his fists and, in the direction of his coaches and substitutes, hissed: 'We've got 'em.'

Mourinho had spent seven hours with his players during the build-up studying tactics, videos, the way Arsenal lined up, how Arsene Wenger's men would play – and how Chelsea could beat them. The Chelsea players had been told that Arsenal's fullbacks would push on, Wenger would leave his midfield undermanned when they swarmed forward, and Mourinho knew his team could drive right through the heart of Arsenal's midfield. The fact that Wenger had chosen just one defensive-minded midfielder in Mikel Arteta played straight into Chelsea's hands.

In that first attack, Arsenal had confirmed everything that

Mourinho had been telling his players and that's why the Chelsea manager, renowned as a meticulous tactician, knew he had Wenger exactly where he wanted him. Never mind it was Wenger's 1,000th game, the self-styled Special One was determined to humiliate his managerial rival.

It's not just a clash of personalities when Mourinho and Wenger meet. It's also a clash of management styles. Wenger puts the onus on the players to win games. Mourinho puts the onus on the tactics to win games. Mourinho's dominance of Wenger in their head-to-head encounters – Wenger failed to beat Mourinho once in their first 13 meetings over the course of five seasons up to the 2014/15 season – perhaps proves a point.

Arteta was supposed to sit in front of Arsenal's back four; Alex Oxlade-Chamberlain was in central midfield; Tomas Rosicky, Santi Cazorla and Lukas Podolski made up the rest of Arsenal's midfield. Chelsea were too strong, they could smell blood, and stormed through the heart of Arsenal's midfield time after time. And to make things worse, Mourinho knew it was going to happen.

Chelsea were 3-0 up after 17 minutes. It was 4-0 by half-time and 6-0 by the end. Instead of being a day that Wenger would never forget because it was his 1,000th game in charge of Arsenal, it was a game he would never forget because it was one of the worst and most humiliating defeats of his entire career. In fact, possibly *the* worst because of whom it was against.

In truth, Mourinho will go to great lengths to get a result; some might even call his methods cynical. For example, when Chelsea played at Liverpool in April 2014, Liverpool needed to win to virtually clinch the Premier League title. Mourinho was still trying to balance an outside hope of a title challenge with the Champions League and felt he had to rest and rotate his squad at Anfield, even fielding rookie Tomas Kalas in defence.

However, there are few better managers than Mourinho at being able to put out teams to get results in one-off games. Mourinho set up to defend in a way that Wenger never would. Mourinho made his team resolute, broke up Liverpool's early momentum with a string of free kicks and stoppages, which prevented them from making the fast start to the game that had been such a feature of their title challenge. Chelsea weathered the early storm and nicked a 2-0 win. There is a stark contrast between Mourinho fielding a weakened team with a tactical strategy and Wenger sending out a full-strength Arsenal team at Anfield that got battered 5-1 by Liverpool.

Wenger's whole managerial philosophy is based on playing attacking football; he puts the onus on the players, does practice set pieces and phases of play, but the principal idea is to give the players freedom. When they had players of the quality of Thierry Henry, Dennis Bergkamp, Patrick Vieira, Robert Pires and Sol Campbell, Arsenal had enough quality to win games and the opposition could do little to curtail their power, pace and creativity. But those players and characters have moved on, and Arsenal no longer enjoy the luxury of being able to just send out an 11 with the notion that if they play at their best then there is little the opposition can do about it.

Only once has Wenger set up a team to frustrate the opposition and that was in the 2005 FA Cup final against Manchester United. 'I've not really been tempted to do it since,' said Wenger. 'Maybe sometimes we have not had much of a choice. We have always tried to attack because we have a team that has that ability.'

Before fans rush to judge him, it's worth remembering that his brand of football not only entertained but it also delivered trophies in the early days. Now, as with Wenger's philosophy on transfers, preparation, training methods and science, other clubs have caught up and arguably overtaken him.

Maybe Barcelona, with their vast array of attacking players, are the only team left in Europe who can send out a team to go all-out attack, play fantasy football and still expect come out on top. TV pundit Paul Scholes, the former England and Manchester United midfielder, has claimed Arsenal are a 'million miles away' from being serious contenders because of their physical and mental approach and they simply 'capitulate' when the pressure is on.

In one of his most cutting pieces of analysis, just three days after the six-goal mauling at Chelsea after they had been held at home by Swansea, Scholes said: 'They go on the pitch with no discipline. It's as though "you four, five midfielders go out there and do what you want – try and score a goal. A few nice one-twos, nice tippy-tappy football – but don't bother running back."'

Chelsea seem to dominate Arsenal physically and maybe that is why Mourinho has had such a hold over Wenger on the pitch. You can no longer simply send out a team and hope they play at their best and win.

One interesting take on Wenger, which perhaps cuts to the heart of the matter, is that he is not good at delegating. He likes to be in complete control of everything, whereas, particularly in the latter days of his reign, Sir Alex Ferguson was a brilliant delegator. The Manchester United manager had strong people around him and they were in charge of different aspects of coaching, fitness and science. Ferguson oversaw the operation, but allowed others to work effectively. The strength of Ferguson's management was his skilful delegation.

The joke doing the rounds in some quarters of the club before the 2014 FA Cup final was that Wenger spent more time on making sure the yellow cup final carnations were what he wanted than on tactics for the game itself. It was an exaggeration, but you get the point. Wenger will take on the smallest of tasks and he is incredibly loyal to staff.

For example, he involved himself in a row over fuel cards for club masseurs – who do not earn much money but often have to travel long distances – taking their case to the board and winning. Similarly, when a long-standing member of his backroom staff was under threat after a reshuffle in the way Arsenal organised their travel, Wenger went to the board and made it very clear that this was a point of principle and under no circumstances could this employee be made redundant. Once again, Wenger won the day. It's no wonder he gets such loyalty from his staff.

While Wenger's own loyalty deserves respect, one former colleague puts it perfectly. 'I think he is an outstanding manager. But he is what I term a micromanager. He manages a lot of very small things so he worries about one hell of a lot of quite small details. He's not a great delegator, not good at getting people around him. But he's a brilliant, brilliant manager. But he's not a good strategist in terms of his squad. That's one of his failings.'

Among the biggest criticisms of Wenger are his approach to tactics, some of the coaches he has around him and also the amount of time he puts into preparation compared to managers at other clubs.

One former player describes him as a 'dictator', who hates confrontation. But that was a player who felt hard done by, who didn't think he got enough game time and who felt that Wenger would even try to avoid eye contact with him rather than discuss it. Other players, like Ray Parlour, Nigel Winterburn and Stephen Hughes, were more complimentary, praising his man management, his willingness to help and discuss issues and – particularly Parlour on this point – the fact that he would involve them even when they weren't in the team. However, others complain that Wenger blanks players who are not in his first-team plans.

Wenger is a contradiction on so many levels. He is incredibly science-minded and yet will overrule scientific advice on resting players when they enter the 'red zone' and are tired, fatigued and liable to injury. Wenger does like to keep a small squad – he believes that it forges good camaraderie and unity rather than carrying a raft of disaffected players – but the downside is not being able to rest and rotate as other big clubs. Players tend to get soft-muscle injuries when they play or train when fatigued. Arsenal seem to have fallen behind on fitness because they have suffered so many injuries. In the ten years since the 2004/05 season, only one team, Newcastle, has lost more players to injuries than Arsenal.

Wenger's training methods were hailed as different and innovative when he first arrived. They were intense and Wenger had a stopwatch on everything. Yet some players told Wenger they felt they weren't doing enough. Now the issue seems to be about getting the balance in training right, particularly when it comes to intensity. Some players don't think it is intense enough and, consequently, they don't feel they are 'in the zone' when it comes to games.

But at other times training can be too intense, when players actually need to be tapering down or building up gradually. For example, Mikel Arteta tore a thigh muscle in training in August 2013. The majority of his team-mates were on international duty; Arteta stayed behind and was given a tough session in which he practised hitting long balls and sustained the injury. Did that session cause the problem?

In September 2014, Arteta and Aaron Ramsey were both rested from Arsenal's Capital One Cup tie with Southampton, but both suffered soft muscle injuries the following Saturday against Tottenham. Arteta, who limped off after 28 minutes, damaged his calf, while Ramsey lasted 45 minutes before pulling a hamstring. So much for the rest. But Arteta and Ramsey were both pushed hard in training that week, so their bodies arguably had a tougher week of training than they would have done had they played the League Cup game.

Of course, much of this comes down to whom Wenger listens to among his coaching staff. Arsenal's physio Colin Lewin and doctor Gary O'Driscoll have excellent reputations but they can only make recommendations: it is up to Wenger whether he listens to them or not.

One of Wenger's most maligned transfers was the signing of Kim Kallstrom on loan from Spartak Moscow in January 2014. Wenger had always liked Kallstrom as a player, ever since his days at French club Lyon. So when Gilles Grimandi, Wenger's French scout, told the Arsenal manager that he was available on loan, Wenger decided to sign him. But when Kallstrom arrived for a medical, it showed up a fracture in his back sustained playing beach football while on a break in the Russian season.

The Arsenal medical staff spotted it and they told Wenger he would be out for weeks, yet Wenger decided to press ahead with the signing. His reasoning was that it was too late to get anyone else and he was better than nothing. The medics suggested that Wenger announce the signing with the caveat that Kallstrom had a pre-existing injury and wouldn't be available straightaway. Wenger insisted he would make the situation clear at his next press conference. Needless to say, news of Kallstrom's injury leaked out and the headlines were all about Arsenal signing a crock, with blame heaped on the medical department. However, it was Wenger's decision to carry on, without going public about the injury, that opened up the club to ridicule. The medical staff had actually spotted the problem so they were certainly not to blame.

Once again in 2013/14, Arsenal's season was dominated by injuries. Wenger promised a full investigation, which many behind the scenes claimed never really happened. Arsenal did, however, appoint the American fitness expert Shad Forsythe in the summer of 2014. Although he had worked with the German national team, there were concerns about whether Wenger would listen to him.

Some managers believe that changing coaches is healthy, and Sir Alex Ferguson regularly switched his assistants at Manchester United. Over the years he worked with Archie Knox, Brian Kidd, Steve McClaren, Carlos Queiroz and Mike Phelan, as well as using Walter Smith, Rene Meulensteen and Jimmy Ryan on his staff. Ferguson enjoyed delegating and was good at it.

Wenger, on the other hand, was so set in his ways that he did not want Pat Rice to retire as his number two in 2012 and admits that he tried to talk him out of it. He promoted Steve Bould and Neil Banfield from the ranks, as both had excellent reputations within the club. Bould is seen as the more senior partner because he is a club legend, and he sits next to Wenger on a match day. However, despite being part of Arsenal's famous back four, questions have often been raised about how close they really are, how much input Bould is allowed to have and whether Wenger actually listens.

Wenger, like every manager, has an ego, and he appeared to resent the praise that Bould received soon after he took over and Arsenal's defending seemed to improve, particularly at set pieces. When Arsenal came from a goal down at West Ham in October 2012 to win impressively 3-1, a friendly question was put to Wenger in the post-match press conference, almost inviting him to commend the impact of his new number two on the defence. Wenger replied: 'Well, I think you'll find we conceded less goals from set pieces before Steve was working as my assistant.'

The answer was a proper put-down and Wenger was perhaps fortunate that more was not made of it. The fact that Arsenal had just won a difficult London derby was the story rather than Wenger's reluctance to give credit to his assistant.

In the same 2012/13 season, when Arsenal played Montpellier in the Champions League, Wenger was banned from the touchline. He'd received the ban for confronting referee Damir Skomina following Arsenal's Champions League exit the previous season. Wenger did his pre-match press conference but, to make a point to UEFA because he felt the ban was unfair, refused to conduct his post-match press conference, leaving the media duties to Bould, who was also in charge on the touchline.

Once again, though, Wenger did not react well to questions in his pre-match press conference about whether Bould – who had only been promoted a few months previously – had made a significant difference. His answer also outlined his coaching philosophy:

No, we've not changed anything. I build the training sessions and it will remain like that. I've been coaching for 30 years, so am not going to change things because Steve Bould arrived in August. But he does a great job. At the end of the day, it's important that we have a style of play and people are convinced of that style of play, coaches and players.

[Bould] is doing his job very well. I believe it's a bit early to speak about our defensive record, because we've played only four games. Don't forget that the basis of our team is a very offensive philosophy. So sometimes, if we concede goals in the future, it will not be Steve Bould's fault. It will only be a consequence of the way we see football.

As the weeks went by that season, Arsenal's results nose-dived, and stories emerged that Bould was being allowed to do less work on the training pitch. Wenger returned home to France on compassionate leave before Arsenal's home game with Swansea on Saturday 1 December, but rather than allow Bould to take training, fitness coach Tony Colbert oversaw the session. It was more of a warm-down than a pre-match training session and some Arsenal players felt they were not in the 'match zone' – they duly lost 2-0.

People are often bemused as to why Bould, such a strong and vocal figure as a player, rarely leaves his seat on the bench to shout instructions or encouragement. He did, however, support his manager when Wenger pushed Jose Mourinho on the touchline at Stamford Bridge in October 2014. When Chelsea's assistant Rui Faria yelled at Wenger, Bould also got involved and shouted at him to be quiet. You wouldn't want to mess with Bould as he is a tough, intimidating figure.

Bould is understandably very touchy about talking about the nature of his relationship with Wenger and, as time has gone by, their trust and rapport has grown, even if Wenger still likes to be in complete control of training. They seem much closer now, and their relationship is stronger. However, because of Wenger's philosophy, the emphasis is on attacking play rather than defensive drills.

Boro Primorac is his long-term trusted coach and, during the Invincibles era, many questioned exactly what he did, apart from often being something of a joker on the team bus with his funny remarks. He is charming and has a good sense of humour, as well as speaking even more languages than Wenger. For years, Primorac has led the warm-ups – the jogs and light stretching – and what a strange sight it makes: a big guy in his sixties taking a session with super-fit 20-year-olds following his instructions. He sits in the stands during games to observe the play and give a different perspective, which Wenger listens to and respects greatly.

But Primorac and fitness coach Tony Colbert are definitely of a mind-set that believes in hard physical work in training. They often encourage Wenger to put on tough sessions, which is seen as 'overloading' by others, putting players at risk of fatigue-related injury.

As a result, Colbert definitely divides opinion among the players. Thierry Henry credited him by name when he got back to match fitness after returning for a short loan spell from New York Red Bulls. By contrast, Cesc Fabregas used his own personal trainer while at Arsenal. One high-profile Arsenal player avoids talking to Colbert.

Former Wales fitness coach Raymond Verheijen described Arsenal's fitness staff as 'amateurs'. The Dutchman has also claimed the players are made to train 'like marines' in pre-season. Verheijen has never met Arsenal's medical staff and, without doubt, is only voicing some concerns about the intensity and level of training shared by others at the club. But his regular outspoken attacks on Arsenal's medical staff and fitness coaches seem to be aimed in the wrong direction, because unless the manager listens and decides to act then the regime won't change. Verheijen has also aimed similar attacks at Manchester United and Manchester City because of the conditioning of their players.

In the latter part of the 2013/14 season, Wenger tapered off training. The injury crisis eased, and Arsenal rediscovered some form, squeezing into fourth place and winning the FA Cup. The pattern was noticed not just at the training ground, but within the club's hierarchy.

Arsenal chief executive Ivan Gazidis used his quarterly update to shareholders in December 2014 to talk about injuries. 'It is frustrating for everyone that the run of injuries we have sustained in the first third of the season has meant we have only seen flashes of this talented squad's true potential. We continue to work hard to improve our prevention of injuries and to accelerate recovery, but it is clear there is no single contributing factor.'

It's an area in which Gazidis has taken a personal interest. He has become proactively involved and is determined to improve the situation. But, once seen as revolutionary when it came to injuries, fitness and injury prevention, Wenger's Arsenal is now painted as a club that has a poor injury record and it is alleged that their own methods have played a part.

Wenger has his own, sometimes bizarre, theories about why Arsenal get so many injuries. Often he will throw in something he's read or been told about. For example, at a press conference in April 2014, he came out with the strange theory that some pills used for hair loss, as slimming aids or even to boost sex drive could be the cause behind some football injuries. Unsurprisingly, Wenger backtracked when asked whether he meant his own players, but his comments provoked a mixture of disbelief, amusement and bewilderment among staff at the training ground.

'Some of them [injuries] are down to the medication that the players take that you don't even know about it. You realise afterwards that they took this medication that's not prudent,' said Wenger. 'The liver doesn't work as well, the toxins don't go as quickly out of the body as they should and they get tired.

'If you lose your hair and take something to make it grow, it might not be good for the rest of your body. Medication always pushes a part of your body and is sometimes detrimental to other parts of your body. At the moment we have not come to any conclusion. We need to analyse deeply why things happen.'

Immediately, of course, we thought about players who have lost their hair and suffered a spate of injuries afterwards. But it left us wondering whether it was more of a deflection tactic than a genuine scientific belief. As we have seen, Wenger will be told when players are nearing or are in the 'red zone', meaning they are in danger of picking up an injury. It's Wenger's choice whether or not to heed the warning. Nine times out of ten, if there is a big game, Wenger will choose to ignore the advice and go with the more experienced player even if they are in the 'red zone'. He has publicly admitted to 'overplaying' Jack Wilshere and Aaron Ramsey when they've been in the 'red zone'.

Former Arsenal defender Sol Campbell believes that there's another factor: they have a smaller pool of top-quality players than some of their main rivals, and that is why Wenger often has to risk playing the likes of Wilshere and Ramsey.

> I think you've got to say that the medical side at Arsenal is really top-notch. If anything, they've got too many people! It's a pretty good set-up. I think you've got to have a few more players in certain situations, so the guys don't have to break their neck every week to be in the side. You can have more players to allow you to rest and rotate and the level doesn't drop. At the moment, I think the first 11 or the 13 is great, but beyond that you need a few more players to take up the slack. So if players are getting tired, or playing too many games, then someone can come in and it doesn't rock the boat.

> Trouble is, when a big player does go then it's a big problem because there's no one to help out, players have to rush back. In their mind, they're thinking: 'Oh God, the team needs me.' That's a good position to be in because it's good that players want to play for the team. But I think, long term, you need more players to fill in and get into a situation where the level doesn't drop. That is where Arsenal have lacked, so that when players do get injured, they don't rush back too quickly. But if they have players to fill the space for two weeks, a month or three months, whatever, that would make a huge difference going forward ...

Up front you need options because otherwise opposition back fours can lock you down. It hurt when Theo [Walcott] got injured, and [Aaron] Ramsey and Jack [Wilshere] as well. But even with that you still need a little bit more to thicken it up, to absorb the injuries, to give them a break, take up the slack when players are not playing as well as they should be.

You need to be able to change it – teams are watching everybody, there are people watching every single move via a computer around the world. That's why you have to be able to switch it, flip it and change it. The top-class players can do that. When it's a bit tight in a game, the best players can find a way to make it happen, to change it within a game. They use their individual skill and Arsenal need a few more like that to be able to go and make the difference, to be able to win the games.

Wenger acknowledged that the arrival of Shad Forsythe would make a difference, particularly when it came to preparation, warm-ups and also tailored personal fitness programmes. Clearly, it will take time for the adjustments to kick in. Whether or not it is down to Forsythe's impact or a combination of better luck and subtle change, things did improve very noticeably towards the end of the 2014/15 season. To prove a point, during the run-in, Arsenal were able to field an unchanged team for six consecutive league games for the first time in Wenger's 19-year reign.

One of Wenger's great qualities is his unerring loyalty to his staff. In February 2011, shortly before the Carling Cup final, a delegation of players – including the captain at the time, Cesc Fabregas, and keeper Wojciech Szczesny – went to see Wenger to talk to him about how they wanted more video preparation and also about the keeper coach Gerry Peyton. Peyton is seen as something of a figure of fun to some at the training ground;

players and coaches laugh that he often tries to sit next to Wenger at mealtimes and they see him as something of a 'yes man'.

Nicknamed 'The Head' because of his large head, Peyton is blamed by some for Arsenal rejecting France keeper Hugo Lloris before he joined Tottenham in 2012 because he claimed he would be poor on crosses and would struggle with the physical side of the game in the Premier League. However, Lloris went on to become one of the best keepers in the league.

Wenger clearly listens to and respects Peyton on keepers, so unsurprisingly the players' delegation didn't get very far when it came to raising questions about his keeper coach. However, Lukasz Fabianski put his return to the first team down to the work he did with academy keeper coach Tony Roberts. When Fabianski eventually left in the summer of 2014 to join Swansea, he told Wenger that he did not enjoy working with Peyton. He and Roberts have now been reunited at Swansea after Roberts left Arsenal in the summer of 2015.

There are other areas where Wenger's methods have been questioned. A new video suite was set up at London Colney, reflecting the greater importance placed on video preparation nowadays. However, one player, who came from another big European club, joked with an international team-mate that his old team would spend hours on video analysis while 'Arsenal spend 20 minutes'.

The comment reflects a sore point with Wenger: the accusation that he doesn't do much coaching. It annoys him greatly. 'Do you think I would have managed for more than 30 years if I did no coaching? Of course we work on coaching.' What is clear is that Wenger's style is different: precise, intense and all aimed to improve technique. In fairness, Arsenal introduced more video analysis during the 2014/15 season and greater emphasis is now put on preparation.

Former Arsenal player Stephen Hughes was a big fan of Wenger's training methods and recalls:

The training was always so intense. I could come up with a million examples of 'they ended up rolling around fighting' and there was an edge to the group. I really enjoyed it. It never boiled over but it was healthy, good and really intense.

We'd go through the set pieces; we'd walk through them and it was always two hours before the game when he'd name the team, talk for about ten minutes, then he'd show us the opposition team, tell us who would mark who and that was for about ten minutes. It doesn't surprise me to hear talk now that he doesn't focus too much on tactics because he had ultimate belief in the lads, he'd believe in his own players.

Others will say that you need to think more about the opposition and the other players. But he'd put the onus on his own players and sometimes they'd let him down, which really hurts him. He'd struggle with that. But it's still a lovely way to be, rather than a manager who hasn't got that belief in you ... He'd just say: 'Don't worry, you can do it.' That, as a player, made you feel good. He didn't want to heap any added pressure on you. I liked that, I admired that, particularly as a young player, and you came in and learned that was the way it was.

I watch all the games now and I'm sure it's been tweaked now, the team talks and everything. He never used to say much at all in the dressing room. He'd let you have five minutes at half-time then go over the basics. He'd tweak things ... He's not a big believer in big long speeches and I asked why once and he said he wanted to keep it short, to the point and didn't want to clog a player's mind with too much.

Hughes also says that Wenger was incredibly hands-on and would trust his own judgement when it came to players and injuries. 'He would crouch down on one knee, watch intently and, one time, I was just coming back from injury, hoping to play but, to be honest,

I wasn't ready. He sent me back in and said: "You're holding back." He'd see everything.'

Ray Parlour is another who refutes the popular accusation that Wenger doesn't do any coaching. 'No, that's rubbish,' he said. 'He's brilliant. He was on that training field every day, every single day.'

Parlour also says Wenger's ability to keep squad members fresh and involved was first-rate. 'If the first team was off and we were doing a warm-down then he'd still be out there on the training pitch with the other boys. He'd be trying to get the other boys ready. He always wanted the other players ready because if suddenly there was an injury or suspension, then the other boys would have to be ready to come into the team.'

But Wenger's main coaching strength, believes Parlour, is his skill at improving players on a technical level. Parlour's energy, desire and work rate were never in doubt. Under Wenger, though, he became a very accomplished midfielder, part of the Invincibles and a key member of the most successful team of Wenger's glorious reign. He explains:

Looking at technical ability, I improved so much in that short space of time. Suddenly, I was competing against the best teams and players in Europe. Going back to the Inter Milan game in the Champions League, we were fantastic on that day. He brought that little bit of buzz into your game. You were confident about getting the ball, passing and really developing your play. That was all down to Arsene Wenger.

A lot of it was down to training. During the week is where, I always say, the manager earns his money. As a player, you should be going across that white line and you should know exactly what you're doing for the team, know what your job is. But during the week it should be about training routines, moves and making you a better player. His training methods are very good. Every 15 or 20 minutes, he would change it, mix it up and he'd always make you think, make your mind work and push you.

Other managers might make you work for 40 or 45 minutes and you lose the quality along the line. His training methods were so important and so good. His catchphrase would always be along the lines of going out there to 'express yourself, you know your job and if you get into the final third, take players and try to do something'.

As a midfielder, he'd never restrict you. He'd never, ever tell you: 'Do this, you can't do that.' All the time, he was always working on movement, telling you to switch inside, for the forward to go outside, and you can see how they play today – there's a lot of interchanging, which is down to training methods and how we worked in training.

The phrase 'I did not see it' has become forever associated with Arsene Wenger. It's now something of a running joke on TV, radio and in the newspapers. But it's a very deliberate ploy: a feature of his management philosophy is his unerring support of his players and he very rarely criticises them in public. He would rather see himself ridiculed and derided as a figure of fun for his selective vision than openly condemn a player.

One former colleague said of Wenger: 'The thing that he gets criticised for, which I think is really unfair, is that he will never, ever criticise his team in front of the press, the media or the public. He's a great believer in things being done behind closed doors. If one of his players does an awful tackle he will simply say: "I did not see it." But what else can he say? "I did see it and it was a fucking awful tackle"? Or "I told him not to hit the bugger"?'

Wenger will protect his players at all costs. After the now infamous Eduardo game with Celtic in the Champions League in August 2009, when the Croatian international was accused of diving to win a penalty, Wenger was told all the questions would be about whether Eduardo was a cheat. Wenger was furious and stormed into the press conference still stewing over what he saw as a blatant dive by Ryan Babel in a Champions League quarter-final in April 2008. 'Why don't they ask about Ryan Babel? They never asked about that,' he fumed.

Youth development and scouting for potential transfers are high up on Wenger's agenda. It's clear that some members of the Arsenal hierarchy think Wenger's reputation as a 'micromanager' means he needs help with delegation. As we have seen, Arsenal have moved towards using their own stats-based company, StatDNA, to evaluate players, while Ivan Gazidis oversaw the appointment of Andries Jonker – originally sourced by former employee Hendrik Almstadt – as the head of Arsenal's academy.

Both departments had struggled in recent times, with the scouting team often despairing of Wenger's apparent indecisiveness when it came to transfers, let alone his perceived lack of a transfer strategy. Arsenal's chief scout Steve Rowley is world renowned, has a brilliant eye for talent and has spotted a whole generation of players for Arsenal as well as deserving credit for Robin van Persie, Thomas Vermaelen and Cesc Fabregas.

Increasingly, however, Wenger listens to the club's French scout Gilles Grimandi and there is some natural tension between the two: both are clearly recommending different players and any scout will be judged on their recommendations.

English-based agents go either to Rowley or to the club's transfer fixer Dick Law, while Grimandi clearly has the French market and strong French links, which in recent times have brought in players such as Kallstrom and France Under-21 striker, Yaya

Sanogo, from Auxerre. His proven successes include Bacary Sagna and Laurent Koscielny.

Whoever the scouts spot, much of Arsenal's transfer dealings and policy are down to Wenger, who certainly has the final say. For example, at the start of the summer of 2014, Wenger had told his scouts to identify a holding midfield player as a priority. By the end of it, Wenger had changed his mind. That, according to one insider, is down to his lack of strategic planning when it comes to transfers:

I don't think that strategy is there because Arsene is not a strategic thinker. If you ask him what his strategy is, he would give an answer, start to think about it – you would see the brain cogs going but ultimately he doesn't have a strategy.

If you think how many outfield midfield players there are, you run out of hands to count them up on. If you go through the Arsene way of developing a squad, it is to have a world-class centre forward, a world-class midfield player, a world-class centre half and to have a world-class goalie. That was the spine of his team.

You go through [the 2014/15 squad] and you end up by saying you haven't got a world-class forward – Sanchez is not really a striker or a midfielder – he doesn't have a world-class midfielder when you compare with Vieira or Gilberto …

Then you've got so many midfielders of the same type. They're all five foot eight inches, all reasonably good, but not world class – there's no stature to them. That all comes back to a lack of planning. He would … have two weeks off to escape, then he'd come back while others are doing transfers. There's no one there doing the business for him.

As we have seen, Wenger passed on Hugo Lloris on the say-so of Gerry Peyton. The club were told about the Spanish striker

Michu, but he was deemed not good enough. He then joined Swansea for a bargain fee and soon was rated as a £20 million player, though he hasn't sustained that level of form.

When Manchester United signed Juan Sebastian Veron in 2001, they already had a wealth of brilliant midfielders including Roy Keane, Paul Scholes and David Beckham. The talk in football was that Manchester United were suddenly moving away from a structured transfer plan towards fantasy football.

The same can surely be said of Wenger's Arsenal in recent seasons: they have moved away from a team of giants in the Invincibles era towards a smaller, more technical brand of player. It does tend to leave Arsenal lightweight at times, and yet Wenger insists it wasn't something that was pre-planned.

'When we buy a player we do not look at how heavy he is, but how good he is,' said Wenger in 2014. 'It is a coincidence that we are a bit lightweight. Maybe because we use more technical players in the middle of the park, especially Arteta. On that front maybe. It depends as well who plays. If I play Cazorla or Podolski, the weight is a bit different. But it's true, we are a bit more lightweight than before, when we had Petit, Vieira, Parlour ...

'You always want to improve technically and sometimes when you want to do that you go a bit more for skill, which can be more lightweight. At the time when Vieira left, we had Fabregas there who was 17 years old. You cannot say you are not heavy enough so you cannot play. He had the quality to play.'

If Arsenal's scouting system has unearthed fewer bargains and gems compared to Wenger's early years, it has also been noticeable in recent times that Arsenal's youth development has declined, at least in the number of players who are progressing towards the first team. Arsenal's academy has been famed for the wonderful players who have come through on the conveyor belt – Jack Wilshere,

David Rocastle, Tony Adams and Paul Davis, to name just a few. For many years, it was run by club legend Liam Brady, arguably the most talented Arsenal graduate of all, who went on to join Juventus.

However, Arsenal struggled to gain top category one status under the Premier League's Elite Player Performance Plan, a scheme intended to improve the quality and quantity of home-grown players. It would have caused huge furore had they failed to meet the required standard.

Wenger and Brady did not always see eye to eye and even Arsenal's former head of coaching, Terry Burton, who worked at the club during the golden age of Adams and Rocastle, admitted after he left in the summer of 2014 that Arsenal had 'fallen behind' and 'were not working hard enough'. Burton was furious that Arsenal had gone for a foreign academy director, but it was Gazidis who supported the decision to recruit Dutchman Andries Jonker, who was assistant manager at Wolfsburg and had also been number two to Louis van Gaal during his time at Bayern Munich.

Arsenal went for a radical change because the youth department was slipping behind. But the question is: was Wenger failing the academy or was the academy failing Wenger? He is proud to produce young players whether or not they make it at Arsenal, and sees that as part of Arsenal's academy role. While they can make money on the sale of players like Steve Sidwell, who left to join Reading, the real test as far as fans are concerned is who makes the Arsenal first team.

Jonker has already ruffled feathers, annoying some by taking credit for the redevelopment of the training ground and the development of the Hale End academy training centre, as well as claiming that Arsenal have not produced enough home-grown players. That may not be wise with Jack Wilshere and Kieran Gibbs as established first-team players.

Jonker is self-confident and forthright. He wants trees to be planted in between pitches, and to produce more first-team-ready players, but his most outspoken remarks are about Arsenal's scouting. In an interview with a Dutch magazine, *Voetbal International*, Jonker explained that his 'massive experience in youth football, [as] a man who can actually develop their own coaches' was why he had been brought in.

He had worked with Louis van Gaal at Bayern Munich where the pair continued their working partnership: 'I owe everything to Louis. After [Ajax] he took me with him everywhere he went. Even to the national team.'

He added: 'The scouting [at Arsenal] must be restructured all over again. The scouting needs to be brought to a level that we can bring in the absolute best talents from abroad and from England at an age that Wenger can immediately work with them in his squad.'

He wasn't complimentary about the quality of player the academy had been producing: 'At this moment, considering the investments the club has done, players have hardly been developed properly. Gazidis wants Arsenal to be the best academy in the world. He realises that will cost money and will take time, but that is his massive ambition.'

He spoke about his working relationship with Wenger, noting how others sought approval from the manager before doing anything, and said how they would discuss things together before training as 'we must not go behind his back'.

He concluded by saying: 'I have a very good feeling about the way Wenger and I are working together. We both think the technical side of the game is very important. So that is something we share. But there are a lot of things in the academy which can be improved or should be done differently.'

There is no doubt that Wenger arrived as a revolutionary at

Arsenal, but certain aspects have lagged behind. The biggest issue for Wenger is whether he can reinvent himself and Arsenal not only to enjoy a second era of sustained success, but also to build a lasting legacy for the club. It would appear that, increasingly, some feel that he needs help to continue his progression at Arsenal.

CHAPTER 17

THE SUMMER OF 2014

'I WILL NOT DANCE ON THE BEACH in Rio, believe me,' said Arsene Wenger, barely managing a smile amid the tension of the build-up to the 2014 FA Cup final. 'Honestly, you win the next game or you lose it. If you win it, what do you think? You think you dance for one week? No, you think about preparing well for the next season, and winning the first game of next season. That's what it has to be ...'

Wenger didn't dance on the beach in Ipanema in Rio de Janeiro – but he did just about everything else. Beach volley-ball, head tennis, swimming, football and even going for the odd run opposite his plush five-star hotel. He had a whale of a time.

If ever there was a man who appeared transformed, then it was Wenger. Gone was the manager showing the signs of stress and feeling the pressure, to be replaced by someone who looked years younger, full of energy and in remarkably good physical shape for a 64-year-old, even when wearing very brief trunks – which, inevitably, the newspapers compared to a pair worn by 007 star Daniel Craig in a James Bond movie.

And no wonder. While Wenger seemed to be having the time of his life on the beach in front of the paparazzi – fooling one columnist into lambasting his lack of transfer activity – the hard work was being done behind the scenes. It was quickly becoming Arsenal's busiest and most exciting transfer window since Wenger arrived at the club.

Wenger does the same at every tournament. As French TV station TF1's star co-commentator, he bases himself at the best location throughout the World Cup or European Championship, whatever it may be. In South Africa in 2010, Wenger was largely in Johannesburg. At the Euros in 2012, he stationed himself in Warsaw. At the 2014 World Cup in Brazil, he was in Rio. Wenger either travelled around with the TV crew or, very often, was given a lift in David Dein's private jet. They remain inseparable. It's also worth remembering that, despite his acrimonious departure from Arsenal, Dein is on friendly terms with the current chief executive Ivan Gazidis and there is certainly no animosity there.

Wenger was very visible throughout the World Cup, warmly greeting familiar faces from the English media, enjoying a casual chat more than being pumped for information. He looked calm and relaxed. While working for TV, he often travels to games in white trainers before changing into smarter shoes to go with the rest of his attire. On passing through an airport he might stop for a chat, or have a drink in a hotel bar, and any hostilities towards the media had vanished. He would even quickly return text messages with an exclamation mark or perhaps even attempt a joke, poking fun at the latest enquiry.

Wenger was also good company for the band of former players, partnering Christian Karembeu in a beach volleyball team and spending time at dinner in the hotel with Fabio Cannavaro. On the final weekend in Rio, he spent a lot of time with Liverpool manager Brendan Rodgers, as they shared a meal, a drink and convivial conversations over the course of a couple of nights.

The previous summer they'd been at loggerheads over the transfer tug-of-war involving Luis Suarez. This summer Arsenal had beaten Liverpool to Alexis Sanchez, a player Rodgers openly admitted he was desperately disappointed not to get to replace Suarez. But this time Wenger, renowned among other managers for not mixing with his peers, not sharing the traditional post-match glass of wine and not even going to the annual end-of-season League Managers' Association dinner, was good company as he and Rodgers recalled the trials and tribulations of the past season and, more tellingly, the test of the summer transfer window.

But Wenger seemed re-energised by the imminent arrival of new players. The wide variety of signings was also perfect for him. Alexis Sanchez, a world-class striker with a fantastic work rate; a young up-and-coming player with real potential in Calum Chambers; a French defender, Mathieu Debuchy; and a Colombian keeper, David Ospina, with much to prove in the Premier League. This was surely the ideal Wenger dynamic.

The signing that took a lot of groundwork was Sanchez. When it was hinted that he was about to become available at Barcelona, Arsenal put him at the top of their list, ahead of the likes of Mario Balotelli, Loic Remy and Mario Mandzukic. Sanchez was the sort of player they had been looking for the previous summer – and he didn't come with the Suarez baggage.

The groundwork was done by Dick Law, who spoke to Sanchez's agent Fernando Felicevich over the course of several phone calls and meetings in Spain and London. Arsenal quickly became extremely confident they were going to get their man, as promises were made on handshakes and it was all done with the blessing of Barcelona, who needed the money to finance a move for Suarez.

The really impressive part was the fee, which was set at £33 million and surprised many observers, though it was typical Wenger, always driving a hard bargain. While other clubs – Juventus, Liverpool and Manchester United – were making enquiries about Sanchez, the deal was already in the bag. Liverpool actually offered around £5 million more but, according to one source, Arsenal 'always knew the player was going to join' them.

Sanchez spoke to Wenger while in Brazil, and the Arsenal manager outlined his vision, the way Arsenal played and that he was central to his plans. He explained that Sanchez would fit into the system and help Arsenal win trophies. Wenger is a very good salesman. He is able to charm players and win them over, as he did with Mesut Ozil the previous summer, and his reputation quickly gains their respect.

Debuchy was an interesting case. Despite being French and succeeding Bacary Sagna as first choice in the French national team, when I first heard of Arsenal's interest and did an internet search, nothing came up linking his name to the club. That is very rare in this day and age.

The story was that Arsenal were sounded out, showed an interest and, the next thing, Debuchy was doing a press conference at the World Cup stressing that he wanted to play Champions League football this coming season. Debuchy was putting the wheels in motion, suggesting he wanted to move on, and he did it knowing it could help grease the wheels. Like it or not, that's how football works.

Arsenal were heavily linked with a move to re-sign Carlos Vela – brilliantly nicknamed Sid The Sexist in the dressing room during his first spell at the club because of his resemblance to the *Viz* cartoon character – but that was never going to happen. They had a buy-back clause in Vela's contract, but it was seen as a bargaining tool rather than a genuine option.

Wenger did not want to lose Lukasz Fabianski as his number two keeper, but his departure forced him to look for a new goalie and the World Cup was the perfect shop window. Fabianski was fed up with being second choice. He wanted to move on, so joined Swansea City on a free transfer. A number of keepers were suggested to Wenger: Cardiff's David Marshall was first choice, but he was priced at £10 million; Reading youngster Alex McCarthy was priced out of a move at £6.5 million; and some loose interest in Norwich's John Ruddy cooled when a price tag of £5 million was put on his head.

Wenger was then besieged by calls about potential keepers, including Mexico's goalie Guillermo Ochoa after his heroic display against Holland. But Wenger said he was not built for the Premier League. Instead, Wenger had made up his mind on Ospina, believing the Colombian to be good enough to challenge first choice Wojciech Szczesny and back him up.

But the signing that probably excited Wenger as much as any was Calum Chambers, who had been scouted tirelessly by Steve Rowley throughout the previous season and spotted during other spying missions to watch Luke Shaw. Chambers had been on Arsenal's radar for a long time but, intriguingly, not necessarily as a right back: he had played centre back and defensive midfield throughout the age groups for England. He took it upon himself to switch to right back to try to hold down a regular place at Southampton – only for Arsenal to spot his versatility and try to change him back.

But the clincher was that Wenger met Chambers and his family, and sold the club to them. He told Chambers he would play 20-odd games in the forthcoming season, either as a back-up right back or, as was the longer-term plan, as a centre half and holding midfielder. The impressive part for any younger player – as Aaron Ramsey or Alex Oxlade-Chamberlain had discovered in the past – was that Wenger knew all about them, their characteristics and where they could play. Sitting before Chambers was one of the great managers of his lifetime – Chambers was born just under 18 months before Wenger took over at Arsenal – telling him he was a big part of Arsenal's future. He made up his mind to join Arsenal, no matter how early it was in his career.

Just as it had with Aaron Ramsey, who was flown out with his family on a private jet to meet Wenger at Euro 2008 in Switzerland, the personal touch won the day. Ramsey told me back in March 2013 that Wenger's faith in him at the time, and during some low points through lack of form and injury, made the Frenchman one of the biggest influences on his career. The Welsh player, who chose Arsenal over Manchester United and Everton, said:

The main factor in joining Arsenal was meeting with Arsene Wenger and to hear what his plans were for me. He has brought through so many youngsters and given them opportunities and turned them into great players.

They flew me over there to have a meeting with him. I was overwhelmed. I was 17, and one of the best managers in the world wants to meet me face to face. It was definitely a hard choice to make at my age, but I've no regrets, I think I made the right choice. I felt more wanted at Arsenal, I felt the plan was better for me and they gave youngsters more opportunities. Manchester United also had a lot of midfielders at the time as well.

It's great that all the British players chose to commit to the club [Arsenal] and it's important to have that.

When talking about the impact Wenger had on persuading him to join Arsenal, Chambers said: 'The great thing about him is that he makes you feel wanted, feel part of it, and gives you the confidence to go and play your game. He is a great manager, has a great history of bringing through young players, so I've got a lot of respect for him. He told me to relax, enjoy myself in training and express myself.

'He's brought through so many players, like Alex [Oxlade-Chamberlain], Theo [Walcott] and so many others. He gives young players a great chance. It's a great place to train, work and improve. I think everyone makes sure that the standard of training is really intense [and] really high every day.'

It is clear that Wenger gets as much – if not more – enjoyment from signing young players as he does world-class ones. He has gained a reputation for flying all over Europe to meet with young players, and convince their families that their youngster is safe in Arsenal's hands. From Cesc Fabregas and Philippe Senderos, to Ramsey, Chambers and whoever – there seems to be a genuine desire to do the right thing by young players in terms of developing them not just as footballers but as young men too.

Suddenly, Arsenal were competing on a more level playing field as they built up their squad, tried to be stronger and were also as active in the transfer market as Gazidis had wanted and spoken about the previous summer. Wenger himself looked revitalised, even if his body didn't feel like it. Fast approaching 65 at the time, he complained of a sore back after playing in a staff football match. Former Arsenal keeper Jens Lehmann, who has been a regular back at the club while doing his coaching badges and remains a very popular figure, is the organiser and when Lehmann calls, you can't say no. Wenger's team drew 2-2 and it was the first time they hadn't won in 13 games. 'It's the worst I've played in a long time. I'd give myself two out of 10.

Jens Lehmann was very upset,' smiled Wenger through the pain of his aching back.

There can be no doubt that his summer of fun in Brazil, combined with a busy and productive transfer window and winning the FA Cup, lifted the pressure from Wenger's shoulders and dispelled the gloom. Wenger was in a good place, even though a couple of issues kept cropping up. One was Cesc Fabregas and Arsenal's failure to re-sign him when they had a first option – written into the original deal when Fabregas was sold to Barcelona – to buy him back should another club bid for him.

Wenger felt sure in his heart of hearts that, despite making all the right noises publicly, Fabregas didn't want to return to Arsenal. Maybe the previous summer, when Manchester United were keen to sign him, it might have been more of a possibility, before Arsenal signed Mesut Ozil. In fact, Wenger spent the whole of that summer 2013 telling those of us on Arsenal's pre-season tour of Asia that they would move for Fabregas if he became available, and it was obvious they were still in touch and friendly. However, Fabregas never really came close to leaving Barcelona in 2013, but the following year he was told very early on that he could leave.

Fabregas's departure from Arsenal hadn't been smooth and, even though he parted on good terms with Wenger, the Spanish midfielder forced the issue and there were those at the club who weren't in a rush to take him back. Similarly, Fabregas clearly fancied a new adventure at a club where he would stand a greater chance of winning trophies. Wenger maintains that by the time Arsenal were told Fabregas was available, the deal with Chelsea had already largely been done.

Fabregas is represented by leading agent Darren Dein, son of Wenger's great friend and the club's former vice-chairman David Dein. Darren Dein has sold a succession of players from the club, including Fabregas, Thierry Henry and Gael Clichy. Dein is a very good agent for his clients and was Thierry Henry's best man, while Henry also went to Dein's wedding, missing an Arsenal game in the process (he was injured and therefore able to attend).

That Fabregas wanted to go to Chelsea rather than Arsenal is a view backed up by both Jose Mourinho and Wenger. The Chelsea manager missed his son's final football match of the season to go and see Fabregas which, to the Spanish midfielder, proved how much he wanted him. Mourinho said in July 2014: 'I spoke with him for 20 minutes. I think he really wanted to come to us. As you know, Arsenal had an option where they could interfere, but I think he was not open to that. I think he was very, very much in our direction, so it was an easy job for me.'

That is echoed by Wenger. 'I believe his decision was already made. I also told you why it was not a subject for us. We were in search of more up front and more defensive opportunities than creative midfielders. We have many. I personally believe that deal was done a long time ago, early 2014. Look, people came out and said he wanted to go to Chelsea, so I don't know who tells the truth. But he landed where he wanted to go.'

It really is, therefore, a nonsense to suggest that Arsenal should have re-signed Fabregas and that they made a mistake by not doing so. Despite the first-option clause, the deal was never a prospect for Arsenal because Fabregas had chosen Chelsea. Wenger smiled when pressed about why he felt the deal with Chelsea was already done. 'My instinct,' he said.

The only consolation for Arsenal was that the complex Fabregas deal not only included a first option – worthless though that proved to be – but also a slice of any transfer fee, which netted them a further £5 million.

In the end, Wenger was left to praise and defend, in equal measure, his own midfield playmaker Mesut Ozil, who had struggled at times during his first season not only to adapt to English football but also against the Fabregas comparisons. The key difference with Fabregas was that he was Premier League ready, having already established himself with Arsenal before joining Chelsea. Fabregas was braced for it. Ozil, by contrast, continued to labour.

It's so easy to forget that Ozil won the World Cup in the summer of 2014, played all the games and had his best game in the final. But of all Wenger's lightweight fancy-Dan players, Ozil is the one, despite his obvious quality, who has struggled to win over some of his critics.

Wenger, ever loyal to his players, insists that the critics of Arsenal's £42 million German midfielder are unfair:

> People are very harsh with Ozil because he's a player who's always very easy on his play, but when you watch the game again after, the next day, you see what a player he is. Everything he does is intelligent. The timing of everything he does is absolutely perfect. You never catch him giving the ball too late. The number of players you catch giving the ball too late is unbelievable. You never get that with Ozil. He's like a guy who plays the music, the timing of what he does is perfect, you don't get many players like that.
>
> He will never be a tackler. But he is not getting enough praise. He came back as a World Cup winner. He played all seven games. He played some good games. There was the same debate in Germany during the World Cup and in other games but, at end of the day, he was always in the team.

The fascinating thing about football is that those in the game tend to hear what's going on not just at their own club, but everywhere else in the Premier League, if not Europe. Wenger is certainly not a manager who is glued to his phone. In fact, one former employee says that, throughout the best part of a decade, they probably only had half a dozen phone conversations. Wenger often responds better to text messages and emails – and if he does ring then you know it's serious.

There have been several occasions when, just in chatting, Wenger has clearly known something about a player, his fitness, perhaps, or whether he's about to sign for someone else. That's how it works in football: it's one big soap opera full of gossip. For example, Wenger let slip in conversation that Juan Mata was going to Chelsea before Mata had been seriously linked with the club. Wenger knew because Arsenal had been on the case, and while they dithered, Chelsea sneaked in and signed him instead.

It's ironic that when Arsenal did their mad 'supermarket sweep' in the summer 2011 transfer window, signing Per Mertesacker, Mikel Arteta, Andre Santos and Yossi Benayoun on loan, Wenger was out of the country at a conference during the final few days. That was also the case at the end of the 2014 summer window, when Arsenal became desperate after Olivier Giroud, the first-choice centre forward, broke his tibia in a 2-2 draw at Everton, was ruled out for three months and, suddenly, they were left with Yaya Sanogo, a powerful but raw France Under-21 forward, leading their attack. They had plenty of good build-up play, but no one to finish it off.

Wenger was adamant in the final week of the window that he wasn't going to buy. Samuel Eto'o, desperate to move to Arsenal, offered to pull out of a move to Everton, but Wenger did not fancy it. Eto'o's big motivation was to move to a club that could threaten Chelsea and to gain revenge on Jose Mourinho, who had questioned his age during an off-the-record chat with TV reporters that was later shown on French television.

But the pressure on Wenger to buy really grew after Arsenal drew at newly promoted Leicester, and their lack of firepower meant they looked as if they were really struggling for goals. As so often in the past, the players were fed up and were complaining privately that Wenger had money but wasn't signing anyone and they needed to. The previous week, Arsenal had put wheels in motion on a few different options, asking about Danny Welbeck and Radamel Falcao among others.

Falcao was an interesting proposition – and Arsenal came very close to bringing him in. The Colombian was at Monaco; he was regarded as one of the finest strikers in the world, but had suffered a serious knee injury and missed the World Cup. In the meantime, Monaco's owner, Dmitry Rybolovlev, appeared to be losing interest in the club following a costly divorce and decided to cut his overheads. Falcao was made available for loan and his agent Jorge Mendes was charged with finding a club – the most likely destination was England, because Premier League clubs like Chelsea, Manchester City or Manchester United could afford him if they could balance up their Financial Fair Play regulations so as not to break UEFA's spending rules.

But the surprise team in the market was Arsenal. The problem with the Falcao deal was that the package was mind-blowing: £20 million for one season, made up of a loan fee and wages of £15.6 million a year – added to which there were doubts about whether and how quickly he could get back to his best and peak fitness after a long lay-off for such a serious knee injury. To further complicate matters, the payment involved a complex method whereby a large proportion of the wages was to be paid to the tax haven of Monaco. Several clubs had concerns about whether the deal would actually break the rules.

But after Arsenal's draw at Leicester, Dick Law pushed ahead to try to make the Falcao deal happen. Arsenal have always had a difficult relationship with Mendes, the majority of whose deals with English clubs have been with Chelsea, Manchester United and Manchester City. Despite the mind-boggling figures, Arsenal were prepared to do a one-year loan deal, having discussed the Falcao transfer at great length. In fact, Dick Law went to bed on Sunday 31 August believing a deal was on. By the time Law woke up the following morning, the day the transfer window shut, the figures had changed as another club, Manchester United, had come in. The knock-on effect of this was that United would have to balance their own books to bring in Falcao and the obvious player out of the door was Danny Welbeck.

Meanwhile, Wenger had long since agreed to referee and manage a team in an all-star fundraising Match for Peace charity game in Rome and, together with his regular adviser Leon Angel, got an early flight to Italy. When pictures of Wenger at an airport and reports of what he was doing hit social media, Arsenal fans were furious at the prospect of the club not signing a striker while Wenger jetted off to Rome, which, as far as they were concerned, was a dereliction of duty.

By sheer fate, Welbeck was on England duty and the team were training at Arsenal's London Colney training ground. It was possibly to be the easiest and quickest scouting mission of Steve Rowley's career, as he simply popped out of his office, watched training and even kidded a couple of journalists that he was just curious to see what they were doing. Rowley was, in fact, taking in every kick of Welbeck's training session and, meanwhile, Arsenal's players were mounting a charm offensive. Jack Wilshere tried to 'tap him up' to come, while Per Mertesacker and Mikel Arteta went one step further – they collared him in the gym, found out his availability and urged him to join the club.

From then on, Ivan Gazidis took matters in his own hands. The deal took various twists and turns throughout the day. At first it looked as if only a loan deal might be on, then Manchester United wanted a permanent deal and, even with only a few hours remaining, it was still very much in the balance. Eventually, with the clock ticking down, Arsenal got it over the line. It was a tense moment for United because Falcao's medical and final negotiations were taking longer than expected, but there was no way they could pull the plug on the Welbeck deal.

Wenger quipped afterwards that the deal would not have gone ahead had he not chosen to go and participate in the charity match in Rome. 'Meeting the Pope was an experience I did not want to miss,' Wenger smiled. 'There were many Argentine people there, because they like Maradona. I had him afterwards in my team.

'I am a Catholic, so it was an experience, and [invitation] I accepted a long time ago and, on top of that, it was a game for peace and multi-religion understanding. I thought as we are a bit in front of an international religious war, it was a very important game. [The Pope] was a great person to meet because he shows humility and is available to meet for everybody. He has a word with everybody. He is a supporter of San Lorenzo in Argentina. He is a football fan. You cannot be born in Argentina and not be a football fan! I wanted to be discreet and say: "It was nice to meet you and bye-bye."'

Wenger then laughed about managing Diego Maradona: 'It was very difficult! He comes late, and he wants to play ...'

Wenger is always at his most entertaining when talking about anything but football. Religion, him being a Catholic and meeting the Pope, gave an insight into Wenger beyond his injury updates or a soundbite for the back page. A bit of small talk always loosens him up as well, before we get down to the nitty-gritty. It is always fascinating to discover what football people think about subjects other than football. Discovering something different about someone in football can completely change your perception of them.

However, it was hard to get a straight answer out of Wenger about whether he wanted a loan deal for Welbeck, or a permanent one, and why exactly the deal wouldn't have happened had he not gone to Rome. He had this to say about the deal:

> If I had not travelled that day, Welbeck would not be here. I'll explain that a bit later, but the coincidence made that because I was on my way. If I stayed at home, Welbeck would not be here today. I will tell you that story one day but that's the truth.
>
> We are in 2014 and you can always be in touch with everybody, even when you travel. The advantage of that day was I had to get up at six o'clock in the morning and I was available the whole day.
>
> At the moment, I thought when Manchester United bought Falcao they had to let somebody go and I was not aware at the start when I heard that he could be available. It was quick because it was on the last day of the transfer window and I had no hesitation to do it.

When asked whether he would have preferred a loan deal for Welbeck, he replied: 'With an option to buy, yes. At the start the player was only available on loan but after he became available to buy, I agreed.'

Wenger also said that he'd met Sir Alex Ferguson at a two-day coaching conference after signing Welbeck. All the press talk was that Ferguson – unlike Louis van Gaal – would never have sold a home-grown player like Welbeck to a direct rival.

'You should ask him,' smiled Wenger. 'I met him [Ferguson] by coincidence on Tuesday and Wednesday, and I would like to keep that conversation to myself! He [Welbeck] can first of all make himself a better player because I can help him. He's a young boy, he's not 24 yet, and let's not forget that some players who arrived here at the age of 23 made huge careers here, so I hope we can contribute and help him.'

By the end of the transfer window, Wenger had, with the funds he'd been given to build and strengthen, assembled his new-look team. Having won the FA Cup in 2014, bought big that summer – including a genuine world-class talent in Alexis Sanchez – and closed the window with a big signing in Welbeck, it was essential that the club showed signs of progress. It was supposed to define Wenger and reveal whether he could reinvent himself at Arsenal in order to help the club scale the heights all over again.

CHAPTER 18

FINAL JUDGEMENT

ARSENE WENGER IS AT HIS BEST when his back is against the wall. It makes him more determined and defiant, while his teams often tend to dig out results when they need them most. He also seems to relish the gallows humour that goes with being under pressure in football.

When Arsenal had, what Wenger might describe as 'a little wobble' after the turn of the year in the 2014/15 season, the familiar rumblings from supporters could be heard again, especially after they lost 3-1 at home to Monaco at the end of February. That defeat brought about the familiar frustrations and questions as to whether it was time for Wenger to stand aside.

Wenger is not foolish. He hears the supporters' moans and groans – even if he often chooses to ignore them. At one of the increasing number of question-and-answer sessions for well-heeled executive fans to keep them onside, Wenger displayed his familiar sense of humour when a supporter asked whether he had an exit strategy.

'Yes, I thought I'd go downstairs, leave by the front door, get a taxi and go home,' smiled Wenger.

Wenger knew the fan was asking whether – and how – he was thinking about leaving his position as Arsenal manager. But his reply made it very clear that he had absolutely no intention of standing down. Anyone who suggests otherwise doesn't know the man. He sees it as a personal insult if people judge him on the back of one defeat and start calling for him to go. That, as Wenger sees it, is to ignore all of the good work that has gone before in the previous 19 years. What is 90 minutes compared to nearly two decades? That is Wenger's mindset and yet it is clearly at odds with the frustrations of supporters who get upset after big defeats. While Wenger has always taken defeat badly, he has also been able to see the bigger picture.

During the three years of gradual decline and break-up of the Invincibles team, he would often stand in the dressing room after a defeat and, in full view of the other players, say to Thierry Henry: 'Don't worry, we played well, we had more shots.'

It was almost as if Wenger was trying to reassure himself as Arsenal went from being champions to also-rans. In his heart of hearts, Wenger must have known his team was no longer good enough to challenge for the top prizes. When you go from Robert Pires to Gervinho, it's difficult to measure up to previous standards. But despite working with lesser players, Wenger has continued to defy the odds and logic by keeping Arsenal in the top four. Yet now, Wenger is driven by a desire to build another successful team with the club's new-found spending power, based on their self-sustaining wealth.

Wenger likes to pontificate and tell people about his philosophy and how his way is the right way. That is why he tends to enjoy the Q&A sessions for supporters, as the club offer these exclusive evenings for wealthy box holders, diamond club members and executive fans. During these events, Wenger drops his guard and many of the less confrontational fans are soon eating out of his hand. He will tell them about player contracts and even revealed that Wojciech Szczesny would be dropped in January 2015 before he had actually told the Arsenal keeper himself.

When asked about Theo Walcott's contract negotiations and whether he thought it was to do with the England winger's desire to play as a more central striker, Wenger leaned back in his chair and gently sang the Abba song: 'Money, Money, Money'.

Every season brings its own funny moments, controversies, highlights and disappointments. They seem to be amplified these days because Arsenal fans are more savvy on social media than most, they are a massive London club and, in Arsene Wenger, they have one of the most high profile and famous managers in world football.

For example, when Newcastle's caretaker manager John Carver had an angry exchange with fans, only one newspaper carried the story with any prominence. The *Sunday Telegraph* put it on the front of their sports pull-out, but every other paper buried it inside somewhere. Compare that to Wenger being abused by angry Arsenal fans at Stoke railway station in December 2014 after a disappointing defeat: it was back-page news for days. One fan filmed the incident and TV pundit Gary Lineker took to Twitter to call the video 'disgusting, inexcusable and disrespectful'.

Wenger is in the spotlight all of the time. He can be spiky and dismissive of questions about things he does not like or want to talk about. The trick is often to word the question in such a way that it draws a response. Two days after those angry scenes at Stoke railway station, Wenger was in Istanbul for the pre-match press conference ahead of Arsenal's final Champions League Group stage fixture.

Wenger knew the questions were coming and handled them brilliantly. And if you analyse what he said and what unfolded in the rest of the campaign, it makes perfect sense:

We are professional footballers and football people, we have to cope with that. I am a competitive person. What is important is the next game and responding in a strong way. It is part of our job. We cannot always look for excuses. We are down. Everyone feels it. When you have a disappointment you have to respond in a strong way.

You cannot guarantee you will never lose a game. But many teams will lose at Stoke. You have to be realistic. The response during the game was strong and everyone is disappointed, but the Premier League is difficult and we want to be judged at the end of the season.

This is my 180th Champions League game and that shows something. Many of those were for this club. We want to be judged at the end of the season. Not after every single game when emotion is very high. Let's get our stability back and see at the end of the season where we are.

Wenger finds it impossible to accept that people can judge him after one bad result, out of more than 1,000 games in charge. He believes that to condemn him on the back of one mistake, an own goal, a refereeing error or moment of pure bad luck would be so harsh. I'm convinced that is why he can be quite dismissive, even after a season-changing defeat, such as the Monaco game at the Emirates in February 2015 which effectively ended their Champions League campaign. However, this response only succeeds in winding up fans even more. It looks as if the manager doesn't care enough when actually he is just trying to put it in context.

After that Galatasaray press conference held in an airport hotel, Wenger walked off the stage and a couple of us went up and had a chat. He was very relaxed, seemed happy that he'd got a strong message out on his terms and actually even told us not just the team line-up but in which formation they would play, which was extremely unusual.

Arsenal beat Galatasaray, Aaron Ramsey scored a wonderful goal and yet pulled a hamstring which ruled him out for a month (a very familiar story of two steps forward and one step back for Arsenal) and, in doing so, prompted Wenger to recall Francis Coquelin from a loan spell at Charlton. Little could he have known that Coquelin, a French midfielder who had failed to make the grade and was preparing to leave when his contract expired, would change the course of Arsenal's season.

Finally, through Ramsey's bad luck, Arsenal had a defensive-minded midfielder, the player the fans had been crying out for since Patrick Vieira and Gilberto Silva had left. Coquelin started at West Ham after Christmas, Arsenal won and, despite a defeat at Southampton on New Year's Day, it signalled an upturn in results and fortunes that gave Wenger new momentum in 2015.

The low point of the 2014/15 season came with the defeat at Southampton. The fall-out from the game at St Mary's had ramifications for the rest of the season. After a disastrous performance during the match, reports filtered out that Szczesny had infuriated Wenger after being caught smoking in the showers, fined and dropped. It was given additional weight by former Arsenal midfielder John Jensen who said on Danish TV station 6'eren that the keeper wouldn't play again that season. I managed to find out what Szczesny had done and the *Daily Mirror* ran a back-page story. The keeper is one of my favourite characters and so there was a tinge of regret that I had to write the story.

Wenger did not deny it at his next press conference, even offering various anecdotes about smoking during his playing days in France and he admitted he smoked during his time as a young coach.

'The other day I was watching French television they showed

me on the bench smoking a cigarette,' said Wenger when a few of us pressed him on his views about smoking. 'I didn't even think it was me ... I grew up in a pub where you did not see from here to the window because of the smoke and I spent my youth selling cigarettes. But times have changed. Society has had an evolution. In some respects in a positive way in others in a negative way; this is one of the positives today that people don't smoke any more. You cannot smoke in public spaces, that means people who are not smokers don't suffer.'

The other noteworthy part of that Southampton defeat was that it meant that, incredibly, Arsenal had yet to win three games in a row in the Premier League. Their form was inconsistent and they were struggling to maintain a push for another top four finish, with the Saints ahead of them in the table, as well as Chelsea and the two Manchester clubs. It prompted Arsenal's senior players to call one of their now-regular team meetings, and it was Per Mertesacker – captain in the absence of Mikel Arteta – who led a delegation to Wenger to outline their concerns of how the team was playing.

The players wanted to be tighter defensively, set up differently and focus more on defence rather than attack. The change was never more obvious than when Arsenal went to Manchester City on Sunday 18 January and pulled off a memorable 2-0 win, which was lauded by Sky Sports pundit Gary Neville.

'We've seen so many examples over the last four or five years of Arsenal capitulating that if you offered me the opportunity to come back as an Arsenal defender, I would have said no. It wouldn't have been much fun,' said Neville. 'I've seen it too many times with Arsenal. Today, the defenders were never exposed; it was one of the best back-four performances I've seen.'

It was viewed as a game changer for Arsenal. And it was the players who persuaded Wenger to change their approach, especially after their heavy defeats to top four rivals the previous season. Wenger admitted that it was the players who persuaded him to go against his attacking principles:

> You can say to the team: 'It's not especially my style of play,' but at some stage you cannot go against the feelings of the team because it's detrimental to the result. The team sometimes needs to be reassured and reassurance comes first from feeling solid and strong, and then you can express your talent and our confidence in the big games had been damaged by those big results [last season].
>
> Of course [I listened to the players]. Your tactics have to be aligned as well with the feeling of the team and with the confidence level of the team. That's why you hear so many times in the papers or on television: 'Let's get back to basics.'
>
> It's not because a team doesn't know the basics, it's just to get the priorities right to reinforce the confidence of the team again, because you gain it slowly back by feeling that you are not going to get blown away.

Arsenal, with Coquelin patrolling midfield, suddenly found a balance in the team and a consistency which propelled them to the FA Cup final, saw them go on their best winning run in the Premier League since the Invincibles days – they won eight in a row – and the questions and doubts among the fans about Wenger were quietened down.

From time to time, there is an explosion on social media. When Borussia Dortmund boss Jurgen Klopp, the darling of the modern 'hipster' fan because of what he has achieved in Germany, announced in April 2015 he would be leaving at the end of the 2014/15 season for a new challenge, it set off another one. Klopp is seen by some as a perfect replacement for Wenger.

Wenger, understandably, became a bit tetchy when asked out-right whether he thought Klopp would be a good replacement. As journalists, we all have to ask daft questions and sometimes we lose sight of what is downright disrespectful. But we ask it all the same. Wenger snapped back: 'I am not an agency to place managers. I find that circus a bit ridiculous, honestly.'

However, the closing few weeks of the 2014/15 season saw Wenger and the club in much happier spirits. In the spring, they invited several sets of players' families to the training ground. On one such occasion, the families of Jack Wilshere, Per Mertesacker and Kieran Gibbs were all given a guided tour of the facilities at London Colney as they saw everything from the media building, changing room, training pitches and players' canteen. The families were charmed by the experience. It highlighted just what a family club Arsenal is and how they try to make their players feel part of it.

Sometimes it works, sometimes it doesn't. Arsenal have always prided themselves on being a club with class and tradition, they tell the players to behave with manners. And, without question, Wenger has bought into that tradition, embraced it and promoted it to his players. It is part of his philosophy on and off the pitch. The atmosphere in the dressing room is one of camaraderie and togetherness. In Wenger's mind, it helps performances because the teamwork is there and they gel on and off the pitch. When there have been a couple of rotten apples in the dressing room, it has tended to coincide with disappointing seasons. They have been moved on quickly.

Wenger had also found a happy balance between homegrown players, clever signings and big stars like Alexis Sanchez and Mesut Ozil. The blend of developing young players, shrewd signings and world-class talent has provided him with a great squad.

Arsenal's form in the 2014/15 run-in was remarkable. One of the most eye-catching results was the FA Cup quarter-final win at Old Trafford, Danny Welbeck – Arsenal's deadline-day signing from Manchester United – scoring the winner against his old club. Welbeck admitted it felt 'weird' warming up at the other end of his old ground, but couldn't help but celebrate with particular delight after keeping a dignified silence when United boss Louis Van Gaal had made several critical remarks about him after selling him.

That was the highlight of Arsenal's FA Cup run which took them to Wembley. Eight days later, they came close but couldn't quite overturn Monaco's first-leg lead when they won 2-0 in France but went out on away goals for another depressing Champions League exit. Of all their wins in the Premier League run-in, few were better than at Hull City on 4 May when Arsenal won 3-1. For part of that game – they desperately needed to win to finish in the top three to qualify automatically for the Champions League – they reached sublime heights with their passing and movement.

Francis Coquelin anchored the midfield, Santi Cazorla provided the impetus in his new 'number eight' role, Aaron Ramsey scored, Alexis Sanchez thrilled, Mesut Ozil glided across the pitch, while Olivier Giroud was the focal point of attack. During spells of that game, Arsenal reached football's equivalent of utopia. The problem was that it was too little, too late. Chelsea had clinched the Premier League title the day before.

Wenger's running war of words with Chelsea boss Jose Mourinho had escalated, their bitterness and feud returned to perhaps underline the fact that the Portuguese once again felt the need to go back on the offensive as he views Arsenal as a genuine threat once more. There could be no better compliment.

Arsenal were in great form when they met Chelsea at the Emirates on 26 April. They had just won eight Premier League games in a row, and Wenger had a great chance of ending his run of never having beaten Mourinho in 12 meetings between the two managers. But Arsenal could not find their free-flowing, rhythmic football just when they needed it most. Chelsea, in the midst of a dip in form but still grinding out results, held on for a draw and celebrated on the pitch afterwards as if they had won the title. To all intents and purposes they had, since they had held off one of their biggest challengers, as Arsenal fans chanted 'Boring, boring Chelsea' in frustration at the goalless stalemate.

Typically, Mourinho didn't let it pass without getting his own back at Arsenal, Wenger and their fans. 'You know, boring I think is ten years without a title. That's very boring,' said Mourinho. 'You support the club and you're waiting, waiting, waiting for so many years without a Premier League title, so that's very boring. But maybe they aren't singing to us.'

A few days later, Wenger picked his moment to give a dignified response, but accused Mourinho of a lack of respect. 'The biggest thing for a manager is to respect each other and some people have to improve on that,' said Wenger pointedly. 'Everybody lives with his own internal problems and I live with mine. That is enough.'

Mourinho could not let it lie and, at Chelsea's end-of-season awards night, made a speech – which he called a 'fiction story' – with the aid of an elaborate video to mock Manchester United, Manchester City and, last of all, Arsenal for only playing between January and April. Wenger was asked about it the next morning at his pre-FA Cup final press conference.

'Forget his speech, and get to something else,' Wenger snapped. 'I'm not interested in his speech. I just don't listen to what people say. I listen to the questions you ask to me and those I don't want to answer, I don't want to answer.'

The simmering rivalry will surely continue. But nothing could distract Wenger from the build-up to the FA Cup final. There was a different atmosphere around the club from 12 months previously, when there had been the nerves and tension surrounding the build-up to the Hull City final, when it felt like Wenger's whole future was on the line.

Arsenal stayed at the Hilton Hotel in Wembley the night before the game. Despite being a stone's throw away from the stadium, the players still have to board a coach to get to the ground. It's a matter of a couple of hundred yards but security insists upon it. But once out on the pitch, Arsenal brought everything together and delivered a brilliant performance to retain the FA Cup, which meant Wenger became the first post-war manager to win the trophy six times.

Wenger was brave and bold by selecting Theo Walcott up front ahead of Giroud, while Sanchez, Ozil and Cazorla all played at their very best as Arsenal completely overwhelmed Aston Villa. The pace, power and movement of Arsenal through their midfield and attack was mesmerising at times. The pitch can be slower than the Emirates, which is kept slick to help Arsenal's play, but for once the Wembley grass was shorter, and Arsenal found their rhythm. Sanchez's wonderful 25-yard strike – which dipped and swerved – will go down as one of the great cup final goals. It typified a great day for Arsenal.

In fact, the 4-0 scoreline doesn't tell the whole story of just how dominant Arsenal were. It's hard to remember a more one-sided FA Cup final – even when Manchester United beat Millwall 3-0 in 2004, when the latter were mid-table in the second tier of English football, it was closer.

Wenger, dressed elegantly in a Lanvin club suit, looked like the cat who had got the cream afterwards. When asked whether finishing the season with another trophy was the best way to answer the critics, Wenger smiled: 'We don't miss the critics.'

Meanwhile, the players took more than an hour to come out of the dressing room as more beer and champagne was shipped in.

The Arsenal hierarchy, including majority shareholder Stan Kroenke, were all at Wembley. Club captain Mikel Arteta, who missed the second half of the season through injury, enjoyed playing to the audience when the bigwigs walked in with Ozil playing hide and seek behind a medical screen. 'Ivan, where are our bonuses?' shouted Arteta in jest at Arsenal's chief executive Ivan Gazidis. Gazidis played along, pointing to his heart to show that's where it should matter.

The traditional post-match press conference rituals took place after the Wembley final. Wenger was content and happy, the questions were as much about the future as the FA Cup success because the campaign had highlighted the fact that Arsenal should be title challengers next season.

When he was told that Arsenal had looked better than a team which finished third in the Premier League, Wenger replied: 'We have to show that next season and we want to do it. I feel that we have moved forward, and people think always it's about buying, but it's as well about cohesion and cohesion is a very important factor that is a bit underrated usually by people. We have to keep that cohesion and maybe add quality. But the quality we have to add is in short numbers. But the other teams – how good will Chelsea be? Who will they buy? I don't know.'

Wenger was also asked as to whether they would compete at the top end of the transfer market this summer, bidding for players over and above the £60 million mark. He answered:

We have not spent that kind of money. People forget that for years we had to sell our best players and that was a very difficult period. That is the reality. Since we buy again, we slowly come back to a more competitive level. You speak maybe about stratospheric numbers where we will not be involved. Not at that level for financial reasons. It's simple.

I do not want to tell you how much money we have. But I have not made a clear decision yet for what I will do. Don't rule anything out and I will not tell you as well how much money we will spend. I'm always more focused on quality.

Santi Cazorla has been voted man of the match. I don't think he has cost £150 million. Coquelin was one of the best players on the pitch. You have to always look at the real quality of people. I am not against spending money. I have shown that recently. But I want a good rapport between price and quality.

If ever Wenger was able to find good value and proven quality in a player, then surely the signing of Petr Cech encapsulated both. Cech has incredible experience, has won every major domestic trophy and, even at 33, is still regarded as a genuine world-class keeper so the £10 million transfer fee can be seen as good value.

It was an incredible signing for Arsenal on many levels. Chelsea, with Thibaut Courtois installed as their No 1, allowed Cech to join a direct title rival, significantly strengthening Arsenal's squad. Mourinho had presented his fiercest managerial rival with a top-class signing. For Arsenal, it could be seen as the missing piece of the jigsaw. Cech also wanted to move to Arsenal, not just to stay in London but because he felt they would be genuine contenders.

Cech said: 'In the first meeting we had, I spoke to the manager, Arsene Wenger, and obviously it was a big difference because I am as hungry as ever and have the same motivation and commitment to win trophies as I had ten or 15 years ago and as a kid. Having spoken to him, I believe I will find a team that wants to be successful and wants to challenge the best in Europe.

'It is an exciting project for me. It was probably the hardest decision for me to go, but last year I realised that I am not in a phase of my career when I would sit on the bench. I want to be playing, I want to have a chance to compete for my position in the team and I want to be useful for the team and do the usual stuff on the pitch week in, week out. I hope I will have that possibility to compete for my place here at Arsenal and I hope that I can bring something a little extra to the team that can help.'

The interesting thing for Arsenal was that they actually tried to sign Cech before he moved to Chelsea in 2004. Wenger was never in any doubt about Cech's quality, but his biggest worry was that Chelsea wouldn't sell to Arsenal. While Wenger continued to talk up his other keepers David Ospina and Wojciech Szczesny even after the FA Cup final, he knew that he wanted Cech and that Cech could strengthen his squad. It is perhaps the first time Arsenal have had a world-class keeper since Jens Lehmann, the No 1 in the Invincibles season. Suddenly, the perception was that Arsenal would be a lot stronger defensively thanks to the signing of Cech. A top keeper can give a defence great confidence.

The finish to the 2014/15 season had brought about more belief for Arsenal even if, at the same time, it has possibly persuaded Wenger that he doesn't need to strengthen the squad as much as he might have thought when they were struggling earlier in the campaign.

Arsenal midfielder Jack Wilshere, as he spoke after the FA Cup final win, provided some insight into that belief and why they feel they can move forward as a club. He said:

I think this season we've made a big step mentally. I remember in previous years going to big games, Man United, City, Chelsea, thinking 'have we really got a chance today?' But this year from the first big game, Man City at home, we've done well. We always thought we had a chance. Even United away we got a point. That's a big step that we needed to do so next year we feel like we're in a better position.

There's a group of us British players and a few of the foreign players, we've been together for a few years now. We know each other, we fight for each other. If a team like Arsenal, with the quality we've got, can fight for each other and win the ball back, we're going to create chances.

I remember [in the past] coming away from games like United away thinking 'we dominated that game' but we never really got anything for it. So I think this year was a big thing. We've got players who can hurt teams with Sanchez and Ozil, world-class players we've added in the last two seasons. Ozil has had a great season, he's settled, and Sanchez's first season was unheard of. So we're looking forward to next season.

Those sentiments were echoed by Wenger. He claimed Arsenal's momentum could be a significant benchmark in his reign as manager.

'We think we have made progress. We were in a bad position in January,' Wenger conceded. 'We were seventh and there were not many people predicting we would finish the season like that. But we have made progress. We still have some things to do, I am conscious of that, but I am conscious as well that mentally and tactically we are stronger. And the technical quality is not bad.'

Arsenal's post-cup final celebration wasn't bad either. After the club's reception, some players partied at London's trendy Libertine club until 6 a.m. But it made for some sore heads and hangovers on the open-top bus parade through the streets of Islington on the Sunday morning.

Wilshere still looked worse for wear when he took to the microphone on stage chanting some anti-Spurs songs and the club was forced to shut down their own broadcast of the victory parade so as not to offend. Wenger spoke to Wilshere about his behavior, as did his assistant Steve Bould and other members of the coaching staff, and the midfielder was eventually fined £40,000 by the FA. It was the final act of Wenger's season, another campaign full of twists and turns.

Throughout Wenger's house, there are very few reminders of what he does for a living. He does not know where many of his medals are, the 2015 FA Cup winner's medal has already been pushed to one side and forgotten. He laughs when I ask whether he's ever copied a few other managers by going to bed and sleeping with one of his trophies. 'I am not a man who collects anything, I'm focused on what's next,' he said.

The past few seasons have been difficult. Wenger's legacy was in danger of being remembered for decline rather than glorious success. But Wenger appears to be back on the right path again, having won back-to-back FA Cups. Wenger can now look back with that familiar 'I told you so' smile.

Wenger was hailed as a genius in the early years, went through tough, lean times while he helped build a football club from the foundations upwards. But his love of Arsenal has never diminished, nor has his unshakeable belief that his way is the right way. Wenger wants to win, but win with style. And if they lose, then expect him to take it badly and sulk, just like he did back in those early days when he was a young manager starting out.

At Arsenal's state-of-the-art training ground which he helped design, Wenger smiled as the morning sun streamed through the windows to light up a glorious day in May. 'I heard you so much telling me that we don't win anything that I'm quite surprised I am suddenly on the other side of it,' he laughed. 'I don't deny I'm a bad loser, because in my job if you're a good loser you don't go far. I have been in this job a long time and I've won more games than I have lost, you know.'

Wenger finished the 2014/15 season, looking forward to entering his 20th year as Arsenal manager. His determination, hunger and desire to succeed have never been greater. He still craves respect as well as more trophies. The Champions League remains the Holy Grail. Yet it has been an incredible – and often turbulent – journey that has brought unprecedented success to Arsenal.

They have moved stadium, faced new wealthy challengers and competed on what has often been an uneven playing field. But Wenger has emerged out of the other side, having built a new team, foundations for long-term success and with a belief that the future can be as successful as the glory days of the past.

INDEX